T0391437

Narrative and Drama in the Book of Revelation

Volume 175

The book of Revelation is one of the most cryptic books of the Bible and one that raises many scholarly questions. What is its literary genre? Why is it considered to be both a narrative and a drama? Why does John disregard time–space coordinates? Why does the audience have such an important role in the text? What literary guidelines has the author designed to facilitate the reading of the book? Applying the methods of literary theory to her study, Lourdes García Ureña argues that John wrote Revelation as a book to be read aloud in a liturgical context. In her reading, John chose a literary form, similar to the short story, that allows him to use time–space coordinates flexibly, to dramatize the text, and to take his time in describing his visions. Through these techniques the audience relives and is made part of the visual and auditory experience every time the book is read.

LOURDES GARCÍA UREÑA is Associate Professor in the Facultad de Humanidades y Ciencias de la Comunicación of CEU-San Pablo University in Madrid (Spain). She holds a PhD in Theology from Pontifical Holy Cross University (2003) and received a second PhD in Classical Philology from the University of Córdoba in 2009.

SOCIETY FOR NEW TESTAMENT STUDIES:

MONOGRAPH SERIES

General Editor: Edward Adams

175   NARRATIVE AND DRAMA IN THE
BOOK OF REVELATION

SOCIETY FOR NEW TESTAMENT STUDIES

MONOGRAPH SERIES

Recent titles in the series:

Narrative and Drama in the Book of Revelation

A Literary Approach

Lourdes García Ureña

CEU-San Pablo University, Madrid

Revised by the author and translated by Donald Murphy

CAMBRIDGE
UNIVERSITY PRESS

CAMBRIDGE
UNIVERSITY PRESS

University Printing House, Cambridge CB2 8BS, United Kingdom

One Liberty Plaza, 20th Floor, New York, NY 10006, USA

477 Williamstown Road, Port Melbourne, VIC 3207, Australia

314–321, 3rd Floor, Plot 3, Splendor Forum, Jasola District Centre,
New Delhi – 110025, India

79 Anson Road, #06–04/06, Singapore 079906

Cambridge University Press is part of the University of Cambridge.

It furthers the University's mission by disseminating knowledge in the pursuit of
education, learning, and research at the highest international levels of excellence.

www.cambridge.org
Information on this title: www.cambridge.org/9781108483865
DOI: 10.1017/9781108594073

Originally published in Spanish as *El Apocalipsis. Pautas literarias de lectura* ©
CSIC (Consejo Superior de Investigaciones Científicas), 2013.

This English edition © Cambridge University Press 2019

First published 2019

Printed in the United Kingdom by TJ International Ltd, Padstow Cornwall

A catalogue record for this publication is available from the British Library.

Library of Congress Cataloging-in-Publication Data
Names: Garcia Urena, Lourdes, author.
Title: Narrative and drama in the Book of Revelation : a literary approach / Lourdes
Garcia Urena, University of Barcelona ; translated by Donald Murphy.
Other titles: Apocalipsis. English
Description: English edition. | New York : Cambridge University Press, 2019. | Series:
Society for New Testament studies monograph series ; 175 | Includes bibliographical
references and index.
Identifiers: LCCN 2019008050 | ISBN 9781108483865
Subjects: LCSH: Bible. Revelation – Criticism, interpretation, etc.
Classification: LCC BS2825.52 .G3713 2019 | DDC 228/.066–dc23
LC record available at https://lccn.loc.gov/2019008050

ISBN 978-1-108-48386-5 Hardback

τὸ σπαρτίον τὸ ἔντριτον οὐ
ταχέως ἀπορραγήσεται (Eccles 4.12)

To Marta and Silvano

CONTENTS

TABLES

PREFACE

Everyone agrees that there are narratives in the New Testament. These narratives are normally identified with the four Gospels and the book of the Acts of the Apostles. The Apocalypse, however, is less obviously a narrative. It certainly contains a number of brief narratives, but its overall structure is less clear. Some see it as a kind of linear narrative, in which one thing follows another. It gives the reader a series of revelations about the present and the future, which are given in a chronological sequence. Others argue that it is not a linear narrative, but one in which the same events are portrayed or predicted several times. Each time, different images are used. These two readings are sometimes combined so that the structure of the book is seen as having metaphorically a spiral form. The same events are described several times, but each time more detail is given, the narrative becomes more dramatic, and thus the action is moved forwards.

In this book, Lourdes García Ureña offers her readers a much more sophisticated narrative analysis of the Apocalypse. Her first move is simple but has profound implications. She observes that the author has chosen to present himself both as the narrator and as a character in the narrative. His role as character allows him as narrator to verify his claim to the reception of revelation. She also points out the author's preference for external focalization. He confines himself for the most part to describing external features, that is, things that any observer would notice, rather than communicating the inner thoughts, feelings, and motivations of the other characters. He emphasizes his role as observer and thus as a reliable reporter of what he has seen and heard. She also shows that the author uses the rhetorical technique of vivid description. Such description places what is seen and heard before the eyes and ears of the lector and audience so that they virtually participate in John's experience of the revelation. She shows in syntactical detail how the author uses this technique so that her readers can fully appreciate the way in which the Apocalypse creates its effect.

Professor García Ureña demonstrates further that the Apocalypse is not only a narrative but also a drama. In its narrative portions, the author describes places, characters, and events. In other parts of the work, the author draws upon the techniques of ancient Greek tragedies. One of these is mimesis, representing speech and events directly, rather than describing them indirectly. He also uses a device similar to the way in which the chorus comments on the action, interpreting it and revealing its significance and consequences for the audience. Another convention from Greek tragedy is the use of messenger speeches. Rather than describe the fall of 'Babylon' (Rome) directly, he presents characters, who give vivid portrayals of it.

Her analysis also draws upon the discipline of linguistics to illuminate the text of the Apocalypse and how it works. For example, she shows how the author communicates the meaning of certain utterances by providing contextual information. It also draws upon orality studies to show how the author ensured that the intended impact of the work would indeed be made upon the audience.

Finally, she shows that the structure of the work as a whole serves to implement the author's intentions, as she reconstructs them. Her thesis that the work has an introductory liturgical dialogue (1.4–8) and a concluding one (22.17–21) illuminates two portions of the work that are otherwise very difficult to understand. With regard to genre, the analogy she makes between the Apocalypse and the short story as we have known it since the nineteenth century is bold but illuminating.

Professor García Ureña has employed a variety of methods in her close reading of the Apocalypse and made a significant contribution to the interpretation and appreciation of this intriguing and cryptic work. We – scholars, teachers, and students alike – are all in her debt.

Adela Yarbro Collins
Yale University Divinity School

ABBREVIATIONS

1   General

col., cols.	column, columns
LXX	Septuagint
ms., mss.	manuscript, manuscripts
MT	Masoretic Text
NT	New Testament
OT	Old Testament

2   Bible Editions and Reference Works

ABD	*The Anchor Bible Dictionary*
ANRW	*Aufstieg und Niedergang der Römischen Welt*
B-UNAV	*Sagrada Biblia*, ed. Professors of the University of Navarra School of Theology
BDAG	*A Greek–English Lexicon of the New Testament and Other Early Christian Literature*
BDB	*A Hebrew and English Lexicon of the Old Testament*
JB	*The Jerusalem Bible*
BNP	*New Pauly Online*
DGE	*Diccionario griego-español*
DGENT	*Diccionario griego-español del Nuevo Testamento*
DPAC	*Diccionario patrístico y de la Antigüedad cristiana*
DRAE	*Diccionario de la lengua española*
GI	*Vocabolario della lingua greca (greco-italiano)*
LOUW and NIDA	*Greek–English Lexicon of the New Testament Based on Semantic Domains*
NBE	*Nueva Biblia Española*
NIDNTT	*The New International Dictionary of New Testament Theology*
NT-BOVER	*Nuevo Testamento Trilingüe*
NT-IGLESIAS	*Nuevo Testamento*, ed. M. Iglesias
PL	*Patrologia Latina*

TDNT	*The Theological Dictionary of the New Testament*
THAYER	*A Greek–English Lexicon of the New Testament:*
	Being Grimm's Wilke's Clavis Novi Testamenti, trad.
	and expanded rev. by J. H. Thayer

3   Journals

AUSS	*Andrews University Seminary Studies*
Bib	*Biblica*
BT	*The Bible Translator*
CBQ	*Catholic Biblical Quarterly*
Greg	*Gregorianum*
HTR	*Harvard Theological Review*
IndTheolStud	*Indian Theological Studies*
Int	*Interpretation*
JBL	*Journal of Biblical Literature*
NT	*Novum Testamentum*
NTS	*New Testament Studies*
RB	*Revue Biblique*
RevThom	*Revue Thomiste*

4   Books of the Bible

4.1   Old Testament (including apocryphal books)

Amos	Amos	1–2 Kings	1–2 Kings
Bar	Baruch	Lam	Lamentations
Bel	Bel and the Dragon	Lev	Leviticus
1–2 Chron	1–2 Chronicles	1–4 Macc	1–4 Maccabees
Dan	Daniel	Mal	Malachi
Deut	Deuteronomy	Mic	Micah
Eccles	Ecclesiastes (Qoheleth)	Nah	Nahum
Esth	Esther	Neh	Nehemiah
Exod	Exodus	Num	Numbers
Ezek	Ezekiel	Obad	Obadiah
Ezr	Ezra (Esdras)	Odes	Odes
Gen	Genesis	Prov	Proverbs
Hab	Habakkuk	Ps	Psalms
Hag	Haggai	PssSol	Psalms of Solomon
Hos	Hosea	Ruth	Ruth
Isa	Isaiah	1–2 Sam	1–2 Samuel
Jdg	Judges	Sir	Sirach (Ecclesiasticus)

Jdth	Judith	Song	Song of Songs
Jer	Jeremiah	Sus	Susanna
Job	Job	Tob	Tobit
Joel	Joel	Wisd	Wisdom
Jon	Jonah	Zech	Zechariah
Josh	Joshua	Zeph	Zephaniah

4.2 New Testament

Acts	Acts	Mark	Mark
Col	Colossians	Matt	Matthew
1–2 Cor	1–2 Corinthians	1–2 Pet	1–2 Peter
Eph	Ephesians	Phil	Philippians
Gal	Galatians	Philem	Philemon
Heb	Hebrews	Rev	Revelation
Jas	James	Rom	Romans
John	John	1–2 Thess	1–2 Thessalonians
1–3 John	1–3 John	1–2 Tim	1–2 Timothy
Jude	Jude	Tit	Titus
Luke	Luke		

5 Pseudepigrapha

Most of these abbreviations are taken from the *Greek OT Pseudepigrapha* module of *Accordance 12.0.2.*

Abraham_B	*Testament of Abraham B*
Adam_Eve	*Apocalypse of Moses (Life of Adam and Eve)*
Aristeas	*Letter of Aristeas Greek*
3 Bar	*Greek Apocalypse of Baruch*
1 Enoch	*Ethiopic Book of Enoch (1 Enoch)*
2 Enoch	*The Secrets of Enoch*
Esdr	*Apocalypse of Ezra*
4 Ezra	*4 Ezra*
Jub	*Book of Jubilees*
Levi	*Testament of Levi*
Prayer_Jac	*Prayer of Jacob*
Pseudo_Hecat	*Pseudo-Hecateus*
Rechab	*History of the Rechabites*
Sedr	*Apocalypse of Sedrach*
SibOr	*Sibylline Oracles*
Sol_A	*Testament of Solomon A*

6   Qumran texts

The abbreviations used for Qumran texts are those found in the list created by F. García Martínez (ed.), *Textos de Qumrán*, Madrid: Trotta, 1993. References are cited as shown for the following example: 4Q266 Fr. 6, col. 2,5–6.

4Q266	name of document
Fr.	number of fragment
col. and number before the comma	column in which it is found
number(s) following the comma	line or lines which contain the quotation

7   Classical and Hellenistic Works

Aristotle	*Po.*	*Poetics*
Catullus	*Catullus*	*Carmina*
Cicero	*Inv.*	*De Inventione*
	Fam.	*Epistulae ad Familiares*
Demetrius of Phaleron	*Eloc.*	*De Elocutione*
Homer	*Il.*	*Iliad*
Horace	*Carm.*	*Carmina*
Philo	*Agric.*	*De Agricultura*
	Contempl.	*De Vita Contemplativa*
Pliny the Elder	*NH*	*Naturalis Historia*
Pliny the Younger	*Epis.*	*Epistulae*
Thucydides	Th.	*Historia*
Vitruvius	Vitr.	*De Architectura*

8   Patristic Literature

Clement of Alexandria	*QDS*	*Quis dives salvetur?*
	Strom.	*Stromata*
Origen	*Cels.*	*Contra Celsus*
	Comm. Joh.	*Commentarius in E. Ioannis*
Tertullian	*Adv. Marc.*	*Adversus Marcionem*

INTRODUCTION

The book of Revelation, the last of the biblical corpus, is also one of the most difficult to understand. Its inherent complexity stems from a variety of factors. Not only does its NT language transgress the norms of both Greek grammar and Greek syntax, but the work itself is comprised of disparate literary forms, in a language saturated with symbolism. At the same time, it possesses a highly complicated plot and theological content of great depth. Even so, in the early days of Christianity, the book of Revelation would come to play an important part in the liturgy of the Eastern churches, and would later become, at least in Spain, one of the most widely read books of the Middle Ages, thanks to Saint Beatus of Liébana's *Commentary on the Apocalypse*. After the Middle Ages, while it did inspire works of art, especially in the Renaissance and Baroque periods, it was little studied. It was only in the second half of the twentieth century that the great specialists finally turned their attention to the book of Revelation; today, it is even disseminated and studied through the Internet.

Current lines of research on the book hinge upon three fundamental areas: its exegesis, its theological content, and its hermeneutics. Generally speaking, a strictly literary analysis has been largely absent from this work. Except for some important linguistic studies, which have shed light on the author's use of Greek, there have been few ventures into the literary dimensions of the book of Revelation. Indeed, although exegetical commentaries may have their basis in literary analysis, these immediately move on to questions of sense and theological interpretation; at the same time, a detailed analysis of each verse frequently makes it difficult to obtain a more general vision of the work. Likewise, the book of Revelation has been studied through the lens of rhetoric, and not surprisingly, as the work is addressed to a specific audience to whom the narrator alludes repeatedly and, in effect, the author makes use of a variety of devices drawn from this discipline. The work itself, however, is not presented as one attempting to persuade the public of certain truths, but as one with the aim of transmitting, making known, and teaching about a revelation that has occurred as a type of religious experience. It is thus difficult to consider rhetoric as the crucial interpretative key to the book, and much less as a device employed by the author to criticize a given society.

One task which has been overlooked, and which I intend to address in this book, is that of defining the guidelines which govern a reading of the book of Revelation and the way in which these guidelines determine the literary forms adopted, the stylistic techniques and devices employed, and how these function within the plot.

A study of reading guidelines such as these in the case of the book of Revelation implies a specific understanding of the act of reading. Reading is a dialogue established between the work and its reader thanks to the 'reading pact', that implicit contract between text and reader according to which the latter accepts the norms offered by the text itself for its own comprehension.

Once concluded by its author, a work acquires its own autonomy. As Johannes Petrus Fokkelman argues, after its dissemination in antiquity (or, in our own time, its publication), the umbilical cord connecting it to its author is broken and, to continue the metaphor, it takes on a life of its own.[1] That is to say, once the author has put the final touches to the work, it may then enter into a dialogue with the reader, as the author has endowed it with a series of characteristics and capabilities that make this possible, i.e., a set of reading guidelines. Among these may be noted: the language chosen, the style, the genre,[2] and, at times, specific indications by the author as to how the text should be read.

In any case, while the work does have a life of its own, it is, in the words of Umberto Eco, *una machina pigra* (a lazy machine) which needs someone to help it operate.[3] Without the intervention of the reader, the text remains mute. Active cooperation is thus required for a dialogue to be established. The reader must approach the text with the right attitude in order for their reading to be effective and to correspond to what the text really transmits; it is therefore a question of contemplating the work as

---

[1] J. Fokkelman, *Reading Biblical Narrative: A Practical Guide*, trans. I. Smit (Leiden: Deo Publishing, 1999), p. 22.
[2] U. Eco, *Lector in fabula: La cooperazione interpretativa nei testi narrativi* (Milan: Bompiani, 1979), p. 55.
[3] *Ibid.*, p. 52.

something 'received' and not something to be 'used'.[4] This act of reading must, accordingly, respect the guidelines which the author has etched, so to speak, into the text. Otherwise, the text will ultimately be forced to communicate what one *wants* it to communicate, and not what the text itself transmits. The task of the reader may therefore be reduced to being sufficiently attentive to detect such indications. Once these are discovered, the reader then creates a 'model' through which the sense is grasped and the text interpreted. If, once this is elaborated, some elements are left unaccounted for, the model may be deemed inadequate and the reader will need to begin the task again.

The elaboration of the model involves a process of 'disassembling the mechanism without ruining it; disassembling it until the keys to its organisation are found'[5]. The means available to the reader for this 'disassembling' is that of formulating questions about the text,[6] so that the text itself provides the answers. It may be the case that the answers in turn give rise to new questions, but there comes a moment when these disconnected pieces begin to fit together. Thus, little by little, the text is reconstructed and presented to the reader's eye as an organically structured whole: one which justifies its harmonies and its dissonances, and from which its sense emerges.

In the case of the book of Revelation, an attitude conducive to viewing the work as something 'received' arises from a particular fact: that the book is not an independent work, like the *Iliad* or the *Odyssey*, but belongs to and closes a larger corpus, the Bible. For this reason, the reader should also keep in mind the intertextuality inherent in the books of the Bible, the function of which is of great relevance to the field of biblical studies.

Alongside these considerations, while the period in which the work was written (the late first century AD) is certainly important for placing the work in context, the exact year is not, as this does not influence the book's literary characteristics. The same is true of its authorship. Although it has traditionally been attributed to John the Apostle,[7] in

---

[4] C. S. Lewis, *An Experiment in Criticism* (Cambridge: Cambridge University Press, 1961, rep. 1995), p. 88.

[5] L. Alonso Schökel, *Treinta salmos: Poesía y oración* (Madrid: Cristiandad, 1981), p. 21.

[6] Fokkelman, *Reading Biblical Narrative*, p. 207.

[7] The first testimony is that of Justin Martyr in the *Dialogue with Trypho* 81.4. Others would follow, from Church Fathers such as Irenaeus (*Adv. Haer.* 5.30), Clement of Alexandria (*QDS* 42.1–2; *Strom.* 6.13.106), Origen, Tertullian (*Adv. Marc.* 4.5), and Jerome (*PL* 23.625a). The testimony of Origen seems particularly relevant, because of the insistence with which he affirms the authorship of John in various of his works (*Cels.*

recent years this claim has been called into question, precisely because the narrator presents himself as John – the name that has been used to refer to him ever since – while apocalyptic works were generally written under pseudonyms.[8] At the same time, if the author of the Fourth Gospel is indeed the same as that of the book of Revelation, it seems surprising that he would in the Gospel try to hide his identity behind the expression ὁ μαθητὴς ἐκεῖνος ὃν ἠγάπα ὁ Ἰησοῦς, 'the disciple whom Jesus loved' (John 13.23; 17.26; 19.26; 21.7–20), but would then in the book of Revelation give special emphasis to his authorship – ἐγὼ Ἰωάννης – both in opening and closing the narrative (Rev 1.4, 9; 22.8). Today, this attribution is still an open question. However, one does not need to identify the author in order to grasp the sense of the text, since, as we have mentioned, a literary work, once written, acquires an autonomy independent of its authorship.

The testimonies – papyri, manuscripts, quotations from the Fathers – which have come down to us show that the book was written originally in Greek. Despite the complexities of the manuscript tradition, and thanks to the meticulous contribution of Joseph Schmid,[9] we have at our disposal a reliable text. For the biblical quotations in this book, I use the text of the twenty-eighth edition of the *Novum Testamentum Graece*, prepared by Nestle and Aland,[10] taking into account the significant variations accepted by the editorial committee of the UBS,[11] as well as other exegetical contributions. The translations, unless otherwise indicated, are my own.

As the text transmits a message through the medium of words, the language used and the way it is articulated prove as important as the

---

6.23.9; 8.17.7; *Comm. Joh.* 1.1.2; 1.22.132; 2.5.45); in *Comm. Joh.* 1.14.84 he would even declare that the author of the book of Revelation was none other than John, son of Zebedee.

[8] D. E. Aune, *Revelation 1–5* (Dallas, TX: Word Books, 1997), pp. xlvii–lvi; J. Roloff, *The Revelation of John: A Continental Commentary*, trans. J. E. Alsup (Minneapolis, MN: Fortress Press, 1993), pp. 8–9; P. Prigent, *Commentary on the Apocalypse of St John*, trans. W. Pradels (Tübingen: Mohr Siebeck, 2001), pp. 36–50. Pseudonymity, however, is not necessarily the defining characteristic of apocalyptic literature, as has been noted by J. J. Collins in *The Apocalyptic Imagination: An Introduction to Jewish Apocalyptic Literature*, 2nd edn (Grand Rapids, MI – Cambridge: William B. Eerdmans, 1998), pp. 270–3.

[9] J. Schmid, *Studien Zur Geschichte des Griechischen Apocalypse-Textes*, 2 vols. (Munich: Karl Zink, 1955–6).

[10] *Novum Testamentum Graece*, E. Nestle and K. Aland, eds., 28th rev. edn (Stuttgart: Deutsche Bibelgesellschaft, 2012). In the notes on textual criticism included here, I am following the abbreviations established in their critical apparatus.

[11] B. M. Metzger, *A Textual Commentary on the Greek New Testament: A Companion Volume to the United Bible Societies' Greek New Testament*, 2nd edn (Stuttgart: Deutsche Bibelgesellschaft, 2002).

message itself; indeed, at times the only way of discovering the true sense of the text is through a detailed analysis of its form; that is, 'how it is said'. This 'how' is not something accidental, but is essential to an adequate interpretation. Though this 'how' is relevant to the analysis of any literary work, it is especially so for the book of Revelation, as, due to the great distance in time and space between its conception and our reading of it, it will be difficult for the reader, if they are not able to perceive how the content is transmitted, to arrive at its sense.

This being said, symbolism, an inherent aspect of the language of the book of Revelation, will not be dealt with in this study, and there is a reason for this. The symbol, by its very nature, possesses two dimensions, one visible to the reader and another *in absentia*, which must be discovered, and which, moreover, allows for multiple interpretations. This element *in absentia* corresponds to what Umberto Eco refers to as the 'unmentioned' element of a work,[12] and its interpretation occurs at the moment when the reader has created the 'model' and proceeds to extract the meaning of the text. This aspect lies beyond the scope of the present study, which focuses only on the development of the model.

---

[12] U. Eco, *Lector in fabula*, p. 51. Along the same lines, D. Marguerat and Y. Bourquin, *Per leggere i racconti biblici: La Bibbia si racconta. Iniziazione all'analisi narrativa*, trans. M. Zappella (Rome: Borla, 2001), p. 126.

1

THE LITERARY FORMS OF THE BOOK OF REVELATION

Even in a first approach to the book of Revelation, the reader wishing to grasp its sense will encounter an initial obstacle in the form of the work's textual heterogeneity. Indeed, unlike other contemporary books, whether of the New Testament or the Pseudepigrapha, or classical Greek and Latin works, the book of Revelation appears at first to be an amalgam of texts.

Such diversity makes understanding its message all the more difficult. In light of this, the reader is left with two options: limiting oneself to the idea that the book is a cryptic text and partially closed to the modern reader; or accepting the challenge it poses and attempting to discover that which might confer unity on this variegated melange of literary forms, unconnected as they may seem. The latter is undoubtedly the best course, as it is only in this way that the reader can place themselves in a position to read the work in depth and thereby understand its sense.

1.1   The Book of Revelation: A Multi-form Text

At the very beginning, the reader is presented with an extensive clausal section (Rev 1.1–2), followed by a 'makarism', or beatitude (Rev 1.3), which situates it within the work as a whole. After this comes a series of statements, with subject matter distinct from the preceding verses, and which, in addition, are listed with no apparent organizing principle (Rev 1.4–8). The reader then finds a long section, spanning nearly the entire length of the work (Rev 1.9–22.5), made up of statements articulated according to what John saw and heard. Finally, the reader distinguishes, together with indicators of a thematic continuity, an alternation of short phrases introduced by *verba dicendi* (Rev 22.6–21) that suggest an interchange of voices and interrupt the temporal succession that has been maintained up to this point.

1.1.1   Rev 1.1–3: A Possible Prologue?

In the opening clausal section, the voice of the narrator is hidden by the use of the third-person singular (Rev 1.1–2). Subsequently, this is broken *ex abrupto* by a makarism addressed to a specific audience of listeners (Rev 1.3). The initial pericope (Rev 1.1–2) is comprised by a short nominal syntagma, accompanied by a series of relative and infinitive clauses that fill out its meaning. The literary form chosen seems to be one that is declarative in nature and allows the narrator gradually to provide the listener/reader with information about the characteristics of the work before them.

First, both the subject of the text and its literary genre are made very clear: Ἀποκάλυψις Ἰησοῦ Χριστοῦ, 'The Revelation of Jesus Christ' (Rev 1.1). The three Greek words synthesize the content of the text and the listener/reader obtains from them enough data to frame the entire work, as they communicate that:

a)   The content of the book will be something previously unknown to them, as they know that ἀποκάλυψις proceeds from ἀποκαλύπτω, 'removing the veil'; that is to say, 'revealing something hidden to someone else'.[1] At the same time, the term ἀποκάλυψις connects the work with a specific type of literature, which had already been circulating for some time and which was presented as revelatory: a genre that would come to be known as 'apocalyptic literature'.

b)   It is Jesus who unveils the mystery, as confirmed by the subjective genitive employed and the following relative clause: ἣν ἔδωκεν αὐτῷ ὁ θεός, 'which God communicated to him' (Rev 1.1b).

c)   The work has a sacred character, as the revelation itself is attributed to Jesus, also referred to as Χριστός, a title that identifies him as the Messiah.

Immediately after this, through more relative clauses, the characteristics of the revelation are enumerated:

a)   Its divine origin: ἣν ἔδωκεν αὐτῷ ὁ θεός, 'which God communicated to him' (Rev 1.1b).

---

[1] *DGENT 3*, col. 868, s.v. ἀποκαλύπτω.

b)   Its audience: τοῖς δούλοις αὐτοῦ, 'to his servants' (Rev 1.1b), i.e., those who constituted the early Christian communities.[2]

c)   Its contents: events that will take place in the near future, ἃ δεῖ γενέσθαι ἐν τάχει, 'which must soon come to pass' (Rev 1.1b), making it a revelation that is completely new and distinct from New Testament texts such as Rom 16.25 or 1 Cor 2.7–8, which speak of the wisdom of God that has always existed.

d)   Its mediators: an angel of God and John himself, καὶ ἐσήμανεν ἀποστείλας διὰ τοῦ ἀγγέλου αὐτοῦ τῷ δούλῳ αὐτοῦ Ἰωάννῃ, 'and made it known by sending it through his angel to his servant, John' (Rev 1.1c).

e)   His qualifications as a witness, ὃς ἐμαρτύρησεν τὸν λόγον τοῦ θεοῦ καὶ τὴν μαρτυρίαν Ἰησοῦ Χριστοῦ ὅσα εἶδεν, 'who has given testimony to the word of God and the testimony of Jesus Christ, to all that he saw' (Rev 1.2).

It is precisely the verbal lexeme[3] μαρτυρέω that implies a first-hand witness, and it is therefore significant that the text specifies that John is witness not only to what he hears, τὸν λόγον τοῦ θεοῦ καὶ τὴν μαρτυρίαν Ἰησοῦ Χριστοῦ, but also to what he sees, ὅσα εἶδεν (Rev 1.2).

The information given to the listener/reader in Rev 1.1–2 is so specific and orientative that it may be considered a small map of the text. Indeed, the author, by means of this varied declarative passage, is offering to the audience a series of guidelines for understanding the work itself.

Next, the makarism suddenly appears, μακάριος ὁ ἀναγινώσκων καὶ οἱ ἀκούοντες, 'blessed is the one who reads aloud and the ones who hear . . .' (Rev 1.3), concluding with the brief but urgent phrase ὁ γὰρ καιρὸς ἐγγύς,

---

[2]   It seems unnecessary to interpret this term beyond its meaning of δοῦλος, 'servant, slave', as some exegetical scholars have done. For example, 'Christian prophets' has been proposed by H. B. Swete, *The Apocalypse of St. John: The Greek Text with Introduction, Notes and Indices* (Eugene, OR: Wipf and Stock, 1906, rep. 1999), p. 2; and R. H. Charles, *A Critical and Exegetical Commentary on the Revelation of St. John: Introduction, Notes and Indices, also the Greek Text and English Translation*, vol. 1 (Edinburgh: T & T Clark, 1920), p. 6. However, the term δοῦλος appears 14 times in 13 different verses of the book of Revelation, and in these verses δοῦλος does not always refer to the prophets. In fact, δοῦλος is also used to indicate the opposite of free men (Rev 6.15; 13.16; 19.18), and in reference to Moses (Rev 15.3), and to John himself (Rev 1.1). What is more, when the author speaks of the prophets, he adds to δοῦλος the term προφήτης, as in Rev 10.7 or 11.18.

[3]   For the definition of 'lexeme', I take as a reference that of Juan Mateos in *Método de análisis semántico* (Córdoba: El Almendro, 1989), p. 6: 'any lexical unit with an independent nucleus of meaning'.

'for the time is near'. The presence of the makarism surprises the reader because, although the expression may seem familiar – because of its similarity to other sayings of Jesus[4] – it disrupts the textual cohesion that has been maintained up to this point. The text here changes from a series of statements listing the characteristics of the revelation (Rev 1.1–2) to an apostrophe, charged with a strong sense of immediacy, in which the narrator addresses a new set of interlocutors: ὁ ἀναγινώσκων καὶ οἱ ἀκούοντες, 'the one who reads aloud and the ones who hear' (Rev 1.3).

In classical Greek, the verbal lexeme ἀναγιγνώσκω has three accepted meanings: 'to know with certainty', 'to read', and 'to induce (an action)'.[5] Nevertheless, only one of these meanings is used in the NT: 'to read',[6] even though the word appears 32 times in 29 different verses. Once analyzed, it can be observed that ἀναγινώσκω is used on 21 occasions to refer to the reading of the OT,[7] on nine occasions to the letters,[8] and on one occasion (John 19.20), to the inscription on the cross of Jesus. From these contexts, one may deduce that the reading to which this verbal lexeme refers is that which is done aloud rather than silently; and, indeed, ancient texts were usually read audibly. Significant in this regard is the episode in which Philip addresses an Ethiopian when he hears him reading aloud from the book of Isaiah (Acts 8.28–30). In the NT, ἀναγινώσκω means 'to interpret a written text by translating into sounds';[9] that is, 'to read aloud', and so it is natural that it is used in the New Testament corpus to allude to public readings in the synagogues (Luke 4.16; Heb 13.27) or in the meeting places of the early Christian communities (1 Thess 5.27; 1 Tim 4.13).

From this we can conclude that when the book's opening makarism is addressed to ὁ ἀναγινώσκων, it refers not to an indeterminate reader, but rather to the one charged with reading the text aloud to the community and, consequently, οἱ ἀκούοντες refers to those who listen to him. Thus, the interlocutors of the makarism are both he who presides over the community and its constituents, i.e., the Christians who are assembled together. As pointed out by M. Eugene Boring and Ugo Vanni,[10] it is as if

[4] Aune, *Revelation 1*, p. 20.
[5] *DGE* 2, p. 228–9, s.v. ἀναγινώσκω; *GI*, p. 165, s.v. ἀναγινώσκω.
[6] *DGENT* 2, col. 452, s.v. ἀναγινώσκω.
[7] Examples include: Matt 12.3; Luke 4.16; Acts 8.28; 2 Cor 3.15.
[8] This is the case for: Acts 15.31; 2 Cor 1.13; Eph 3.4; 1 Thess 5.27; Col 4.16(3).
[9] *DGENT* 2, col. 452, s.v. ἀναγινώσκω.
[10] M. E. Boring, *Revelation: Interpretation. A Bible Commentary for Teaching and Preaching* (Louisville, KY: John Knox Press, 1989), p. 67; U. Vanni, 'Liturgical Dialogue as a Literary Form in the Book of Revelation', *NTS* 37 (1991), 348.

the author of the book knew that the text would be read in a particular setting, within a community, as was done with the letters of Paul (Col 4.16; 1 Thess 5.27), and sought to differentiate it from those Jewish apocalyptic writings that were usually read in private.[11]

Together with the presence of these new interlocutors, the listener/reader also perceives the temporal shift that has taken place. The past tense that was maintained in Rev 1.1–2 is abandoned, and the present, an immediate present, invades the makarism completely through the use of participial forms (ἀναγινώσκων, ἀκούοντες, τηροῦντες) and the eloquent nominal clause ὁ γὰρ καιρὸς ἐγγύς. The latter confers to the pericope an inarguable sense of imminence and urgency, and therefore of present time.

With this change in discourse, the listener/reader discovers a new guideline for reading the work. The generic οἱ δοῦλοι (Rev 1.1) is transformed in Rev 1.3 into ὁ ἀναγινώσκων καὶ οἱ ἀκούοντες, the community that is now listening to the content of the book. This 'now', given the reiterated use of present participles (ἀναγινώσκων, ἀκούοντες, τηροῦντες) and a total absence of personal forms, endows the makarism with a timeliness that in a sense transcends the text itself; it may even be said that this constitutes a performative act of language.[12] It is thus logical that the listener/reader, upon hearing it, should feel that they are being addressed directly, given that each reader may identify themselves with ὁ ἀναγινώσκων, 'the one who reads aloud', or with οἱ ἀκούοντες, 'the ones who hear' (Rev 1.3). It is as though the implicit readership, to whom the author has directed the work, has been widened; the reader is no longer identified exclusively with those early Christians who assembled together in the past, but also with the present-day readers of the text.

The formal discontinuity between Rev 1.1–2 and 1.3, then, is quite marked. In spite of this, however, both pericopes serve the same function within the work; i.e., they provide the listener/reader with guidelines for

---

[11]   Aune, *Revelation 1*, p. 21.

[12]   John L. Austin establishes three conditions necessary for an act to be performative: a) the acceptance of the statement by the community; b) its complete and correct diction; c) its reception in the appropriate circumstances and by the appropriate persons; see J. L. Austin, *Palabras y acciones. Cómo hacer cosas con palabras*, compiled by J. O. Urmson, trans. G. R. Carrio and E. A. Rabossi (Buenos Aires: Paidós, 1971), pp. 66–80. All three of these requirements are met in Rev 1.3: makarisms are frequent in both the OT (1 Kings 10.8; Ps 1.1) and the NT (Matt 5.3-11), from which it can be deduced that they were accepted by the society; they begin with the adjectival lexeme μακάριος, as in Rev 1.3, and were pronounced by figures of authority; in the case of the book of Revelation, this is John, the mediator of the revelation.

reading. This common purpose allows us to conclude that Rev 1.1–3, its diversity notwithstanding, has a unity within the totality of the book.

Furthermore, its function, to provide the listener/reader with guidelines for understanding the work, is the same as that of the prologue of any work,[13] and so it may be argued that Rev 1.1–3 in fact constitutes the prologue to the book of Revelation.[14]

What is more, Rev 1.1–3 does indeed bring together some of the other requirements of a good prologue. These include: establishing the novelty or degree of originality of the text, as the pericope indicates that the work is a new revelation; the importance or repercussions of the work in terms of its documentary, intellectual, or religious use (Rev 1.1–3 states expressly that blessedness will come to whoever reads it); the unity that Rev 1.1–3 reflects, by its avowal that what the book contains is a unique revelation; and its truthfulness,[15] that is to say, the effort taken to show that the text is true, as in the opening expression Ἀποκάλυψις Ἰησοῦ Χριστοῦ, by which Jesus is presented as the author of the revelation, and John as its visual and auditory witness.

1.1.2   Rev 1.4–8: From Textual Amalgam to Initial Liturgical Dialogue

After the prologue, the listener/reader expects the revelation to begin, above all, given the sense of urgency transmitted by the makarism. However, what they find in place of this is a series of literary units that are very different from each other (at least at first glance): units that lack a temporal or causal nexus and whose subject matter is somewhat different from that of the prologue (Rev 1.1–3).

The *incipit,*[16] Ἰωάννης ταῖς ἑπτὰ ἐκκλησίαις ταῖς ἐν τῇ Ἀσίᾳ, 'John to the seven churches of Asia' (Rev 1.4a), in itself constitutes a novelty. For the first time, an individual voice, i.e., John's, is identified. Along with

---

[13] G. Genette, *Seuils* (Paris: Éditions du Seuil, 1987), pp. 7–8.

[14] See: *NBE, JB, B-UNAV*, Rev 1.1.

[15] Genette, *Seuils*, pp. 202–10, 184–5, 186–192. Genette refers to this quality as *véridicité,* a term that does not correspond exactly either to 'veracity' or to 'credibility'. I have chosen to use here the approximation 'truthfulness', which I believe is closer to the French author's meaning.

[16] The *incipit* is the first phrase of the text that makes the narrator's intention known and functions as a type of reading protocol by providing information to the reader; see Marguerat and Bourquin, *Per leggere, Glossario*, pp. 129, 175, s.v. *incipit.*

this, further new addressees of the text are mentioned: the seven churches of Asia.

The opening salutation continues (Rev 1.4b–5) and is extended by means of a triple ἀπό. The preposition imposes homogeneity on the pericope, at the same time that this anomalous use demands attention from the listener/reader:

> [4b] χάρις ὑμῖν καὶ εἰρήνη [4c] ἀπὸ ὁ ὢν καὶ ὁ ἦν καὶ ὁ ἐρχόμενος [4d] καὶ ἀπὸ τῶν ἑπτὰ πνευμάτων ἃ ἐνώπιον τοῦ θρόνου αὐτοῦ [5a] καὶ ἀπὸ Ἰησοῦ Χριστοῦ, ὁ μάρτυς, ὁ πιστός, [5b] ὁ πρωτότοκος τῶν νεκρῶν [5c] καὶ ὁ ἄρχων τῶν βασιλέων τῆς γῆς (Rev 1.4b–5).

> [4b] Grace and peace to you [4c] from the One who is, who was, and who is to come, [4d] and from the seven spirits who are before his throne, and [5a] from Jesus Christ, the faithful witness, [5b] firstborn from among the dead [5c] and the ruler of the kings of the earth.

Both the *incipit* and the salutation bear a great similarity to the way in which NT letters usually begin.[17] They include the name of the author of the text, Ἰωάννης, 'John'; its addressees, ταῖς ἑπτὰ ἐκκλησίαις ταῖς ἐν τῇ Ἀσίᾳ, 'the seven churches of Asia'; and a phrase that corresponds strictly to the initial salutation, χάρις ὑμῖν καὶ εἰρήνη ἀπὸ . . ., 'grace and peace from . . .'.[18] This type of opening recalls the *praescriptio* common to the epistolary genre, which consists of three elements: a) the *superscriptio*, the name of the sender, in the nominative case; b) the *adscriptio*, the recipients in dative; and c) the *salutatio*.[19] Nor is it surprising that the author of the book of Revelation has adopted this literary form to make his revelation known, as letters were one of the means through which the Apostles supported each other and strengthened the faith of the early Christian communities. It is logical, then, that he should use the

[17] Rom 1.7; 1 Cor 1.3; 2 Cor 1.2; Gal 1.3; Eph 1.2; Phil 1.2; Col 1.2; 1 Thess 1.1; 2 Thess 1.2; 1 Tim 1.2; 2 Tim 1.2; Titus 1.4; Philem 3; 1 Pet 1.2; 2 Pet 1.2.

[18] Although the second-person plural pronoun in Rev 1.4 has traditionally been translated into Latin and the Romance languages as masculine (see *NBE, NT-BOVER, B-UNAV, JB*), in the Spanish version of the present work I use the feminine, as the referent of this pronoun is feminine: αἱ ἐκκλησίαι.

[19] J. W. Bowman, *The Drama of the Book of Revelation: An Account of the Book with a New Translation in the Language of Today* (Philadelphia, PA: The Westminster Press, 1955), p. 12; Roloff, *Revelation*, pp. 22–3; Aune, *Revelation 1*, p. 26; G. K. Beale, *The Book of Revelation: A Commentary on the Greek Text* (Grand Rapids, MI – Cambridge – Carlisle: The Paternoster Press, 1999), p. 186; A. Yarbro Collins, 'Revelation, Book of', *ABD 5*, pp. 694–708.

epistolary genre to disseminate his text, defined as οἱ λόγοι τῆς προφητείας, 'the words of the prophecy' (Rev 1.3).

The *praescriptio* is followed by a doxology, ending with an ἀμήν, a formula pronounced by the community at the end of a prayer:[20]

> ⁵ᵈ Τῷ ἀγαπῶντι ἡμᾶς καὶ λύσαντι ἡμᾶς ἐκ τῶν ἁμαρτιῶν ἡμῶν ἐν τῷ αἵματι αὐτοῦ,
> ⁶ᵃ καὶ ἐποίησεν ἡμᾶς βασιλείαν, ἱερεῖς τῷ θεῷ καὶ πατρὶ αὐτοῦ, ⁶ᵇ αὐτῷ ἡ δόξα καὶ τὸ κράτος εἰς τοὺς αἰῶνας [τῶν αἰώνων]· ἀμήν (Rev 1.5d–6).

> ⁵ᵈ To him who loves us, who freed us from our sins by his blood
> ⁶ᵃ and made us a royal lineage, priests to his God and Father,
> ⁶ᵇ to him is the glory and the power for ever and ever. Amen.

Although doxologies also appear in the New Testament letters,[21] this one presents certain distinguishing peculiarities. It begins with an unexpected dative, τῷ ἀγαπῶντι, which does not exist in any other doxology.[22] It is also dominated by the use of the first-person plural pronoun, as opposed to the second-person plural found in the opening salutation.[23] Lastly, the opening dative, τῷ ἀγαπῶντι, reappears at the end of the doxology in the pronominal lexeme of the third-person singular, αὐτῷ.

Once the doxology has concluded, a new clausal section begins. It opens with the expression ἰδού, addressing a clear appeal to an interlocutor who, in turn, responds with the affirmation ναί, ἀμήν. Literary unity, led by ἰδού, is developed through the use of the third person, dominated by the future tenses ἔρχεται,[24] ὄψεται, κόψονται:

> Ἰδοὺ ἔρχεται μετὰ τῶν νεφελῶν, ᵇ καὶ ὄψεται αὐτὸν πᾶς ὀφθαλμὸς ᶜ καὶ οἵτινες αὐτὸν ἐξεκέντησαν, ᵈ καὶ κόψονται ἐπ' αὐτὸν πᾶσαι αἱ φυλαὶ τῆς γῆς.
> ᵉ ναί, ἀμήν (Rev 1.7).

---

[20] This is the transcription of the Hebrew word אָמֵן, which in turn corresponds to the expression ἀληθῶς γένοιτο, found in LXX. According to David E. Aune, *Revelation 1*, p. 44, ἀμήν is one of the four elements of which doxologies are comprised.

[21] See: Rom 16.26–27; Gal 1.5; Phil 4.20; 2 Tim 4.18; Heb 13.21; Jude 24–25.

[22] Aune, *Revelation 1*, p. 46.

[23] U. Vanni, 'Un esempio di dialogo liturgico in Ap 1,4–8', *Bib* 57 (1976), 459; 'Liturgical Dialogue', 350.

[24] The verb form ἔρχεται with a future value is frequent in New Testament Greek, especially in prophetic texts, see *ibid.*, note 8.

Look! He is coming with the clouds, [b] and every eye will see him, [c] even those who pierced him; [d] and all the peoples of the earth will wail for him.
[e] Yes, Amen!

In terms of content, another change is also at work here, as the acclamation of Christ is abandoned and a prophetic oracle appears in its place.[25] Finally, however, the voice of God is heard in the first person, breaking unexpectedly into the text and introduced by a reporting verb:

Ἐγώ εἰμι τὸ ἄλφα καὶ τὸ ὦ, λέγει κύριος ὁ θεός, ὁ ὢν καὶ ὁ ἦν καὶ ὁ ἐρχόμενος, ὁ παντοκράτωρ (Rev 1.8).

'I am the Alpha and the Omega,' says the Lord God, 'the One who is, who was and who is to come, the Almighty.'

In synthesis, Rev 1.4–8 is made up of four distinct literary units: an initial salutation similar to that of a letter (Rev 1.4–5c); a doxology (Rev 1.5d–6); a prophetic oracle responded to with ναὶ ἀμήν (Rev 1.7); and, finally, a discourse in tagged direct speech (Rev 1.8).

The only nexus of union with the prologue in this amalgam of textual units is the *incipit,* in which the voice we hear is introduced as John's, as not even the addressees of the revelation are consistent: these are now the seven churches. In any case, despite this diversity of literary units and their heterogeneous content, there is a strong sense of textual cohesion in Rev 1.4–8, achieved through co-referentiality, the repeated use of the connector καί, lexical cohesion, and the verb tenses employed.[26]

Co-referentiality in Rev 1.4–8 is established by the use of personal pronouns, which both pervade the text and fight for attention. Thus, following the *incipit,* the pronominal lexeme is insterted into the pericope in the dative second-person plural, ὑμῖν (Rev 1.4b), a pronoun that has as referent αἱ ἑπτὰ ἐκκλησίαι, 'the seven churches' (Rev 1.4a), the reference here being anaphoric. This pronoun is then substituted by the first-person plural pronoun in the accusative and genitive, ἡμᾶς/ἡμῶν (Rev 1.5d[3], 6a), which has the same referent as the dative ὑμῖν (Rev 1.4b): the seven churches. In this way, a close link is created between Rev 1.4 and 1.5, as

---

[25] Vanni, 'Un esempio di dialogo', 455.

[26] M. A. K. Halliday and R. Hasan, 'Dimensions of Discourse Analysis: Grammar', in T. Van Dijk (ed.), *Handbook of Discourse Analysis,* vol. 2 (London: Academic Press, 1985), p. 48.

both refer to the seven churches, which appear first as the addressees of the salutation and then as voices within the text itself.

Another recurring pronominal lexeme is that of the third-person singular αὐτός, whose referent is in most cases Jesus (Rev 1.5d, 6ab, 7bcd), and on one occasion God (Rev 1.4d).

Lastly, in the final section, there is the first-person singular pronoun. Ἐγώ, unlike the other pronominal lexemes, has a later referent, κύριος ὁ θεός, 'the Lord God', and is thus the only cataphoric reference.

Despite the wide range of pronouns used, their referents may be reduced to three: the seven churches, Jesus, and God. This gives strong cohesion to the text in terms of subject matter, as the three appear at significant moments of the pericope: the seven churches in the first part – the *incipit*, the opening salutation, and the doxology; Jesus throughout the entire section, except at the end, when the referent is God, who is also mentioned earlier in the opening salutation. Thus, it may be said that a reference to God both opens and closes the pericope.

The conjunction καί acts as a connector in Rev 1.4–8, appearing 16 times. Its function, like that of the rest of the connectors employed, is to indicate the relationship between discourse segments[27] and to specify how they are linked.[28]

In effect, καί is used especially to coordinate elements, as occurs in: the opening salutation,[29] χάρις ὑμῖν καὶ εἰρήνη, 'Grace and peace to you'; in the titles of God, ὁ ὢν καὶ ὁ ἦν καὶ ὁ ἐρχόμενος, 'the One who is, who was, and who is to come'; τὸ ἄλφα καὶ τὸ ὦ, 'the Alpha and the Omega'; and in those of Christ, ὁ πρωτότοκος τῶν νεκρῶν καὶ ὁ ἄρχων τῶν βασιλέων τῆς γῆς, 'firstborn from among the dead and the ruler of the kings of the earth'. However, the most notable function of καί is to establish unifying links, either additive or clarifying,[30] within each discourse unit. Thus, in the opening salutation, the triple ἀπό is united by two instances of καί, which have an additive value:

---

[27] M. M. Rivas Carmona, 'El concepto de cohesión', in G. Álvarez, *et al.* (eds.), *Comunicación y discurso* (Seville: Mergablum, 2003), p. 51.
[28] M. A. K. Halliday and R. Hasan, *Cohesion in English* (London: Longman, 1976), p. 227.
[29] LOUW and NIDA, 89.92, s.v. καί.
[30] M. A. K. Halliday and R. Hasan, *An Introduction to Functional Grammar*, 2nd edn (London: Edward Arnold, 1994), pp. 323–30. LOUW and NIDA, 89.93, s.v. καί have also suggested this value for the conjunction καί.

⁴ᶜ ἀπὸ ὁ ὢν καὶ ὁ ἦν καὶ ὁ ἐρχόμενος
⁴ᵈ καὶ ἀπὸ τῶν ἑπτὰ πνευμάτων . . .
⁵ᵃ καὶ ἀπὸ Ἰησοῦ Χριστοῦ . . . (Rev 1.4–5a).

⁴ᶜ from the One who is, who was, and who is to come,
⁴ᵈ and from the seven spirits . . .
⁵ᵃ and from Jesus Christ . . .

The same structure occurs in the doxology, where two copulative conjunctions are used to unite the reference to Jesus through his powers of salvation. The second καί maintains the strong unity of the section, which could have been broken by the grammatical shift that takes place with the appearance of a personal form of the verb, ἐποίησεν, rather than the participial form that has been used up to this point, ἀγαπῶντι/ λύσαντι:[31]

⁵ᵈ Τῷ ἀγαπῶντι ἡμᾶς
καὶ λύσαντι ἡμᾶς ἐκ τῶν ἁμαρτιῶν ἡμῶν . . .
⁶ καὶ ἐποίησεν ἡμᾶς βασιλείαν . . . (Rev 1.5d–6).

⁵ᵈ To him who loves us
And freed us from our sins by his blood,
⁶ and made us a royal lineage . . .

Finally, the prophetic oracle is also structured in accordance with the additive καί, except when it precedes οἵτινες, where it has a clarifying value:

Ἰδοὺ ἔρχεται μετὰ τῶν νεφελῶν,
καὶ ὄψεται αὐτὸν πᾶς ὀφθαλμὸς
καὶ οἵτινες αὐτὸν ἐξεκέντησαν,
καὶ κόψονται ἐπ᾽ αὐτὸν πᾶσαι αἱ φυλαὶ τῆς γῆς (Rev 1.7).

Look! He is coming with the clouds,
and every eye will see him,
even those who pierced him;
and all the peoples of the earth will wail for him.

The connector καί, then, enhances the textual cohesion not only of the pericope as a whole, but also of each of the literary units of which it is comprised.

---

[31] This grammatical discordance is intended to emphasize the expression it introduces; see Vanni, 'Un esempio di dialogo', 459.

Lexical cohesion is made visible in Rev 1.4–8 through the repetition of isolated lexemes and a formular expression. Examples of the former include the use of:

–   The preposition ἀπό, which appears three times (Rev 1.4 cd, 5a).
–   The first-person plural pronoun, used on three occasions (Rev 1.5d).
–   The lexeme ἀμήν, occurring twice (Rev 1.6b, 7e).

Both the prepositional lexeme ἀπό and the pronominal ἡμεῖς reinforce the cohesion of the literary units that include the opening salutation and the doxology, respectively. At the same time, the repetition of the lexeme ἀμήν shows that, despite the difference in content of the units – praise of Jesus and prophetic oracle – each constitutes a form of prayer. They are, therefore, similar types of literary units.

As for the formula, ὁ ὢν καὶ ὁ ἦν καὶ ὁ ἐρχόμενος, 'the One who is, who was, and who is to come', it is used to open and close Rev 1.4–8. Its repetition, at precisely the beginning and end of this pericope, demonstrates, among other things, the intention of the author to unify the various statements into a single section.

Lastly, as relates to time, the present, already established by the initial makarism, is maintained in Rev 1.4–8 through the use of nominal clauses and the indicative present-tense forms, εἰμί and λέγει. It becomes in this way another source of textual cohesion, situating the listener/reader within an action *in fieri*. Here, perhaps, lies the reason behind the sharp temporal shift that we find in the initial makarism, Rev 1.3; that is, to serve as a nexus between Rev 1.1–2 and Rev 1.4–8.

In Rev 1.7, however, there appears a present tense with a future value, ἔρχεται, and a pair of futures, ὄψεται and κόψονται. This feature does not affect textual cohesion, as it corresponds to the type of discourse employed. Rev 1.7 is a prophetic oracle foreseeing a future event (the second coming of Jesus), hence the use of this particular verb tense. Once the oracle has concluded, the present tense is resumed explicitly, with εἰμί and λέγει.

It is evident that these factors contributing to textual cohesion act in two ways in Rev 1.4–8: they make each literary unit a compact element endowed with its own autonomy, at the same time that they link the various units together, providing continuity to the whole and producing, in turn, a larger unit (Rev 1.4–8). It can thus be observed that the author has a clear intention: to create a homogeneous textual unit while

Table 1 Voices in Rev 1.4–8

VOICES	CITATIONS
first-person singular	Rev 1.4a
second-person plural	Rev 1.4b
first-person plural	Rev 1.5d–6
third-person singular	Rev 1.7
first-person singular introduced by the third person	Rev 1.8ac/b

preserving the distinct character of each one of its parts (salutation, doxology, oracle, and divine discourse). The literary form of Rev 1.4–8 must therefore respect this same peculiarity.

It should not be forgotten that earlier analysis has noted the allusion to a second interlocutor. This element, along with the alternation of pronominal forms, will prove crucial in determining the literary form of Rev 1.4–8.[32] The pronominal alternation found here suggests the presence of different voices speaking throughout the pericope, as shown in Table 1.

Most of these voices can be identified. It is John who begins the unit of discourse contained in Rev 1.4a, as he states directly: Ἰωάννης, 'John'; and it is John himself who introduces the other interlocutor or recipient of his message: ταῖς ἑπτὰ ἐκκλησίαις, 'the seven churches'; these are mentioned again in the initial salutation by means of the pronominal lexeme in the dative, ὑμῖν (Rev 1.4b). Then, without warning, there is a change of voice. The pronoun in the second-person plural, ὑμῖν, a co-referent of the seven churches (Rev 1.4b), becomes first-person plural, this time in the accusative ἡμᾶς. It is thus the seven churches that, in the first person, present the doxology (Rev 1.5d–6), concluding with ἀμήν, 'amen'. After this, the interjection ἰδού (Rev 1.7) leads to a statement in the third person, ἔρχεται μετὰ τῶν νεφελῶν, 'he is coming with the clouds'. This time, it is not easy to determine to whom the voice of the prophetic oracle corresponds, as it seems not to be the seven churches, whose discourse ended with the ἀμήν. Indeed, this question remains unresolved. Finally, God speaks (Rev 1.8ac), and his declaration is made in the formula proper to tagged direct speech, λέγει κύριος ὁ θεός, 'says the Lord

---

[32] Along general lines, the argument here follows the proposal of Vanni in 'Un esempio di dialogo', 453–67 and 'Liturgical Dialogue', 349–55, later continued by M. A. Kavanagh, *Apocalypse 22:6–21 as Concluding Liturgical Dialogue* (Rome: Pontifical Gregorian University, 1984).

Table 2 Identification of voices in Rev 1.4–8

PERSON	IDENTIFIED VOICE	CITATIONS
first-person singular	John	Rev 1.4a
second-person plural	You = the churches	Rev 1.4b
first-person plural	We = the churches	Rev 1.5d–6
third-person singular	Unknown	Rev 1.7
first-person singular	God	Rev 1.8ac
third-person singular	Unknown	Rev 1.8b

God' (Rev 1.8b), but we do not know, at least at first, whose voice it is that pronounces λέγει κύριος ὁ θεός. This is synthesized in Table 2.

It is important to point out that some of these voices indicate the presence of an interlocutor. This is the case for John, who requires the implicit or explicit presence of his addressees, the seven churches; for the call to attention contained in ἰδού, 'look', which involves the listener/reader;[33] and for the utterer of the emphatic particle ναί, 'yes', which, followed by a conclusive ἀμήν, 'amen', demands the existence of a previous message transmitted by another interlocutor, as is well illustrated by Rev 16.7 and 22.20.

From the indications of the text itself, the pericope may be seen to be ordered thusly: John takes the floor and addresses the churches (Rev 1.4–5c), first explicitly, mentioning them by name, ταῖς ἑπτὰ ἐκκλησίαις ταῖς ἐν τῇ Ἀσίᾳ, 'the seven churches of Asia', and later through a pronominal form in the dative, ὑμῖν, 'you'. Next, with the appearance of the first-person plural pronoun, the churches, John's interlocutors, speak in Rev 1.5d. Their declaration concludes with the end of the doxology (Rev 1.6).

If, up to this point, indications of the identity of the voices that alternate between John and the community have been clearly observable, these now disappear. However, the very coherence of the text itself, and the absence of any marker indicating a change, seem to indicate that this interchange between interlocutors continues. It may, therefore, be assumed that the voice that pronounces the oracle is again John (Rev 1.7a–d) and that it is the community that answers in the affirmative by saying ναὶ ἀμήν, 'yes, amen' (Rev 1.7e). As the lexeme ἀμήν, 'amen',

---

[33] Ἰδού, 'Look!', is a demonstrative particle that gives great vividness to the text by inciting the reader to pay close attention to what is being said; *BDAG*, 3658.1, s.v. ἰδού; THAYER, 2538, s.v. ἰδού.

Table 3 Alternation of voices in Rev 1.4–8

SPEAKER	LISTENER	CITATIONS
John	The seven churches	Rev 1.4–5c
The seven churches	John	Rev 1.5d–6
John	The seven churches	Rev 1.7a–d
The seven churches	John	Rev 1.7e
God/John	The seven churches	Rev 1.8ac/b

has a conclusive value, the speaker then changes again; it is thus John who introduces the divine discourse (Rev 1.8b), all of which is consistent with the structure of Old Testament texts. In such texts, the words of God are introduced by means of the so-called 'messenger formula',[34] spoken by figures who act as intermediaries between God and men – prophets (Deut 10.1; Isa 8.11; Jer 13.1); kings (2 Kings 18.25; Ps 2.7); and so forth. This is precisely how John himself was presented in Rev 1.1–2. Table 3 outlines this structure in more detail.

Having laid down this framework, we may proceed to determine the literary form of Rev 1.4–8. The pericope contains some short statements, with a continual change of interlocutors but with strong textual cohesion throughout, as well as in each of its parts, and it employs direct speech. These are features typical of dialogue,[35] and not of letters, which the initial *praescriptio* seemed to suggest we would be dealing with (Rev 1.4).

It is, in any case, a particular type of dialogue in that both the messages and their responses have content that is specifically religious in theme: a doxology, a prophetic oracle, the amen, and the final oracle. That is to say, they are the dialogical statements typical of an assembly that has gathered to pray together. This type of communal prayer, as Ugo Vanni shows,[36] was practised in synagogues and later carried over into the early Christian communities.[37] It is not surprising, then, that Rev 1.4–8 reveals the same type of scheme.

---

[34] J. L. Sicre, *Profetismo en Israel: El Profeta. Los Profetas. El Mensaje* (Estella: Verbo Divino, 1992), p. 159, note 5.

[35] G. R. Cardona, *Diccionario de lingüística*, trans. M. T. Cabello (Barcelona: Ariel, 1991), p. 81, s.v. *diálogo*.

[36] Vanni, 'Liturgical Dialogue', 348–9, note 4. Along the same lines, D. L. Barr, 'The Apocalypse of John as Oral Enactment', *Int* 40 (1986), 254–5.

[37] The *Didache* 10.6 and Pliny's well-known letter (*Epis.* 10.96.7) informing the emperor Trajan about the Christians provide good examples of this.

Another characteristic of this kind of communal interchange, generally referred to as liturgical dialogue,[38] is the predominance of the present tense, which frames the discourses as occurring in the moment that they are pronounced. This is also characteristic of Rev 1.4–8. It may be thus affirmed, following Ugo Vanni, that the dialogue in Rev 1.4–8 is an example of a liturgical dialogue,[39] which explains both its unity and disparity, its continuity and discontinuity.

1.1.3   Rev 1.9–22.5: The Presence of the Narrative

Upon reaching Rev 1.9, the listener/reader realizes that the liturgical dialogue has concluded, and begins to hear the ἀποκάλυψις, which was foretold earlier and which will extend to Rev 22.5. The first voice to be heard is again John's, in the first person and addressing the recipients of the text (the seven churches): Ἐγὼ Ἰωάννης, ὁ ἀδελφὸς ὑμῶν, 'I, John, your brother' (Rev 1.9). It is, then, apparent that this new section is not completely disconnected from the initial liturgical dialogue, as it maintains a continuity with it through the presence of John and the seven churches.

Immediately after this, the seer informs us of the spatial–temporal framework in which he finds himself: ἐγενόμην ἐν τῇ νήσῳ τῇ καλουμένῃ Πάτμῳ . . . ἐν τῇ κυριακῇ ἡμέρᾳ, 'I . . . was on the island called Patmos . . . on the Lord's day' (Rev 1.9d–10), and recounts to us what happened: ἐγενόμην ἐν πνεύματι, 'I fell into ecstasy' (Rev 1.10).[40] From here, a series of extraordinary events unfolds: a voice is heard, which reveals

---

[38] A liturgical dialogue is composed of an invitation or monition, followed by a response from the assembly; see A. Chumpungeo, 'Diálogo litúrgico y didascalia', *DPAC 1*, pp. 591–3. It generally employs the present indicative and the imperative, which help to give the dialogue a performative character; see Austin, *Palabras y acciones*, pp. 96–110. A detailed study may be found in J. Ladrière, 'La performatividad del lenguaje litúrgico', *Concilium* 82 (1973), 215–29.

[39] Vanni, 'Liturgical Dialogue', 370–1.

[40] The objection may be raised that the expression is repeated in other places in the narrative (Rev 4.2 and 17.3; 21.10, employing another verbal lexeme: ἀπήνεγκέν με . . . ἐν πνεύματι) and so John would have had other experiences that arose at different times and in different places; see R. C. H. Lenski, *The Interpretation of St. John's Revelation* (Minneapolis, MN: Augsburg, 1963), p. 167. Nevertheless, the fact that this mystical phenomenon is framed with other time–space coordinates as well, and that this does not happen anywhere else in the book of Revelation, suggests that the experience is both unique and complex; cf. R. J. Korner, '"And I Saw . . ." An Apocalyptic Literary Convention for Structural Identification in the Apocalypse', *NT* 42 (2000), 176–7.

itself to be that of a son of man and then dictates various messages to the churches (Rev 1.11–3); after this, the throne of God is contemplated (Rev 4), as are the Lamb and the sealed book (Rev 5). That is to say, a narrative ensues in which John tells how he came to receive the revelation of Jesus Christ and of what it consists.

In Rev 1.9–22.5, the listener/reader distinguishes the presence of both a narrator, John, and a story, i.e., that which he saw and heard. These two elements are the two essential features of this story, according to Robert Scholes and Robert Kellogg.[41] Other elements that help to structure the text as a narrative also appear: the temporal succession of facts (the story begins on a Sunday); the presence of a hero dominated by an intention that drives the story on to its finale (John, messenger to the early Christian communities); a plot that arches over the various chains of events and integrates them into the unity of a single action (the seer explains how he has received the revelation of Jesus Christ and its contents); and, lastly, a relationship of causality–consequentiality that structures the plot through the play of cause and effect (as a result of the grace John receives [Rev 1.10], he hears a voice, and from this the entire narrative plot unfolds).[42]

It seems, then, that the literary form of Rev 1.9–22.5 is that of a narrative.[43] However, some anomalies may be observed in both the relationship between causality and consequentiality and in the chronological dimension.

With respect to causality–consequentiality, it will be useful here to point out a few examples that are, to my mind, significant. After the first vision, in which John beholds Jesus and receives from him a series of messages for the churches (Rev 1.10–3.22), he sees a door opening to heaven and hears a voice commanding him to climb through it (Rev 4.1). Here begins the vision of the throne of God in all its glory (Rev 4.2–11.19), during which Jesus disappears and what has happened to the seven letters is unknown; that is to say, the listener/reader is unable to discover the relationship of

[41] R. Scholes and R. Kellogg, *The Nature of Narrative* (Oxford: Oxford University Press, 1966), p. 4.

[42] Marguerat and Bourquin, *Per leggere*, pp. 23–4, based on studies by U. Eco, P. Ricoeur, and J. M. Adam.

[43] This explains the studies based on narrative methodology that have been carried out recently. Outstanding among these are: D. L. Barr, *Tales of the End: A Narrative Commentary on the Book of Revelation* (Santa Rosa, CA: Polebridge Press, 1998); J. L. Resseguie, *Revelation Unsealed: A Narrative Critical Approach to John's Apocalypse* (Leiden – Boston – Cologne: Brill, 1998).

cause and effect that links the first vision to the second, knowing only that one has concluded and the other begun. The same occurs with the episode of the woman and the dragon (Rev 12). The vision begins ἐν τῷ οὐρανῷ, 'in heaven' (Rev 12.1), and concludes ἐπὶ τὴν ἄμμον τῆς θαλάσσης, 'on the sand of the sea' (Rev 12.18), with the episode describing how the dragon becomes enraged by the woman. She then disappears completely from the narrative, while the dragon remains on the beach. When this episode is over, the listener/reader does not know what has in fact happened to the woman, nor why the dragon is left there, as the text does not explain further. The story then goes on to recount how John saw a beast rising from the sea, καὶ εἶδον ἐκ τῆς θαλάσσης θηρίον ἀναβαῖνον (Rev 13.1). Once again, the listener/reader knows that one vision has ended and a new one has begun, but is left ignorant as to the cause–effect relationship between the two.

Something similar occurs in the temporal dimension. While it is true that this is alluded to with the expression ἐν τῇ κυριακῇ ἡμέρᾳ, 'on the Lord's day' (Rev 1.10), the subsequent time indicators – ὥρα, 'hour'; ἡμέρα, 'day'; μήν, 'month'; and ἐνιαυτός, 'year' – cease to be explicit, at least as far as their capacity to link the visions and auditions is concerned, once the experience of ecstasy has taken place; the most explicit indicator of a temporal relationship used is the syntagma μετὰ ταῦτα, 'after these things'. But even when such indicators appear within the account of a vision, they shed no light on the precise moment at which the events recounted take place. When, for example, the angel blows the sixth trumpet and the angels are liberated, οἱ ἡτοιμασμένοι εἰς τὴν ὥραν καὶ ἡμέραν καὶ μῆνα καὶ ἐνιαυτόν, ἵνα ἀποκτείνωσιν τὸ τρίτον τῶν ἀνθρώπων, 'prepared for the hour, the day, the month, and the year to kill a third of humanity' (Rev 9.15), the listener/reader is not told any specific date. The same is true of the fall of Babylon, of which it is said that the destruction will take place ἐν μιᾷ ἡμέρᾳ, 'in one day' (Rev 18.8): the listener/reader does not know precisely which day this will be. As D. L. Barr has pointed out, it is sometimes even difficult to tell whether one event has taken place before or after another.[44]

---

[44] Barr gives the example that the dragon probably does not attack the woman's son (Rev 12) after Jesus has dictated the seven letters, nor after the heavenly celebration described in Rev 11; see D. L. Barr, 'The Story John Told: Reading Revelation for its Plots', in D. L. Barr (ed.), *Reading the Book of Revelation: A Resource for Students* (Leiden – Boston: Brill, 2004), p. 18.

This is, then, a peculiar sort of narrative, in which a crucial role is given to the descriptions and the statements in tagged direct speech (introduced by a declarative verb) that appear throughout Rev 1.9–22.5.[45] Indeed, these two elements break the narrative thread, or at least they seem to; the descriptions arrest or slow the action, while direct speech causes the narrator to disappear partially or completely. Based on this feature, given the continual presence of direct speech, some authors have suggested that the literary form of the book of Revelation is in fact drama, and have even divided the work into acts.[46]

The dramatic character of the book is inarguable, not only because of the use of direct speech, an aspect that will be discussed in depth later, but also because it presents other traits characteristic of the dramatic genre. Both the transmission and the reception of the work, for example, are essentially collective.[47] Just as a theatrical work is conceived to be performed, the book of Revelation was written to be read aloud (transmission) within an assembled community (reception). What is more, it possesses what Kurt Spang has called the 'autarchy' of drama; that is to say, when it is performed – or, in this case, read – 'the fiction that there is no author or public is verified'.[48] It is also the nature of drama to present conflict,[49] and this is certainly what occurs in the visions of John; one has only to recall the celestial combat of Michael and the dragon (Rev 12.7–9) or the sending of the seven plagues (Rev 15–16).

In spite of this, however, there are also elements that distance the book of Revelation from the dramatic form. First of all, there is the presence of

---

[45] I offer only a few examples here. The text describes human individuals and collectives (Rev 1.13–16; 4.2–4; 7.9; 12.1–2; 14.14; 15.2–3; 19.11–16), angels (Rev 5.2; 7.2; 14.6; 18.1–2; 19.17), animals (Rev 4.6–8; 5.6; 9.7–11; 12.3; 13.1–2), natural phenomena (Rev 6.12–15; 16.18–21), and cities (Rev 17.3–6; 21.10–14, 18–27; 22.1–5). Examples of tagged direct speech include the instructions John receives (Rev 1.11; 4.1; 11.1–12; 14.13), prayers (Rev 4.8; 5.9–10.12), and statements spoken by angels or heavenly voices (Rev 5.2; 6.6; 19.17c–18).

[46] See, for example, E. Dansk, *The Drama of the Apocalypse* (London: Fisher Unwin, 1894), p. 11; E. W. Benson, *The Apocalypse: An Introductory Study of the Revelation of St John the Divine* (London: Macmillan & Co., 1900), pp. 57–109; J. W. Bowman, 'The Revelation to John: Its Dramatic Structure and Message', *Int* 9 (1955), 440–4; J. L. Blevins, *Revelation as Drama* (Nashville, TN: Broadman Press, 1984), pp. 7–10; S. S. Smalley, *Thunder and Love: John's Revelation and John's Community* (Milton Keynes: Word Publishing, 1994), pp. 108–10.

[47] K. Spang, *Teoría del drama: Lectura y análisis de la obra teatral* (Pamplona: EUNSA, 1991), pp. 27–8.

[48] 'Se verifica la ficción de que se prescinde de autor y de público', *ibid.*, p. 28.

[49] Arist. *Po.* 1450a.

a narrator who tells the story; while he does this in the first person, he himself appears neither as messenger, nor as an actor in the work,[50] but rather as an intermediary between the message and its recipients. The narrator tells the story and the characters speak when he decides,[51] hence the use of tagged direct speech.

Second, it is the seven churches that constitute the recipient of the narrator's text. This recipient is also referred to as the 'narratee',[52] and is an element more characteristic of narrative discourse.

Third, the book of Revelation is not built only and exclusively upon dialogue, as occurs in drama,[53] nor does it resort to drama's non-verbal codes, such as sets, props, costumes, gestures, lighting, and so forth.[54] In Rev 1.9–22.5, these non-verbal codes are present only, so to speak, verbally; they are created through description, as in the opening vision, where John describes the garments and the aura of splendour in which Jesus Christ is clothed (Rev 1.13–16); or through the narration itself, as when he speaks of the darkness that envelops the earth after the fourth trumpet is sounded (Rev 8.12).

Fourth, a dramatic text is meant to be performed, and while this does not exclude its being read, the reader would feel called upon to verify any possible representation of the work he is reading.[55] This is something that would be unthinkable here, as the listener/reader is always aware that what he is hearing is in fact a revelation given to a chosen few by God himself.

As for its anomalies in time and causality, the book of Revelation itself seems to offer an explanation of these at the very outset:

> ἐν τῇ νήσῳ τῇ καλουμένῃ Πάτμῳ ... ἐγενόμην ἐν πνεύματι ἐν τῇ κυριακῇ ἡμέρᾳ ... (Rev 1.9d–10)

> On the island called Patmos ... I fell into ecstasy on the Lord's day ...

---

[50] P. Pavis, *Diccionario del teatro: Dramaturgia, estética, semiología*, trans. J. Melendres (Barcelona: Paidós, 1998), p. 162, s.v. *épico (teatro . . .)*.

[51] Spang, *Teoría del drama*, p. 30.

[52] Marguerat and Bourquin, *Per leggere, Glossario*, p. 176, s.v. *narratario*.

[53] Spang, *Teoría del drama*, p. 32; J. L. García Barrientos (ed.), *Análisis de la dramaturgia: Nueve obras y un método* (Madrid: Fundamentos, 2007), p. 14.

[54] Spang, *Teoría del drama*, pp. 25–6.

[55] M. Á. Garrido Gallardo, *Nueva Introducción a la Teoría de la Literatura*, 3rd edn (Madrid: Síntesis, 2004), p. 337; Spang, *Teoría del drama*, pp. 24–5.

These words seem to be a key to the apparent chaos. John declares that what he is going to recount is something that happened one Sunday on Patmos, through the action of the Spirit: ἐγενόμην ἐν πνεύματι. Thus, the coordinates of the rest of the work may then move away from referents that are real, and operate according to another order (one marked by the Spirit), without damaging the story's verisimilitude. It might even be said that the reading pact is sealed with the expression ἐγενόμην ἐν πνεύματι. The text is indeed verisimilar, as it relates what John saw and heard as the result of the action of the Spirit.

Rev 1.9–22.5, then, takes the literary form of a narrative, a peculiar story comprising a succession of events that are interconnected in various ways and presented as a detailed enumeration of what John saw and heard.

1.1.4   Rev 22.6–21: The Voices Reappear. A New Dialogue?

After the narrative has concluded, diverse voices break into the text – some in tagged direct speech and others in untagged direct speech[56] – and these once again perplex the listener/reader, even if they recognize the similarity of this section to the introductory part of the book (Rev 1.4–8). Grouped together, the voices in Rev 22.6–21 may be divided into two sections:

a)   Rev 22.6–16, in which Jesus, John, and the angel speak.
b)   Rev 22.17–21, in which the voice of the angel disappears and others are heard in its place, such as those of the Spirit and the bride, and the voice of ὁ ἀκούων, 'the one who hears', mentioned to some extent in Rev 1.3.

Given the disparity of opinions regarding the structure and function of Rev 22.6–21 within the work as a whole,[57] each section will here be examined individually.

---

[56] The interlocutor appears in the text *ex abrupto,* without being introduced by a *verbum dicendi*; see Garrido Gallardo, *Nueva introducción,* pp. 176–7.

[57] The *NBE* generally supports this proposal. In contrast, *JB* and *B-UNAV* maintain that Rev 22.6–15 constitutes the conclusion of the narrative and Rev 22.16–21 the epilogue. David E. Aune excludes Rev 22.21 from the epilogue, as he considers it to be a type of postscript; see *Revelation 17–22* (Nashville, TN: T. Nelson, 1998), pp. 1236, 1238–9. In any case, the *communis opinio* is that Rev 22.6–21 constitutes the epilogue; see W. J. Harrington, *Revelation* (Collegeville, MN: The Liturgical Press, 1993), p. 220; R. H. Mounce, *The Book of Revelation* (Grand Rapids, MI: William B. Eerdmans, 1977), p. 388; while Kavanagh, *Apocalypse 22.6–21*, pp. 71–96, and Vanni, 'Liturgical Dialogue',

a) *Rev 22.6–16: The Epilogue of the Narrative*

Rev 22.6–16 begins after John's vision of the New Jerusalem (Rev 21.1–22.5). To be precise, the final part of that vision concludes with an intrusion by the narrator (Rev 22.3–5), preceded by a statement from the angel, who reveals to John the interior of the city (Rev 22.1–2). Immediately after this, we hear a succession of voices in direct speech, similar to what in today's narrative style is referred to as 'direct narrativized discourse',[58] a type of discourse in which a diversity of voices enters into direct contact with each other after external indicators have disappeared.

These voices are in this case embedded within a specific narrative context, i.e., the final vision of the New Jerusalem (Rev 21.1–22.5).[59] The first voice is that of the narrator, hidden by the declarative verb in καὶ εἶπέν μοι, 'and he said to me' (Rev 22.6).[60] By this method, the narrator manages to recapture the thread that was interrupted by his own intrusion (Rev 22.3–5) as well as to hide his own voice to make way for that of the angel. The presence of the latter is obvious, as the subject of εἶπέν μοι could be no other than that of καὶ ἔδειξέν μοι (Rev 22.1), i.e., the angel.

Then, without warning, we hear the voice of Jesus in untagged direct speech (Rev 22.7). It is possible to identify this voice because the expression ἔρχομαι ταχύ, 'I will come soon', has already been used twice at the beginning of the narrative (Rev 2.16; 3.11) by Jesus himself. It is logical, therefore, to assume that ἔρχομαι ταχύ (Rev 22.7) is also spoken by Jesus.

Following this, there is a new change of voice. The narrator is now heard speaking directly, affirming that he has heard and seen these things

---

356–64, feel that it is a final liturgical dialogue. I believe that such disparity stems from Rev 22.6–16 and 17–21 sharing the same literary form.

[58] A. Garrido Domínguez, *El texto narrativo* (Madrid: Síntesis, 1996), p. 264.

[59] There has been much debate as to the identity of the voices heard in this part of the book of Revelation. After studying the various proposals, I have divided these into two groups. For some scholars, there are three voices: an angel, Jesus, and John; see Aune, *Revelation 3*, pp. 1182–3, 1236; Beale, *Revelation*, pp. 1123, 1127, 1131, 1136, 1143; Charles, *Commentary 2*, pp. 214–15; Vanni, 'Liturgical Dialogue', 356–63. For others, there are only two: John, and the angel or Jesus; see *JB*, note on 22.6; A. Yarbro Collins, *The Apocalypse* (Collegeville, MN: The Liturgical Press, 1979, rep. 1990), pp. 152–3.

[60] It is the nature of dialogue to distinguish between the discourse of the narrator and that of a character, and it is for this reason that the narrator here employs a *verbum dicendi* or *sentiendi*; see Garrido Domínguez, *El texto narrativo*, p. 260.

(Rev 22.8). That is to say, in the terminology used by Mieke Bal, the narrator is here transformed into an actor, inasmuch as he is testifying;[61] to achieve this, the first-person pronominal lexeme is used, with even greater emphasis gained through its placement at the beginning of the statement κἀγὼ Ἰωάννης (Rev 22.8). In any case, he is here referring to the past, recounting what has happened and resuming the narrative, ὅτε ἤκουσα καὶ ἔβλεψα, ἔπεσα προσκυνῆσαι, 'when I had heard and seen, I fell down to worship' (Rev 22.8b).

The voice of John is then hidden again by tagged direct speech, καὶ λέγει μοι (Rev 22.9a), which once again announces the appearance of the angel. In this case, the angel's presence can be deduced from his own statement, as he gives himself the title of σύνδουλος, 'fellow servant', and does not allow John to kneel before him (Rev 22.9b). After this brief interruption, John continues speaking (Rev 22.10–11), although his words are likewise preceded by καὶ λέγει μοι.

Finally, unexpectedly and *ex abrupto*, Jesus begins to speak, announcing his coming, ἔρχομαι ταχύ, 'I will come soon', and confirming that it is his own mandate that the angel has revealed to John (Rev 22.12–16).

In other words, John uses tagged direct speech to introduce the voice of the angel and untagged direct speech for the words of Jesus. The use of direct speech gives continuity to the vision's narrative, as it recreates specific scenes of dramatization, and thereby achieves a greater sense of realism.

However, despite the predominant use of direct speech, it is the narrator who sustains the narrative, as, when he does speak, he does so in the past tense, rather than the present: ὅτε ἤκουσα καὶ ἔβλεψα, ἔπεσα προσκυνῆσαι, 'when I had heard and seen this, I fell down to worship' (Rev 22.8b). The literary form of Rev 22.6–16 is thus closer to that of narrativized discourse than to that of liturgical dialogue.[62] The appearance of this type of discourse just when the narration seems to have concluded (Rev 1.9–22.5) is not casual. The form adopted in Rev 22.6–16, embedded within the narrative, marks the extradiegetic position of the story, at the same time that it creates an effect of verisimilitude (with two qualified witnesses corroborating the fact that the revelation John recounts is true, as was stated earlier, in the prologue, Rev 1.1–3);

---

[61] M. Bal, *Teoría de la narrativa: Una introducción a la narratología*, trans. J. Franco, 5th edn (Madrid: Cátedra, 1998), p. 141.
[62] Vanni, 'Liturgical Dialogue', 356–64; Kavanagh, *Apocalypse 22:6–21*, pp. 71–96.

these are features characteristic of the epilogue of a literary work.[63] Rev 22.6–16, then, can be said to constitute the epilogue of this particular narrative (Rev 1.9–22.5).

b)   *Rev 22.17–21: The Final Liturgical Dialogue*

Rev 22.17–21 is also constructed of a combination of segments of tagged and untagged direct speech. Its novelty lies not only in the appearance of new voices, but also in the fact that the narrative has now concluded; indeed, past tenses are almost completely absent here, and added emphasis is given to elements characteristic of direct discourse, such as the use of the first person, deictic expressions, and the 'now' aspect that it conveys.[64]

The narrator is once again hidden behind declarative verbs – λέγουσιν, εἰπάτω, λέγει – so as to make way for three different voices: τὸ πνεῦμα καὶ ἡ νύμφη, 'the Spirit and the bride', who speak in unison, and ὁ ἀκούων, 'the one who hears' (Rev 22.17). Jesus reappears with the expression ἔρχομαι ταχύ, 'I will come soon' (Rev 22.20b), creating a nexus of union with Rev 22.6–16.

Other voices are also heard in Rev 22.17–21. First, there is the voice of the narrator, who, although hidden behind the *verba dicendi*, resumes his role as protagonist through the present and aorist imperative forms, ἐρχέσθω and λαβέτω, that connect with the jussive of the declarative verb εἰπάτω. After this, the 'integrity formula' is established, through which the fidelity of the text is meant to be preserved.[65] In this case, it is difficult to determine whether it is John who is speaking,[66] or Jesus.[67]

---

[63] C. Reis and A. C. M. Lopes, *Diccionario de narratología*, trans. Á. Marcos de Dios, 2nd edn (Salamanca: Almar, 2002), p. 76, s.v. *epílogo*.

[64] *Ibid.*, p. 201, s.v. *personaje, discurso del.*

[65] Aune, *Revelation 3*, pp. 1208–9.

[66] This has been proposed by I. T. Beckwith, *The Apocalypse of John: Studies in Introduction with a Critical and Exegetical Commentary* (Eugene, OR: Wipf and Stock, 1919, rep. 2001), p. 778; Roloff, *Revelation*, p. 253; Vanni, 'Liturgical Dialogue', 361; Prigent, *Commentary*, p. 648.

[67] A hypothesis supported by: Swete, *Apocalypse*, p. 307; Aune, *Revelation 3*, p. 1230; R. L. Thomas, *Revelation 8–22. An Exegetical Commentary* (Chicago, IL: Moody Press, 1995), p. 514. Generally speaking, arguments supporting this proposal maintain, on the one hand, that the book is more logically the testimony of Jesus, as it is the angel who has spoken before this; and, on the other, that John refers to Jesus as ὁ μαρτυρῶν ταῦτα (Rev 2.20). In contrast to this, Charles, *Commentary 2*, p. 222, considers Rev 22.18–19 to be the work of a later author.

Considering that the work is about to conclude, it is not illogical that John should now make his presence felt by means of the first-person singular, expressed not only by the verb form μαρτυρῶ (Rev 22.18a), but also by the pronominal lexeme ἐγώ, which helps to highlight his presence even more.[68] At the same time, as Ugo Vanni points out,[69] his insistence that the text is now written, γεγραμμένας (Rev 22.18), and that the book itself is now a reality (Rev 22.18–19), seems to indicate that the voice we hear is in fact John, the author of the work.

Two other voices appear after this, and an attempt should be made to identify them. The first is heard after Jesus speaks (Rev 22.20b), in a brief statement that repeats his words in the form of a short prayer addressed to him and reproducing the well-known Aramaic liturgical formula, *marana tha*:[70] Ἀμήν, ἔρχου κύριε Ἰησοῦ, 'Amen. Come, Lord Jesus' (Rev 22.20c). The context suggests that this voice can be identified as that of ὁ ἀκούων, 'the one who hears', as these same words have already been pronounced at the beginning of the pericope (Rev 22.17).

The second voice delivers a blessing, Ἡ χάρις τοῦ κυρίου Ἰησοῦ μετὰ πάντων, 'the grace of the Lord Jesus be with all' (Rev 22.21). With this, the book of Revelation concludes, recalling the closing salutation of many of the Pauline Epistles.[71] This final voice is not difficult to identify, as it is addressed to 'all', wishing upon them the grace of Jesus; by exclusion, the context itself points to John as the one who closes the work. In addition, if it was indeed John who began the book with the epistolary salutation Ἰωάννης ταῖς ἑπτὰ ἐκκλησίαις, 'John to the seven churches' (Rev 1.4), it is logical that he should conclude it in the same way.

As with Rev 1.4–8, Rev 22.17–22 is organized into statements of varying lengths, introduced in some cases by *verba dicendi*, in which there is constant change from the second to the first person (Rev

---

[68] F. Blass and A. Debrunner, *A Greek Grammar of the New Testament and Other Early Christian Literature*, trans. and rev. R. W. Funk (Chicago – London: University of Chicago Press, 1961), § 277.

[69] Vanni, 'Liturgical Dialogue', 361.

[70] *Marana tha* is an expression that appears in 1 Cor 16.22 and the *Didache* 10.6, in liturgical contexts. It is a transliteration of the Aramaic *marana*, 'our lord', and *tha*, the imperative of the verb 'to come'.

[71] 1 Cor 16.23; 2 Cor 13.13; Phil 4.23; Philem 25. While the Pauline Epistles conclude by addressing an explicitly plural 'you', the book of Revelation is addressed to 'all' or 'everyone'. Kavanagh is inclined to think that this is a final blessing pronounced by the lector in the name of Christ; see Kavanagh, *Apocalypse 22.6–21*, pp. 132–3; prior to this, Bowman had proposed a similar idea in *Drama*, pp. 12–13.

22.17–18) and from the first to the second person (Rev 22.20bc). These statements are made by different interlocutors, so that we can once again observe the characteristic features of dialogue: alternating voices, direct speech, and short statements. It may thus be affirmed that the literary form of Rev 22.17–21 is indeed that of a dialogue.

It is, however, a dialogue that reinforces certain characteristics of the form. It is, for example, situated in the present and structured by a succession of imperatives both at the beginning – ἔρχου, εἰπάτω, ἐρχέσθω, λαβέτω, Rev 22.17 – and at the end – ἔρχου, Rev 22.20. This is a continuous and immediate present, one that takes place at the moment of speaking. The use of the aorist imperative, here given an ingressive value, is especially vital in this regard. The form εἰπάτω also plays a fundamental role, as it represents the voice of the narrator, John, who exhorts the listener not only to speak, but to do so now, at this very moment. Indeed, we immediately hear him say: ἔρχου, 'come'. This same sense of immediacy is also strengthened by the words that John proceeds to pronounce in the first person (Rev 22.18–19) and to address to παντὶ τῷ ἀκούοντι τοὺς λόγους τῆς προφητείας, 'all who hear the words of the prophecy'. In other words, the seer is referring not to a single listener, but rather to all who are listening to him;[72] indeed, at the end he will refer again to πάντες, 'all' (Rev 22.21).

Likewise, frequent use is made of pronominal and demonstrative lexemes.[73] These, given their characteristic deictic value, help to reinforce the pericope's dialogical aspect, particularly the pronominal form τοῦτο, which directly or indirectly accompanies βίβλος, 'scroll' (Rev 22.18, 19ab). The presence of the demonstrative shows that the revelation has in fact been put down in writing and is compiled here in the βίβλος, 'scroll'. It is as if the listener/reader were able to view it at the same moment that John points to it.

The pericope's various allusions to Rev 1.4–8, both in content and in form, should also be mentioned here. In terms of content, both pericopes deal with the parousia. In the introductory dialogue, this is referred to in the prophetic oracle (Rev 1.7), while in Rev 22.17–21, it is mentioned by Jesus himself (Rev 22.20b) and in the petition to the assembly, which cries out for his coming (Rev 22.17ab, 20c).

---

[72] Vanni, 'Liturgical Dialogue', 360.

[73] Along with the first-person singular pronominal lexeme, which I have already alluded to, there also appears the third-person αὐτός (Rev 22.18[2], 19). Demonstratives are reduced to forms of οὗτος, both neuter (Rev 22.18[2], 19, 20) and feminine in gender (Rev 22.19).

On the formal level, we find various types of repetition, with structures repeated at the beginning and end of each pericope in inverse fashion. While Rev 1.4–8 begins with an epistolary greeting, χάρις ὑμῖν καὶ εἰρήνη, 'grace and peace to you', Rev 22.21 uses a similar form in closing: Ἡ χάρις τοῦ κυρίου Ἰησοῦ μετὰ πάντων, 'the grace of the Lord Jesus be with all'. And while Rev 1.4–8 ends with a *verbum dicendi* to introduce a segment of direct speech, λέγει κύριος ὁ θεός, 'the Lord God says' (Rev 1.8b), Rev 22.17 opens with one: τὸ πνεῦμα καὶ ἡ νύμφη λέγουσιν, 'the Spirit and the bride say'. In both pericopes, a prayer is offered in response (Rev 1.5d–6, 7e; 22.17ab, 20c).

Other lexemes are also repeated: ἀμήν, 'amen' (Rev 1.6b, 7e; 22.20c); κύριος, 'Lord' (Rev 1.8; 22.20, 21); θεός, 'God' (Rev 1.8; 22.18c, 19b); Jesus is referred to as ὁ μάρτυς, 'the witness' (Rev 1.5) and, later, as ὁ μαρτυρῶν, 'the one who testifies to these things' (Rev 22.20a). All of these repetitions serve to reinforce the connection between Rev 1.4–8 and Rev 22.17–21.

It may be concluded that Rev 22.17–21, given the context of an immediate present as transmitted by dialogue – a feature which reinforces its mimesis even more – and given its similarity to Rev 1.4–8, also constitutes, as argued by both Ugo Vanni and Michael J. A. Kavanagh,[74] a liturgical dialogue. Rev 1.4–8 serves to introduce the intervening narrative (Rev 1.9–22.16), and Rev 22.17–21 to conclude it.

1.1.5   Conclusion: Homogeneity in Diversity and What it Means

By this point, the reader is aware that the textual heterogeneity observable in the book of Revelation is neither accidental nor indicative of the author's lack of skill. It is truer to say that this diversity of textual units corresponds to the different demands that the author imposes on them. The initial prologue (Rev 1.3) allows him to offer essential guidelines that make clear to the listener/reader the nature of the work he is reading and its basic characteristics. The liturgical dialogues that open and close the work, meanwhile, manifest the author's desire that it be read aloud in an assembly. Accordingly, he organizes his text by obliging, to some extent, the listener/reader to experience it as a series of alternating voices: the voice of the lector, and those of the audience who respond. This explains the particularity of the dialogues: the *praescriptio*, Ἰωάννης ταῖς ἑπτὰ ἐκκλησίαις (Rev 1.4), and the formulaic closing farewell, Ἡ χάρις

---

[74] Vanni, 'Liturgical Dialogue', 356–64; Kavanagh, *Apocalypse 22.6–21*, pp. 132–3.

τοῦ κυρίου Ἰησοῦ μετὰ πάντων (Rev 22.21), both of which are specific to the New Testament epistolary genre and are here used to frame the dialogues. These devices ensured that the work would be read in assembly by the early Christian communities. At the same time, they indicate the broad range of its addressees: ταῖς ἑπτὰ ἐκκλησίαις, 'the seven churches' that we hear of at the beginning, expand by the end to include πάντες, 'all'. Finally, the narrative itself (Rev 1.9–22.5) presents the revelation that John saw and heard, while the brief epilogue (Rev 22.6–16) testifies to its veracity.

1.2   Rev 1.9–22.5: A Unique Narrative

While the nucleus of the book of Revelation (Rev 1.9–22.5) takes the literary form of a narrative, what is less obvious is the type of narrative that structures the work, as this work does present some peculiarities. As well as being a text conceived to be transmitted and received in public, it features an unconventional treatment of time and space as well as a recurrent use of description and dialogue.

The fact that the book of Revelation was written to be read publicly, and that the author makes this so clear in the prologue (Rev 1.3), seems crucial to the way in which the work is structured. Among the various types of narrative, one is characterized precisely by the degree of attention given to it by the reader; indeed, this is such a determining factor in narratives of this type that their effectiveness depends largely on the reader's attention being captured and maintained from the opening lines to the very end. The recipient of the text must be held in constant suspense, and not given any possibility of respite.[75] Such narratives, then, 'must be read all in one sitting, as any extended pause would spoil the emotional and aesthetic effect of the narration'.[76] This is clearly the case for the book of Revelation. The attention of the listener/reader is appealed to by the opening makarism (Rev 1.3), before the story proper even begins, and then maintained thanks to the initial liturgical dialogue, which, through their being called upon to respond to the lector, involves the listeners/readers directly in the story (Rev 1.4–8). By presenting the

[75] This was part of the advice given by the great Russian writer Anton Chekhov to Ivan Schcheglov in a letter dated January 22, 1888; see A. Chekhov, 'Letters on the Short Story', quoted by J. M. Pozuelo Yvancos, 'Escritores y teóricos: La estabilidad del cuento', in C. Becerra, *et al.* (eds.), *Asedio ó conto* (Vigo: Universidad de Vigo, 1999), p. 41.

[76] M. Baquero Goyanes, *Qué es la novela: Qué es el cuento* (Murcia: Universidad de Murcia, 1988), p. 150.

revelation gradually, the narrator manages to create a great feeling of suspense. Indeed, even once the narrative has begun, the narrator takes his time in getting to the revelation itself; thus, after John is introduced (Rev 1.9), he begins a step-by-step account of what happened to him (Rev 1.10ff.) from which it is difficult for the listener/reader to be distracted. The narrative type I am referring to here is that of the short story, in which the author tells a story[77] by choosing images that are meaningful enough to act upon the reader as 'a sort of aperture', and by projecting his own intelligence and sensibility toward something that transcends mere literary anecdote.[78]

Despite its chronological distance from the modern genre, something similar is at work in the book of Revelation. Upon hearing the account, the listener/reader is incited to search for its meaning, and this search extends beyond the anecdotal. The listener/reader contemplates the plot not for its own sake, but for what it may signify and for the repercussions it may have on their own life. This is, in effect, the aim of apocalyptic literature: to interpret the present in the light of a supernatural world and to influence its listeners by calling on divine authority.[79]

Among the various definitions of the short story form, that of the writer and essayist Anderson Imbert seems to me especially significant:

> The story would come to be a brief narrative in prose that, however much it would be based on a real event, would always reveal the imagination of an individual narrator. The action – whose agents might be men, personified animals or animate things – consists of a series of interwoven events in a plot where tensions and distensions, graduated to maintain the mood of the reader in suspense, ends by resolving itself in an aesthetically satisfying denouement.[80]

Rev 1.9–22.5 is in fact presented as a brief narration in prose. The 'action' is performed by various 'agents', which include: men, such as John, the 24 elders (Rev 4.10–11), or the kings of the earth (Rev 6.15); animate objects, for example, the altar that speaks (Rev 16.7); personified

---

[77] The popular folk tale, by contrast, is characterized by its anonymity and oral transmission; see Baquero Goyanes, *Qué es el cuento*, p. 107; E. Serra, *Tipología del cuento* (Madrid: Cupsa, 1978), p. 21.

[78] J. Cortázar, 'Algunos aspectos del cuento', *Casa de las Américas* pp. 15–16 (1963), quoted by Baquero Goyanes, *Qué es el cuento*, p. 135.

[79] A. Yarbro Collins, 'Early Christian Apocalypticism', *Semeia* 36 (1986), 7.

[80] E. Anderson Imbert, *Teoría y técnica del cuento* (Barcelona: Ariel, 1992), p. 40.

animals, the cast of which is rich and varied: the Lamb (Rev 5.6–7), who picks up a book and opens it (Rev 6.1), becomes angry (Rev 6.16–17), herds his chosen (Rev 7.17), triumphs in the battles waged between the kings and the beast (Rev 17.14), and even marries, with a traditional wedding banquet to celebrate (Rev 19.9; 21.9); the beast, who has the ability to speak and to seduce men (Rev 13.14), as well as to make war (Rev 19.19); and the locusts, which are organized into an army to punish men (Rev 9.7–11).

As for what can be termed the 'plot', its basic structure is constituted of a series of events in which moments of tension and drama are interspersed with those of peace and authentic jubilation for the listener/reader. Hence, after the opening of the first six seals and the appearance of the three horsemen who scourge the earth with war, famine, and plague (Rev 6.1–8), the lament of the immolated souls is heard (Rev 6.9–11), followed by a devastating earthquake (Rev 6.12–17). John then witnesses a multitude of souls praising God (Rev 7.9–13), which provides welcome solace to the listener/reader.

The 'satisfying denouement' may be found in the fact that the book of Revelation has, in effect, a happy ending. This is the vision of the New Jerusalem and the bride of the Lamb, at a time when ὁ θάνατος οὐκ ἔσται ἔτι οὔτε πένθος οὔτε κραυγὴ οὔτε πόνος οὐκ ἔσται ἔτι, 'death will no longer exist, nor weeping, nor lamentation, nor even pain' (Rev 21.4).

Alongside these aspects, the fact that the short story is aimed at a specific recipient gives it some privileges that are denied to other narrative forms. Mariano Baquero Goyanes expresses it like this:

> It is, then, a genre that falls in between poetry and the novel, having a semi-poetic, semi-novelistic dimension that can only be expressed through the medium of the short story. ... It departs from the normal narrative style ... to seek the effects of verse, without actually resorting to it.[81]

This is why time and space both have a relative value in the short story form, why adjectives may be used with specific connotations, and why description and dialogue may either be absent or, on the other hand, play a crucial role in such a story. I will, therefore, now turn my attention to a spatial/temporal analysis of the short story and the use of adjectival lexemes.

---

[81] Baquero Goyanes, *Qué es el cuento*, pp. 139, 133.

The short story grants the narrator a great amount of freedom and flexibility in establishing the place and the exact space in which the story unfolds. In fact, once these space/time coordinates have been established, the narrator may then widen or reduce this space, to the point of dispensing with its corresponding chronological development altogether,[82] while space itself may cease to be a key element in the narration.[83] These features can be observed quite clearly in the book of Revelation.

At the very beginning of the narrative (Rev 1.9–22.5), the first thing the narrator does, besides introducing himself, is to situate the religious experience he has had in a specific place: ἐγενόμην ἐν τῇ νήσῳ τῇ καλουμένῃ Πάτμῳ, 'I was on the island called Patmos' (Rev 1.9d). Patmos, mentioned in antiquity by authors such as Thucydides and Pliny,[84] is a small island of the Sporades archipelago, in the eastern Aegean, close to Miletus and the coast of Asia Minor. As shown by the inscriptions and the Greek ruins found there,[85] it was not uninhabited, as there is evidence of a second-century AD gymnasium and a flourishing cult of Artemis.[86] This indicates that John has set his experience in a place that is not imaginary, but real, geographically specific, and apparently civilized.

The narrator's method of presenting the place where the story takes place is significant, as he does not say, 'I was on Patmos', but rather 'I was on the island called Patmos'. That is to say, before giving the name, he specifies the place as ἐν τῇ νήσῳ, 'on the island'. Although the place was known, it is as if the island were not familiar to his interlocutors, and the narrator therefore felt obliged to explain that it is in fact an island.[87] It is also possible that the author is trying to establish an opposition between the island and the seven churches of Asia,[88] to highlight the isolation and solitude of the seer in contrast to the churches, which were

---

[82] *Ibid.*, p. 149.

[83] Serra, *Tipología del cuento*, p. 21.

[84] Th. 3.33: μέχρι μὲν Πάτμου τῆς νήσου ἐπεδίωξεν . . .; Plin. *NH* 4.23.69.

[85] S. T. Carroll, 'Patmos', *ABD* 5, 178–9.

[86] H. D. Saffrey, 'Relire l'Apocalypse à Patmos', *RB* 82 (1975), 397–8, 410; Aune, *Revelation 1*, p. 77.

[87] At least in New Testament texts, when reference is made to places that are known to readers, the tendency is not to specify whether these are cities, islands, or villages. Examples include: Matt 2.1; 3.5; 4.12; Mark 1.9; Luke 7.1; John 2.12; Heb 7.43.

[88] E. S. Malbon, 'Narrative Criticism: How Does the Story Mean?', in J. C. Anderson and S. D. Moore (eds.), *Mark and Method: New Approaches in Biblical Studies* (Minneapolis, MN: Fortress, 1992), p. 31.

located in the same geographical area and were well connected with each other.[89]

Immediately after this, however, the seven churches become no longer an indeterminate narratee but rather the churches of seven specific cities: Ephesus, Smyrna, Pergamum, Thyatira, Sardis, Philadelphia, and Laodicea (Rev 1.11). These cities, far from imaginary, were real places in western Asia Minor and, at the time when the book of Revelation was written, important economic centres.[90]

In any case, the spatial framework changes completely after the account of the first vision. The narrator abandons the precision that he has maintained up to this point and situates what he sees and hears in indefinite spaces, such as heaven (Rev 4–5; 12.1, 7), the desert from which he contemplates Babylon (Rev 17.3), the high mountain from which he views the New Jerusalem (Rev 21.10), and so on. Even so, at many points in the narrative the listener/reader is not sure where John is, or even where the events he describes are happening. The opening of seals (Rev 6.1–17), for example, seems to take place in heaven, where John sees the Lamb (Rev 5.6–8); however, after the sixth seal is opened, there is an earthquake that devastates the earth, causing the great and powerful to cry out (Rev 6.12–17), and the listener/reader does not know whether or not John has perhaps left heaven to witness first-hand what is taking place on earth.

In other words, the narrator uses spatial coordinates with great flexibility. He first frames his story in a real space, Patmos, which allows him to give it credibility and, at the same time, to arouse an aesthetic emotion in the listener/reader of his time in response to his mentioning the seven churches and the seven cities, which would have undoubtedly been familiar.[91] Then, beginning with the vision of God in his glory (Rev 4), he reduces spatial indicators to a minimum, and uses them very freely. As a result, throughout the narrative there is an oscillation in the spatial context and, as content becomes more important, location becomes less and less relevant; thus, the references made to heaven, the desert, and the mountain are sufficient for the purpose of visualizing the narrative

---

[89] W. M. Ramsay, *The Letters to the Seven Churches*, rev. edn (Peabody, MA: Hendrickson, 1994), pp. 132, 136–41; C. J. Hemer, *The Letters to the Seven Churches of Asia in Their Local Setting* (Sheffield: JSOT Sheffield, 1986), p. 15.

[90] Ramsay, *Letters*, pp. 151–71, 182–94, 205–12, 231–9, 259–70, 286–93, 303–12.

[91] The aesthetic emotion arises when the experience of the character concurs with that of the reader; see Anderson Imbert, *Teoría y técnica del cuento*, p. 233.

action.[92] This is precisely what happens in a short story, where both space and time must be compressed.[93]

The temporal framework of a story is what may be called 'story time', which may be expressed in terms of chronological units such as hour, day, or year,[94] or through a 'type of time': at night, in the winter, on a Saturday.[95] In the short story, in any case, these units are always fictitious, as the real becomes unreal within the form itself.[96]

In Rev 1.9–22.5, the narrator provides us with a time frame by using an expression that is unique in the NT: ἐν τῇ κυριακῇ ἡμέρᾳ, 'on the Lord's day' (Rev 1.10).[97] This is a paralexeme that was used in early Christian literature[98] to refer to Sunday.[99] John situates his experience in a specific temporal unit, or 'type of time', i.e., on a Sunday. After this, as the account of what John heard and saw gradually unfolds, specific time indicators disappear from the narrative. Not only this, but beginning with ἐγενόμην ἐν πνεύματι ἐν τῇ κυριακῇ ἡμέρᾳ (Rev 1.10), a gradual recounting of all that was heard takes place, without the mediation of any specific time indicator other than μετὰ ταῦτα. Naturally, the listener/ reader may find this bewildering; however, if we consider the similarity of Rev 1.9–22.5 to a short story, this confusion subsides. In the

---

[92] These types of setting have been called 'scenes properly speaking', as few elements are required in order to visualize the action that is taking place in them; *ibid.*, p. 234.

[93] J. Cortázar, 'Algunos aspectos del cuento', cited by Baquero Goyanes, *Qué es el cuento*, p. 136.

[94] D. Villanueva, 'Glosario de narratología', in *Comentario de textos narrativos: La novela* (Gijón: Ediciones Júcar, 1989), pp. 181–201. Available at: https://glosarios.servidor -alicante.com/narratologia/tiempo-de-la-historia [Consulted: 03/09/2019], s.v. *tiempo de la historia*.

[95] Marguerat and Bourquin, *Per leggere*, p. 85.

[96] Anderson Imbert, *Teoría y técnica del cuento*, p. 186.

[97] U. Vanni, *L'Apocalisse: Ermeneutica, esegesi e teologia* (Bologna: Dehoniane, 1988), p. 87.

[98] Examples are found in: *Didache* 14.1; *Strom.* 5.14.106.2

[99] The expression ἡ κυριακὴ ἡμέρα was a locution employed in bureaucratic writing to refer to the emperor, in which contexts κυριακὴ may be translated as 'imperial'. It was later adopted by Christians to refer to the day on which Christian assemblies were held and the resurrection of Jesus commemorated: Sunday; see A. Deissmann, 'Lord's Day', in T. K. Cheyne and J. S. Black, *Encyclopedia Biblica: A Dictionary of the Bible. A Critical Dictionary of the Literary, Political and Religious History, the Archaeology, Geography and Natural History of the Bible*, vol. 3 (London: Macmillan & Co., 1902), cols. 2813–16. Today, this interpretation is the *communis opinio* among exegetes: E. B. Allo, *L'Apocalypse* (Paris: Lecoffre, 1933), p. 41; W. Stott, 'A Note on the Word KYPIAKH in Rev 1:10', *NTS* 12 (1965–6), 70–5; Vanni, *Apocalisse*, p. 90–7; Boring, *Revelation*, p. 82; Harrington, *Revelation*, p. 52; Aune, *Revelation 1*, p. 84; Beale, *Revelation*, p. 203.

etymology of 'account'[100] we find a meaning that enables us to understand the author's intention in the book of Revelation: i.e., that a short story is in effect an enumerated account of the facts.[101] This is precisely what the listener/reader finds in Rev 1.9–22.5: an account of John's visions and oral revelations.

Another characteristic of the short story is that it 'typically jars the sensibility of the reader in an abrupt manner'.[102] Qualifying adjectives help to achieve this effect, not only because they make the narrative more precise – by nuancing, dramatizing, or amplifying – but because they provide the listener/reader with valuable information about the characters, illustrating their moral disposition, i.e., their goodness – and, consequently, beauty – or their wickedness and corresponding ugliness.[103] This function of the adjective aids the listener/reader's reception of the text, as, given its oral character, on many occasions it allows them to recapture the thread of the plot when their attention has been distracted. The adjectives thus serve as a useful tool for capturing the reader's attention.

Although qualifying adjectives are not used in abundance in Rev 1.9–22.5, they do help to create a sort of climax. In the consideration of their semantic content that follows, they are classified into three groups: colours; qualities or defects; and the materials from which things are made.

1.2.1   Colours

The adjectival lexemes that denote colour are: λευκός, 'white' (Rev 1.14 [2]; 2.17; 3.4, 5, 18; 4.4; 6.2, 11; 7.9, 13; 14.14; 19.11, 14[2]; 20.11); κόκκινος, 'scarlet' (Rev 17.3, 4; 18.12, 16); πορφυροῦς, 'purple' (Rev 17.4; 18.16); πύρινος, 'fiery red' (Rev 9.17); πυρρός, 'bright red' (Rev 6.4; 12.3); χλωρός, 'pale greenish grey' (Rev 6.8; 8.7; 9.4); μέλας, 'black' (Rev 6.5, 12); ὑακίνθινος, 'sapphire blue' (Rev 9.17); θειώδης,

---

[100] Translator's Note: In the original Spanish text, the author is here linking the etymology of *cuento* ('story') with the verb *contar* ('to tell a story', but also 'to count'). To approximate this in English, I have used the noun 'account', which has a similar etymological link to the act of enumerating.

[101] Baquero Goyanes, *Qué es el cuento*, p. 99.

[102] *Ibid.*, p. 134; A. García Berrio and T. Hernández Fernández, *Crítica literaria: Iniciación al estudio de la literatura* (Madrid: Cátedra, 2004), p. 322.

[103] J. R. R. Tolkien, 'On Fairy-Stories', in C. Tolkien (ed.), *The Monsters and the Critics and Other Essays* (London – Boston – Sydney: Allen & Unwin, 1983), p. 151.

'sulphurous yellow' (Rev 9.17). This varied range of colours helps the listener/reader to visualize what is being narrated, at the same time that each transmits the sensations and emotions connected with it.

As well as the colour white, λευκός denotes radiance,[104] and in those passages where white is mentioned it also connotes some type of brightness or splendour. Indeed, when λευκός appears for the first time, to describe the hair of one who is 'like a son of man' (Rev 1.14[2]), the whole context exudes a certain radiance, from Christ's golden girdle (Rev 1.13) to his flaming eyes (Rev 1.14). This same brightness is later seen to emanate from the garments of the elders (Rev 4.4), from the heavenly armies (Rev 19.14), and from the throne of God (Rev 20.11).

Jesus is the first to be associated with white and, curiously, this will be the colour of everything closely related to him: of the small stone received by the church of Pergamum (Rev 2.17); of the garments of those who remain faithful to Christ (Rev 3.4, 5, 18; 6.11; 7.9, 13; 19.14),[105] and of the elders (Rev 4.4); of the conquering horse and those who follow the heavenly armies (Rev 19.14); of the cloud on which the son of man appears (Rev 14.14); and of the throne of God (Rev 20.11). Thus, λευκός, apart from its typical connotations, has a special significance in Rev 1.9–22.5, which is to indicate to the listener/reader those characters that belong to the context of good, i.e., the context of heaven. From here on, I will use the phrase 'the heavenly context' to refer to that which corresponds to God, to the Lamb, and to those figures that have a positive relation to God.

The colour red is presented in four different shades: πυρρός, 'bright red';[106] πύρινος, 'fiery red';[107] κόκκινος, 'scarlet'; and πορφυροῦς, 'purple'. For each of these, an intense reddish coloration infuses the contexts in which it appears, and serves an appellative function for the listener/reader. Apart from this, the colour red, with its fleshly hues, seems to lack any special connotation, but, as various shades of it appear again and again, and are associated with creatures that cause harm, the

---

[104] *GI*, 1181, s.v. λευκός; *BDAG*, 4555, s.v. λευκός; THAYER, 3201, s.v. λευκός.

[105] Rev 3.4 is included here, as ἱματίοις is understood implicitly.

[106] LOUW and NIDA, 79,31, s.v. πυρρός: 'Probably with a tinge of yellow or orange'; D. Romero González, *El adjetivo en el Nuevo Testamento: Clasificación semántica. Tesis Doctoral* (Córdoba: Universidad de Córdoba, 2007), p. 119. Available at: https://helvia .uco.es/xmlui/handle/10396/3535 [Consulted: 03/09/2019].

[107] I here followed the second meaning proposed by LOUW and NIDA, 79,33, s.v. πύρινος, referring precisely to Rev 9.17. Along the same lines, see *BDAG*, 6441, s.v. πύρινος.

listener/reader perceives that the figures presented in this colour are to be feared. They belong to what we might call 'the evil context', comprising those who oppose God and the Lamb. Thus, the second horse that bursts onto the scene upon the opening of the second seal, bringing war, is described as πυρρός, 'bright red' (Rev 6.4), as is the dragon that attacks the woman in Rev 12.3. It is logical, then, that when the armour of the horses of the last plague (Rev 9.17) is described as πύρινος, 'fiery red', the listener/reader experiences a feeling of terror, just as when he or she hears that the colour of the beast is κόκκινος, 'scarlet' (Rev 17.3). This colour also contributes to the suspicion that arises when the listener/reader hears the description of the prostitute's garments (Rev 17.4; 18.12, 16).

Something similar occurs with the colour black. The adjectival lexeme μέλας, 'black', describes the colour of the horse of the third seal, by which famine is sent to plague the human race (Rev 6.5). Thus, when the sun turns black (Rev 6.12), an unusual occurrence in itself, the listener/reader readies themselves to hear of an impending catastrophe.

As for χλωρός, 'pale greenish grey', this is the colour of the fourth horse, which immediately receives the name of Θάνατος, 'Death' (Rev 6.8). For this reason, the listener/reader understands that the colour of this horse, χλωρός, cannot be a 'living' green of the type found in trees and plants (Rev 8.7; 9.4), but one signifying that which is dead. Indeed, χλωρός refers to the greenish skin tone of someone who is ill; and so, the colour of the fourth horse is here described as 'pale greenish grey',[108] a use of the word that can also be found in Homer, Hippocrates, and Thucydides.[109]

Lastly, with regard to ὑακίνθινος, 'sapphire blue', and θειώδης, 'sulphurous yellow', both appear in the same context as πύρινος, 'fiery red'; that is, to describe the breastplates of the monstrous horses of the final plague (Rev 9.17). In this case, the varied colour spectrum of these horses heightens the terrifying aspect that John portrays them as having.

1.2.2 Qualities and Defects

The qualities and defects mentioned are rendered with great expressiveness, as they provide shading or highlighting to one or more characteristics of the subjects they describe. These commonly appear as epithets and constitute the

[108] LOUW and NIDA, 79,34.35, s.v. χλωρός; *BDAG*, 7938.2, s.v. χλωρός. Romero González, *El adjetivo*, p. 118.

[109] THAYER, 5718.2, s.v. χλωρός; *BDAG*, 7938.2, s.v. χλωρός; *GI*, 2235, s.v. χλωρός.

most numerous group of adjectives used, with twenty-five lexemes: ἅγιος, 'holy'; αἰώνιος, 'eternal'; ἄκρατος, 'pure'; ἀληθινός, 'true'; ἄμωμος, 'blameless'; ἄξιος, 'worthy'; γλυκύς, 'sweet'; διαυγής, 'transparent'; δίκαιος, 'just'; δίστομος, 'double-edged'; ἐκλεκτός, 'chosen'; ἔσχατος, 'last'; ἰσχυρός, 'strong, powerful, vigorous'; θαυμαστός, 'admirable'; καινός, 'new'; κυριακός, 'of the Lord'; λαμπρός, 'clear'; μόνος, 'only'; πιστός, 'faithful'; πρῶτος, 'first'; ὅλος, 'whole'; ὀξύς, 'sharp'; ὅσιος, 'devout'; τίμιος, 'precious'; ὑψηλός, 'high'.

Most of these epithets are applied to God or Jesus, or to characters and realities close to them. This is the case for: ἅγιος, 'holy'; ἀληθινός, 'true'; δίκαιος, 'just'; καινός, 'new'; and πιστός, 'faithful'. Consequently, when these epithets are applied to characters other than God or Jesus, they enable the listener/reader quickly to place them within the heavenly context. The adjectival lexeme ἅγιος, for example, is a quality of God. It is, in fact, used frequently in the *Septuagint* as a translation of קָדוֹשׁ, a specific attribute of God.[110] In the book of Revelation, it is applied first to God – being used three consecutive times in praise of the four living beings (Rev 4.8) – and then, later, to the angels (Rev 14.10), to the followers of God (Rev 20.6), and above all to the New Jerusalem (Rev 11.2; 21.2, 10); the narrator thus gives to this adjective a significant expressive value, as it shows how everything close to God participates in a quality that belongs to him, i.e., holiness.

The same can be said of the adjectives ἀληθινός, 'true', and πιστός, 'faithful'. The first denotes an adaptation to a particular reality,[111] i.e., that which is genuine.[112] As an attribute of God, it is closely related to the Hebrew term אֱמֶת (Exod 34.6; 2 Chron 15.3).[113] Hence, it is used to describe God (Rev 6.10), his judgments and designs (Rev 15.3; 16.7; 19.2, 9), and Jesus (Rev 3.14; 19.11). That it is also applied to the words of the book of Revelation (Rev 21.5; 22.6) lends them power in a singularly expressive way, as it effectively places the book on the same level as the judgments of God. With the use of the epithet ἀληθινός, what is being affirmed is that the words of the book of Revelation are indeed the authentic words of God.

---

[110] O. Procksch, 'ἅγιος, ἁγιάζω, ἁγιασμός, ἁγιότης, ἁγιωσύνη. E. ἅγιος in the NT. The Holiness of God', *TDNT 1*, 88–97, 100–15.
[111] Romero González, *El adjetivo*, p. 381.
[112] Beckwith, *Apocalypse*, p. 479.
[113] R. Bultmann, 'ἀλήθεια, ἀληθής, ἀληθινός, ἀληθεύω', *TDNT 1*, p. 238–51.

Πιστός, 'faithful',[114] is an epithet that is applied to Jesus. It is used even before the narrative proper has begun, when the chorus in the opening liturgical dialogue is heard using it as one of the titles of Jesus (Rev 1.5). In the narrative itself, πιστός is applied not only to Jesus, but also to those who are faithful, such as Antipas, the church of Smyrna, and those who fight alongside the Lamb (Rev 2.10, 13; 17.14), as well as to the words of God (Rev 21.5), and the book of Revelation itself (Rev 22.6). That is to say, the expressiveness of this epithet, once it has been applied to Jesus and, later, to other subjects of attribution, increases more and more, acquiring a marked relevance for the listener/reader, and, as it is a title that is applied to Jesus, such a connection is difficult to overlook. What is more, adjectival lexemes like this usually appear within a double or even triple set of adjectives,[115] so that their power is maximized. This explains expressions such as: πιστὸς καὶ ἀληθινός, 'faithful and true', applied to Jesus (Rev 3.14; 19.11); πιστοὶ καὶ ἀληθινοί, 'faithful and true', used to describe the words of God and the book of Revelation (Rev 21.5; 22.6); ἅγιος καὶ ἀληθινός, 'holy and true', to refer to God (Rev 6.10); and ἀληθιναὶ καὶ δίκαιαι, 'true and just', applied to the judgments and designs of God (Rev 15.3; 16.7; 19.2).

Not all of these qualities are applied to figures belonging to the heavenly context, however; there are some whose subject of attribution may belong to either context – heavenly or evil. For example, the adjectival lexeme ἰσχυρός, 'strong, mighty', is presented in the narrative as being an attribute of God (Rev 18.8), of the angels (Rev 5.2; 10.1; 18.21), of an angel's voice (Rev 18.2), and of thunder (Rev 19.6). But it is also applied to Babylon (Rev 18.10), and applied in the same context in which ἰσχυρός has God and the angels as subjects of attribution. It is interesting here to determine which speakers actually use this adjective. First, it is the narrator, John, who employs ἰσχυρός to describe both the angels[116] and the voices; later, the kings of the earth refer to Babylon as ἡ πόλις ἡ ἰσχυρά when lamenting its destruction (Rev 18.10); and, finally, a voice from heaven designates God as ἰσχυρός. This is the argument that is used to justify the fall of Babylon: ὅτι ἰσχυρὸς κύριος ὁ θεὸς,

---

[114] THAYER, 4244.1, s.v. πιστός.

[115] K. Spang, *Persuasión: Fundamentos de retórica* (Pamplona: EUNSA, 2005), p. 238.

[116] In any case, this adjectival lexeme, as it is applied to the angels, refers to a quality that is not spiritual, but rather physical – vigour – as emanates from its context. Rev 18.21 is indeed revealing in this sense, as it recounts that John saw an ἰσχυρός angel throw a stone the size of a millstone. The adjectival lexeme, in this case, might therefore be best translated as 'vigorous'.

'because mighty is the Lord God' (Rev 18.8). The application of ἰσχυρός to Babylon has an implicitly expressive value: the city is seen by the kings of the earth as possessing an attribute proper to God, hence its imminent destruction.

I have up to now been referring to the qualities of persons, but other qualities must also be mentioned, and these are those whose subjects of attribution are other entities. These include ὅλος, 'whole, complete, entire', and ὀξύς, 'sharp'. Ὅλος, 'whole, complete, entire', is particularly powerful as a means of suggesting the vast scale of disasters. Its subjects of attribution are ἡ σελήνη, 'the moon', ἡ γῆ, 'the earth', and ἡ οἰκουμένη, 'the inhabited earth'.[117] Thus, ὅλος is applied to the moon when John tells how, during the earthquake, it takes on the aspect of blood (Rev 6.12). He also applies it to ἡ γῆ to express the great admiration that is inspired by the beast (Rev 13.3). Finally, it is applied to ἡ οἰκουμένη to explain the magnitude of the test that men will suffer (Rev 3.10), the damage that will be wrought by the devil (Rev 12.9), and the preparations for the battle against God (Rev 16.14). The epithet ὅλος, then, expresses the enormity of the catastrophe.

Finally, ὀξύς, 'sharp', is the epithet applied both to ῥομφαία, 'sword' (Rev 1.16; 2.12; 19.15), and to δρέπανον, 'sickle' (Rev 14.14, 17, 18[2]). The use of ὀξύς intensifies the action of these items, in addition to heightening the drama of their context. At the same time, the sword is usually given a double attribution: ῥομφαία δίστομος ὀξεῖα, 'sharp, double-edged sword' (Rev 1.16; 2.12), which, by *amplificatio*, further emphasizes this effect.

As for defects, with the exception of the message addressed by Christ to the church of Laodicea, in which he employs a wide range of adjectives to censure that particular church, the adjectives used to this effect are in fact few. A common feature of those that do appear is that their subjects of attribution belong not to the heavenly but to the evil context; thus, when they are used, the listener/reader is being warned of something that is going to happen. Three such adjectives are antonyms of their respective qualities: ἀκάθαρτος, 'unclean, impure', is the opposite of καθαρός, 'clean, pure'; ἀρχαῖος, 'ancient, old', of καινός, 'new'; and ψευδής, 'untruthful', of πιστός, 'faithful'. The expressive value of each is heightened by the antithesis it creates.

The first of these adjectival lexemes, ἀκάθαρτος, 'unclean, impure', denotes the absence of purity or cleanliness. Those deemed ἀκάθαρτοι are those who oppose the kingdom of Christ, and include spirits (Rev 16.13;

---

[117] THAYER, 3725, s.v. οἰκουμένη.

18.2), birds, and wild beasts (Rev 18.2[2]). The epithet thus creates a reaction of revulsion in the listener/reader in regard to this aspect of its subjects of attribution. Ἀρχαῖος, 'ancient, old', is applied invariably to the serpent (Rev 12.9; 20.2), intensifying the duration of its action and increasing its dramatic impact. Lastly, ψευδής, 'untruthful, false', is used in Jesus' message to Ephesus to designate those he does not consider to be true apostles (Rev 2.2), as opposed to those who are πιστοί, 'faithful' (Rev 2.10). Ψευδής, 'untruthful', acquires a pejorative value, especially in contrast to πιστός, 'faithful', which occurs frequently in the narrative.

The lexemes κακός, 'harmful', and πονηρός, 'painful', are epithets used to describe the noun ἕλκος, 'sore', as produced by the first of the plagues (Rev 16.2). This use of a pair of adjectives reinforces the harmful character of ἕλκος, creating for the listener/reader both a dramatic climax and a feeling of dread.

The adjectival lexemes used by Jesus to reproach the church of Laodicea are as follows: ἐλεεινός, 'pitiful' (Rev 3.17); γυμνός, 'naked' (Rev 3.17); ζεστός, 'hot' (Rev 3.15, 16); πτωχός, 'poor' (Rev 3.17); ταλαίπωρος, 'wretched' (Rev 3.17); τυφλός, 'blind' (Rev 3.17); ψυχρός, 'cold' (Rev 3.15[2], 16); and χλιαρός, 'lukewarm' (Rev 3.16). Not all of these lexemes have a negative connotation in themselves, but they acquire this from the contexts in which they appear. This is the case for ζεστός and ψυχρός (Rev 3.15[2], 16), which become defects through the lack of these qualities: οὔτε ζεστός, 'not hot'; οὔτε ψυχρός, 'not cold'. This does not, however, reduce the expressive value of these adjectival lexemes. The insistent repetition of οὔτε ψυχρός and οὔτε ζεστός, until Jesus finally uses χλιαρός, 'lukewarm', is undoubtedly jarring to the sensibilities of the listener/reader. This same effect is then intensified by the use of antithesis and enumeration. An antithesis is established between what the church thinks of itself, believing that it is πλούσιος, 'rich', while Jesus describes it by its antonym: πτωχός, 'poor'. This censure becomes more and more dramatic as, one by one, the adjectives are enunciated, creating an effect of *amplificatio*: ὅτι σὺ εἶ ὁ ταλαίπωρος καὶ ἐλεεινὸς καὶ πτωχὸς καὶ τυφλὸς καὶ γυμνός, 'because you are wretched, and pitiful, and poor, and blind, and naked'. The detailed enumeration of these different defects serves to intensify the negative connotation of each one and so influences the listener/reader's mood.

1.2.3 Materials from Which Things are Made

Finally, the book of Revelation presents a wide range of adjectives that refer to the materials that things are made of. These are always spoken by the narrator. Their function is informative, allowing the listener/reader to visualize what John sees in a way that is realistic in a tactile sense, as the materials described are familiar ones and form part of their daily reality (wood, stone, iron), or are appreciated for their quality (gold, linen, emerald).

Fourteen adjectival lexemes are used to refer to such materials: χρυσοῦς, 'golden' (Rev 1.12, 13, 20; 2.1; 4.4; 5.8; 8.3[2]; 9.13, 20; 14.14; 15.6, 7; 17.4; 21.15); βύσσινος, 'linen' (Rev 18.12, 16; 19.8, 14); ὑάλινος, 'of glass' (Rev 4.6; 15.2[2]); σμαράγδινος, 'consisting of emerald' (Rev 4.3); ἀργυροῦς, 'of silver, made of silver'; λίθινος, 'stone, made of stone'; ξύλινος, 'wooden'; χαλκοῦς, 'consisting of bronze' (Rev 9.20); ἐλεφάντινος, 'of ivory' (Rev 18.12); θύϊνος, 'made of citron-wood' (Rev 18.12);[118] μύλινος, 'made of millstone' (Rev 18.21); τρίχινος, 'made of hair' (Rev 6.12); σιδηροῦς, 'made of iron' (Rev 2.27; 9.9; 12.5; 19.15); κεραμικός, 'made of clay, earthen' (Rev 2.27). I will examine the most representative of these here.

Of this group, the adjectival lexeme that is used most often is χρυσοῦς 'golden'. In the OT, gold was associated with cult worship, but was also used for jewellery and, in times of monarchy, for crowns, thrones, and cups.[119] In the book of Revelation, the adjective χρυσοῦς is used to describe cult objects, such as the cups used to hold incense (Rev 5.8) or the ones received by the angels (Rev 15.7), as well as the altar (Rev 8.3; 9.13), the censer (Rev 8.3), and the idols (Rev 9.20). Also χρυσοῦς are the crowns of Jesus (Rev 14.14) and of the elders (Rev 4.4), and some of the clothing and objects belonging to Jesus (Rev 1.12, 13, 20; 2.1), the angels (Rev 15.6; 21.15), and the great whore (Rev 17.4).

As for βύσσινος, it is known that linen was a fabric prized for its quality. It was used to make priestly ornaments and cult objects, but in other contexts as well; it was an element of furniture decoration, appeared on book covers, and was used to protect carpets, as well as being a luxury gift item appreciated by women.[120] In the book of Revelation, βύσσινος has as a subject of attribution, on the one hand, Babylon (Rev 18.16) and the goods sold there (Rev 18.12); and, on the other, the New Jerusalem (Rev 19.8) and the heavenly armies. The narrator takes care, however, to show the listener/reader that these are

---

[118] This was a tree much appreciated in antiquity for the quality of its wood and for its multicoloured roots. It was considered a luxury item; see Aune, *Revelation 3*, pp. 999–1000.

[119] J. G. Baldwin, 'Gold, Silver, Bronze, Iron. s.v. χρυσός', *NIDNTT* 2, 95–6.

[120] I. H. Marshall, *et al.* (eds.), *New Bible Dictionary*, 3rd edn (Leicester – Downers Grove, IL: InterVarsity Press, 1996), s.v. *linen*.

different types of linen. The linen of the New Jerusalem and the heavenly armies is accompanied by two adjectival lexemes, one suggesting quality – καθαρός, 'pure' – and the other splendour, by the use of either λαμπρός, 'bright', or λευκός, 'white'. In other words, the adjective βύσσινος is yet another example of an epithet to which a pair of adjectives is attached, here specifying the type of linen used: βύσσινον λαμπρὸν καθαρόν, 'fine linen, bright and pure' (Rev 19.8), or βύσσινον λευκὸν καθαρόν, 'fine linen, white and pure' (Rev 19.14). In contrast, the linen of Babylon is accompanied by πορφυροῦν . . . καὶ κόκκινον, 'purple . . . and scarlet' (Rev 18.12, 16). In any case, to assure the readers that the difference between the two is made clear, a voice from heaven describes the linen of the New Jerusalem in these terms: τὸ γὰρ βύσσινον τὰ δικαιώματα τῶν ἁγίων ἐστίν, 'fine linen is the righteous deeds of the saints' (Rev 19.8).

The lexeme σιδηροῦς, 'made of iron', is also among the most used. Iron is a metal characterized by both its hardness and its malleability when forged: features that make it ideal for weapons of war such as swords, spears, and axes, as well as farming and construction implements.[121] In the book of Revelation, σιδηροῦς, 'made of iron', denotes both the material itself and its strength, whether the subject of attribution is the θώρακες, 'breastplates', of the locusts (Rev 9.9), or the ῥάβδος, 'rod', carried by the conqueror, the woman's newborn child, and the horseman (Rev 2.27; 12.5; 19.15). In addition, the expression ῥάβδος σιδηροῦς, preceded by the verbal lexeme ποιμαίνω, 'to herd' is a direct allusion to Ps 2.9, which also mentions ceramic vessels. By means of this intertextual echo, the pericopes using the phrase are infused with a strong messianic sense, as the second Psalm is one of the royal psalms, which allude explicitly to a messiah-king.

Lastly, the use of adjectives such as ὑάλινος, 'made of glass', σμαράγδινος, 'made of emerald', μύλινος, 'made of millstone', and τρίχινος, 'made of hair', is also significant. The first two are used to express what the narrator considers to be ineffable; that is, all that surrounds the throne of God. For this reason, he uses two adjectival lexemes which, along with the simile in which they appear, facilitate analogy: ὡς θάλασσα ὑαλίνη, 'like a sea of glass' (Rev 4.6; 15.2[2]), and ἶρις κυκλόθεν τοῦ θρόνου ὅμοιος ὁράσει σμαραγδίνῳ, 'a rainbow around the throne that looks as if it were made of emerald' (Rev 4.3).

---

[121] E. E. Platt, 'Jewellery, Ancient Israelite. 3. Copper/Bronze and Iron', *ABD 3*, 823–34.

In contrast, the other two lexemes, μύλινος, 'made of millstone', and τρίχινος, 'made of hair', provide the means for the narrator to translate his vision into visual form, describing the stone that is thrown at Babylon (Rev 18.21) and the aspect of the sun when the sixth seal is opened (Rev 6.12), respectively. The size of the stone and the appearance of the sun are intensified by these adjectives, which provoke in the listener/reader a feeling of awe and dread at what they see happening.

The three types of adjectival lexemes that appear in Rev 1.9–22.5 thus help to give realism to the objects that John describes, as they facilitate the listener/reader's visualization of them. At the same time, they evoke a series of emotions and sensations in the listener/reader and even provide information about the morality of the characters described, so that the recipient quickly identifies them as belonging to either the heavenly or the evil context. It may thus be concluded that the function of such adjectives is very similar to that found in short stories.

So far, the analogy has been made between Rev 1.9–22.5 and the short story form, both in the construction of plot and the choice of characters, and in the use of narrative strategies. Such parallelism, however, remains an open question until it is seen whether the descriptions and discourse employed are indeed adapted to this literary form.

1.3   A Truthful Narrative

One aspect that should not be overlooked here is one that is present throughout the entire narrative, including the epilogue (Rev 22.6–16), and one that the narrator insists on again and again. This is his intention to convey the truth. While it is presented in the book of Revelation with unique force, it is a characteristic that underpins literature in general, and especially the narrative. Aristotle, in his *Poetics*, refers to realism as an element essential to the structure of the action, the *anagnorisis*, the *peripeteia*, and so on.[122] It may be described as being similar to what is true and having the appearance of being so.[123] This aspect of verisimilitude is especially important in short stories. The recipient, upon hearing or reading them, is made to wonder if what is being told is true, as the narrator creates a world that the listener/reader is then allowed to enter.[124]

---

[122] Arist. *Po.* 1451a; 1452a; 1454a; 1455a; 1456a; etc.
[123] P. Ricoeur, *Tiempo y narración II: Configuración del tiempo en el relato de ficción*, trans. A. Neira (Madrid: Cristiandad, 1987), p. 32.
[124] Tolkien, 'On Fairy-Stories', p. 133.

The narrator of Rev 1.9–22.16 stresses that what he is narrating is true through several different strategies:

1.   An authentification of the book (Rev 22.6–16).
2.   A first-person narrative, based upon what John saw and heard.
3.   The use of numerical adjectives.

1.3.1   Authentification of the Book (Rev 22.6–16)

Rev 22.6–16, as the epilogue of the narrative, is invested with a special significance, as it is the part of the narration that allows the listener/reader both to draw conclusions about it[125] and to test its verisimilitude.

In both the OT (Deut 19.15) and the NT (John 8.17), a testimony is valid and recognized as such when it is supported by at least two witnesses. This may clarify the function of the *ex abrupto* intrusion of different voices in direct speech at the end of the narrative. The only way of proving that John's narrative is in fact true is by turning to two witnesses who can confirm its veracity. It is precisely in the prologue that the revelation is affirmed to have taken place, through an angel and by Jesus himself (Rev 1.1–2). The angel and Jesus, then, appear as qualified witnesses who testify to the truthfulness of the narrative; hence it is Christ's voice that is heard again at the end.

The angel and Jesus speak at the beginning and the end of the epilogue, framing the testimony of John at its centre. The angel is the first to speak (Rev 22.6). His testimony is a direct confirmation of the veracity of John's written words. The formula proper to sworn pacts and declarations is used,[126] guaranteeing the truth of what was narrated earlier: οὗτοι οἱ λόγοι πιστοὶ καὶ ἀληθινοί, 'these words are faithful and true' (Rev 22.6a). The adjectival lexemes πιστοὶ καὶ ἀληθινοί are significant as well, as they are the means by which the angel states that the content of the book is the word of God. The angel reveals to the listener/reader that what is narrated in Rev 1.9–22.5 is not merely an invention of John's, but

---

[125] D. Estébanez Calderón, *Diccionario de términos literarios* (Madrid: Alianza, 1996), pp. 342–3, s.v. *epílogo*; E. González de Gambier, *Diccionario de terminología literaria* (Madrid: Síntesis, 2002), p. 140, s.v. *epílogo*.

[126] Formulas like these are occasionally found in Jewish apocalyptic literature, as well as in works of Greco-Roman antiquity; see Aune, *Revelation 3*, pp. 1182, 1229–30.

is indeed the revelation of Jesus Christ that was announced in the prologue (Rev 1.1–3). His affirmation is ratified by alluding specifically to Rev 1.1–2.

While the angel begins the testimony, it is Jesus who concludes it (Rev 22.12–16). His words are here given a special degree of solemnity.[127] It is Jesus in person, ἐγὼ Ἰησοῦς, 'I, Jesus', who speaks. His testimony serves a double function: to confirm the veracity of what is written – by means of a beatitude that gathers together elements of the description of the New Jerusalem (Rev 22.14) – and to support the angel's testimony: Ἐγὼ Ἰησοῦς ἔπεμψα τὸν ἄγγελόν μου μαρτυρῆσαι ὑμῖν ταῦτα ἐπὶ ταῖς ἐκκλησίαις, 'I, Jesus, have sent my angel to testify to you about these things to the churches' (Rev 22.16). His testimony, therefore, serves to corroborate both John's and the angel's.

John's own declaration is completely different, as it aims to prove that he is the direct witness of what he has just recounted. What is more, it affirms that he is the witness not only of what he has heard, but what he has seen with his own eyes, as claimed in the prologue (Rev 1.1–3). For this reason, he employs, insistently and with a certain emphasis, two specific verbal lexemes – ὁράω, 'to see', and 'ἀκούω, 'to hear' – and begins his discourse with a personal pronoun in the first-person singular, κἀγὼ Ἰωάννης, 'I, John', as at the beginning of the narrative (Rev 1.9). John uses all the resources at his disposal to demonstrate to the listener/reader that he is the visual and auditory witness of what he recounts. This is why the story he tells in Rev 1.9–22.16 is not presented as if it were a dream or the product of his imagination. The fact of having seen and heard is the guarantee that Rev 1.9–22.5 is a true account.[128]

John continues his testimony by telling us what he did immediately after this: ἔπεσα προσκυνῆσαι ἔμπροσθεν τῶν ποδῶν τοῦ ἀγγέλου, 'I fell down to worship before the feet of the angel' (Rev 22.8b). In this way, he insists that, although the angel has witnessed these facts, they have their origin exclusively in God.

It may be concluded that the epilogue (Rev 22.6–16) serves to authenticate the work. It is essential to the narrative, as it ratifies its veracity and divine origin, as well as showing John to be the visual and auditory witness of the events he describes.

---

[127] A. T. Robertson, *Comentario al texto griego del Nuevo Testamento*, trans. and notes S. Escuain (Terrassa: Clie, 2003), p. 765.

[128] Aune, *Revelation 3*, p. 1185.

1.3.2   First-Person Narration: John Saw and Heard

Another strategy that gives the narrative its verisimilitude is the fact that it is narrated in the first-person singular from beginning, ἐγὼ Ἰωάννης, . . . ἐγενόμην ἐν τῇ νήσῳ, 'I, John . . . was on the island' (Rev 1.9), to end, κἀγὼ Ἰωάννης ὁ ἀκούων καὶ βλέπων ταῦτα, 'It was I, John, who heard and saw these things' (Rev 22.8). This first-person narrator, identified as John, opens his account by introducing himself as its protagonist, and tells us himself of the religious experience he had on Patmos. However, from this moment onwards, John not only maintains his role as a character in the story, but also becomes the witness of certain events. Indeed, most of the time it is this focalization of the witness that predominates,[129] and only sporadically does he shift to the 'narrated I' focalization.[130]

The narrator's capacity of dividing himself into two selves is a feature of what is called the 'homodiegetic narrator'. This type of narration is characterized precisely by the ability of the narrator to be present in the story he is telling, not only as protagonist, but also as a secondary character in the role of observer and witness.[131]

Logically, the use of the homodiegetic narrator reinforces the story's verisimilitude, as John retells a story that he has witnessed personally. It is thus significant that the narrator makes himself visible through the repeated use of two verbal forms: εἶδον, 'I saw', and ἤκουσα, 'I heard'. In effect, having seen and having heard are the requirements needed for someone to be considered the witness of an event. The choice of these lexemes to express visual and auditory perception, and their repeated use and distribution throughout the narrative, is not accidental, but rather an essential element that reflects the narrator's desire to present himself as the visual and auditory witness of the revelation.

Curiously, in the book of Revelation there is little use of the rich lexical range of the Greek language for expressing visual perception,[132]

---

[129] This aspect is particularly interesting in regard to the descriptions introduced by καὶ εἶδον, which are built upon John's visual perceptions of the figures presented to him.

[130] Characteristic of the homodiegetic narrator is this 'oscillation between the two "I"'s (the "narrating I" and the "narrated I")'; see Reis and Lopes, *Diccionario*, p. 162, s.v. *narrador homodiegético*. A clear example of the 'narrated I' can be found in the εἶδον-λέγων descriptions.

[131] G. Genette, *Figures III* (Paris: Éditions du Seuil, 1972), pp. 252–3.

[132] Examples of this varied range of verbal lexemes for the act of visual perception include: ἐποπτεύω, 'to observe'; θεάομαι, 'to be a spectator of'; σκοπέω, 'to watch'; etc. To this list must then be added derived verbs such as: ἀναβλέπω, 'to look up'; διαβλέπω, 'to see

which is here restricted to only three verbal lexemes: ὁράω, βλέπω, and θεωρέω. Although their meanings are almost identical,[133] 'to perceive objects with the eyes through the action of light',[134] there is a great difference in the use that the narrator makes of each one. And so, in Rev 1.9–22.16, the verbal lexeme ὁράω appears 61 times, while βλέπω occurs 13 times, and θεωρέω twice. John thus seems to have a predilection for ὁράω over βλέπω and θεωρέω.

The verbal lexeme ὁράω has a unique use in the narrative (Rev 1.9–22.16). Predominant here is the aorist indicative, and more precisely, the first-person singular, εἶδον. Indeed, it appears 45 times in reference to the same subject: John. If this were not enough, further insistence is given to the fact that John saw through the use of other verbal forms that are proper, once again, to the seer-as-subject: i.e., the second-person singular of the aorist indicative εἶδες (Rev 1.19, 20; 17.8, 12, 15, 16, 18), or the present imperative ὅρα (Rev 19.10; 22.9)[135] and aorist participle ἰδών (Rev 17.6). And so, of the 61 times that the verb ὁράω appears, 55 are applied to John and only six to other subjects: the ark (Rev 11.19), the woman (Rev 12.1), the dragon (Rev 12.3, 13), the prostitute (Rev 18.7), and the saved (Rev 22.4). It is thus evident that there is an express desire to emphasize that John is the one who saw.[136]

---

clearly'; ἐμβλέπω, 'to look straight at'; περιβλέπομαι, 'to look around, to glance around'; ἀφοράω, 'to direct one's attention without distraction'; ἐφοράω, 'to look upon, to regard'; etc.

[133] *DRAE*, s.v. *ver*.

[134] However, as pointed out by E. Delebecque in '"Je vis" dans l'Apocalypse', *RevThom* 3 (1998), 460, there is a slight difference between them. The lexeme ὁράω refers to the act of seeing more as an active than a passive process; βλέπω, on the other hand, is an expressive verb, as it suggests an intense gaze directed at a specific object; while θεωρέω refers to the kind of observation that arises from curiosity and interest in the object of perception.

[135] The present imperative could be excluded from this count, as, when it is linked to the conjunction μή (ὅρα μή, Rev 19.10; 22.9), the meaning of the verb ὁράω changes from 'to perceive reality through the sense of vision' to 'to pay attention, to be on guard'; that is to say, it acquires a figurative sense; see *BDAG*, 5358.B.2, s.v. ὁράω.

[136] I am not, therefore, in agreement with Allo, *Apocalypse*, p. clxvii, who considers the repetition of εἶδον to be a monotonous device that the author does not know how to control. Furthermore, Korner ('And I saw ... ', 160–83), after a comparative study of 4 Ezra, 1 Enoch, the book of Daniel, and the book of Revelation, argues that καὶ εἶδον and μετὰ ταῦτα εἶδον constitute a literary convention that structures the narration in Rev 1.9–22.15. This hypothesis had already been proposed by Charles. In any case, the author of that particular exegesis stresses that the use of these structures in apocalyptic literature is not as relevant as it is in the Revelation of John; see Charles, *Commentary 1*, pp. 106–7.

This desire is made manifest in the way that εἶδον appears in the text. In most cases (37 times), this verb form is preceded by the copulative conjunction καί,[137] as in Rev 5.1:

Καὶ εἶδον ἐπὶ τὴν δεξιὰν τοῦ καθημένου ἐπὶ τοῦ θρόνου . . .

And I saw in the right hand of the One seated upon the throne . . .

The syntagma καὶ εἶδον is sometimes followed by others such as καὶ ἰδού (Rev 6.2, 5, 8; 14.1, 14), or καὶ ἤκουσα (Rev 5.11; 8.13). At other times, it is preceded by or interspersed with new terms: participles (καὶ ἐπιστρέψας εἶδον, 'and turning round I saw', Rev 1.12); adverbs (καὶ οὕτως εἶδον, 'and so I saw', Rev 9.17); direct objects (καὶ τὴν πόλιν τὴν ἁγίαν Ἰερουσαλὴμ καινὴν εἶδον, 'and . . . I saw the holy city, the New Jerusalem', Rev 21.2); or conjunctions (ὅτε εἶδον, 'when I saw', Rev 1.17). On a few occasions, instead of καὶ εἶδον we find μετὰ ταῦτα εἶδον, 'after these things I saw' (Rev 4.1; 7.1, 9; 15.5; 18.1). The verb form εἶδον appears without an introductory link on only two occasions, when it is used within a relative clause (Rev 10.5 and 13.2).

In this context, the presence of δείκνυμι cannot be overlooked. Properly speaking, the lexeme itself does not mean 'to see', but rather 'to show, i.e. *expose to the eyes*',[138] and John uses it to insist once again that he sees, but that in this case he does so through an intermediary who facilitates visual perception. Hence, δείκνυμι is usually employed in Rev 1.9–22.16 with an angel as agent and John as recipient (Rev 17.1; 21.9, 10; 22.1): δείξω σοι, 'I will show you', or ἔδειξέν μοι, 'he showed me'. Once again, it is insisted that John saw with his own eyes, albeit indirectly, i.e., as the angel instructed him. Exceptions to this are Rev 4.1, in which the agent is not the angel, but the first voice that John hears; and Rev 22.6, where the recipient is not John, but the 'servants', as it refers back to the prologue.

As for the verbal lexemes βλέπω and θεωρέω, the narrator reserves these for expressing the visual perception of other characters that appear in the story, such as the church of Laodicea, ἵνα βλέπῃς, 'so that you see' (Rev 3.18), and those who contemplate (βλέπουσιν/θεωροῦντας/ἐθεώρησαν) the bodies of the two witnesses (Rev 11.9, 11, 12c). Similarly, during the fall of Babylon, the kings of the earth see (βλέπωσιν/βλέποντες) the smoke rising from it (Rev 18.9), as do those labouring at sea (Rev 18.18).

---

[137] Rev 1.12, 17; 5.1, 2, 6, 11; 6.1, 2, 5b, 8, 12; 7.2; 8.2, 13; 9.1b, 17; 10.1; 13.1, 11; 14.1, 6, 14; 15.1, 2; 16.13; 17.3b, 6; 19.11, 17, 19; 20.1, 4, 11, 12; 21.1, 2, 22.

[138] THAYER, 1222.1, s.v. δεικνύω.

There are, however, three exceptions in which John presents himself as the subject of the verbal lexeme βλέπω:

1.   Rev 1.11, which belongs to the beginning of the narrative, where John begins to explain what he saw. Here the seer recalls the first words that he heard spoken: ὃ βλέπεις γράψον εἰς βιβλίον, 'Write what you see in a roll'.

2.   Rev 1.12, which describes John's behaviour immediately after hearing the message: ἐπέστρεψα βλέπειν, 'I turned to see'.

3.   Rev 22.8, which belongs to John's final discourse, and which is used to close the narrative. Together with the present participle, βλέπων, there appears its aorist, ἔβλεψα, both of which have John as their subject. This use departs from the habitual praxis of New Testament Greek, as, when the aorist indicative is used, the author chooses εἶδον,[139] which would be the expected form in the book of Revelation. This intentional use of the verbal lexeme βλέπω, precisely in the epilogue, suggests that the narrator reserves the use of the verbal lexeme βλέπω for opening and closing the narration of that which John saw (Rev 1.9–22.16); that is to say, for those moments when he acts as a character in the story, functioning in the narrative at the intradiegetic level, and not as narrator.

Finally, it should be noted that, while the book of Revelation stresses this act of seeing by John, it also avoids all verbs that have opposite meanings, such as: 'to conceal', 'to hide', 'to disappear', etc. Indeed, lexemes of this kind scarcely appear at all. There is a sporadic use of only two such verbs, and one adjective: φεύγω[140] (Rev 9.6; 12.6; 16.20; 20.11), κρύπτω (Rev 2.17; 6.15, 16), and τυφλός (Rev 3.17). They are used in specific contexts in which their agents are characters that stand in enmity with God and the Lamb (Rev 3.17; 6.15; 16.20).

The only exceptions to this are Rev 2.17 and Rev 12.6. The first of these, τῷ νικῶντι δώσω αὐτῷ τοῦ μάννα τοῦ κεκρυμμένου, 'To the one who conquers I will give the hidden manna', is found in the letter to the Church of Pergamum and, while it alludes to the manna as hidden, the

---

[139]   *BDAG*, 5358, s.v. ὁράω.

[140]   The verbal lexeme φεύγω is included here because, although it does not literally signify 'to hide oneself', but rather 'to flee', in the contexts in which it appears the connotation of 'to hide oneself' is implicit.

fact that it will be given over to the conqueror causes the connotation of concealment to disappear. Something similar occurs in Rev 12.6. This is in regard to the first sign seen in heaven, καὶ ἡ γυνὴ ἔφυγεν εἰς τὴν ἔρημον, 'and the woman fled into the wilderness ... '. Flight is, in this case, a quest for salvation, something that does not appear in earlier texts.

Visual perception, then, plays a significant role in the narrative, as it allows John to present himself as a visual witness, and in this way confirms what was announced in the prologue: that the revelation is also transmitted through visions, ὅσα εἶδεν (Rev 1.2). This explains the intentional use of εἶδον and βλέπω; the first shows the narrator as witness, while βλέπω presents him as protagonist (Rev 1.11, 12; 22.8).

For expressing the auditory side of peception, the Greek language does not present as much variety as it does for the visual.[141] In the book of Revelation, this vocabulary is basically limited to the repeated use of the verbal lexeme ἀκούω, 'to hear'.

Ἀκούω appears 43 times in the narrative (Rev 1.9–22.16), with various subjects. Thus, the verbal form ἤκουσα, first-person singular of the aorist indicative, is predominant in the text (occurring 27 times),[142] and is always applied to the same subject; i.e., John. The remaining verb forms, except for the present participle ἀκούων, which also refers to John (Rev 22.8), have other subjects: ἀκουσάτω (Rev 2.7, 11, 17, 29; 3.6, 13, 22), those who have ears; ἤκουσας (Rev 3.3), the church of Sardis; ἀκούσῃ (Rev 3.20), the church of Laodicea; ἤκουσαν (Rev 11.12), those who see the witnesses; ἀκουσθῇ (Rev 18.22[2], 23), the sound of music, the mill, the bride, and the bridegroom; and, lastly, ἀκουεῖν (Rev 9.20), the idols. What is more, these verbal forms appear in specific contexts, such as the messages given to the churches (Rev 2.3), the enumeration of the types of idols (Rev 9.20), the story of the two witnesses (Rev 11.12), and the destruction of Babylon (Rev 18.22 [2], 23).

It can therefore be said that the verb ἀκούω is used with a preference for John as subject. As with εἶδον, ἤκουσα is the other form through which the presence of the narrator, John, is made patent at the intradiegetic level. The

---

[141] These are limited to the verbal lexeme ἀκούω, 'to hear, to listen', and its derivates: ἐπακούω, 'to give ear to'; παρακούω, 'to hear aside, i.e. casually'; and ὑπακούω, 'to listen, to obey'.

[142] Rev 1.10; 4.1; 5.11, 13; 6.1, 3, 5, 6, 7; 7.4; 8.13; 9.13, 16; 10.4, 8; 12.10; 14.2(2), 13; 16.1, 5, 7; 18.4; 19.1, 6; 21.3; 22.8.

characteristics of the aorist also facilitate this, as in that aspect of the verb the speaker places emphasis on the termination of the action.[143]

Like εἶδον, the verbal form ἤκουσα is associated with an unusual construction, which is repeated throughout the length of the narrative. Thus, ἤκουσα is followed, in most cases (23 times), by the participle of the verb λέγω:[144]

> ἤκουσα ... φωνὴν μεγάλην ὡς σάλπιγγος [11] λεγούσης ... (Rev 1.10–11)

> I heard ... a loud voice like a trumpet [11] saying ...

Direct speech is introduced, making what John heard audible to the listener/reader, and once again helping to reinforce the veracity of the story. In a sense, it enables them to hear the message afresh each time they read the book.

When the form ἤκουσα is found alone, without the widening effect of the verb λέγω (Rev 7.4; 9.16; 14.2[2]; 22.8), its function is not so much to communicate what was heard, as to reaffirm the veracity of what was said. Thus, for example, in Rev 22.8, after it is made clear that it is John who heard these things, this is immediately reaffirmed: καὶ ὅτε ἤκουσα, 'and when I heard it'.

For the expression of visual perception, the verb δείκνυμι is used sporadically to show that it is thanks to the mediation of the angel that John sees. In the case of what he hears, something similar occurs with the use of λέγω, 'to say', to express this reciprocal action.

Λέγω appears 101 times in 94 different verses. On 83 occasions,[145] it is used to introduce direct speech. Up to this point, λέγω can be seen to complete ἤκουσα on 23 occasions; in seven of these cases, it appears in the formula expression τάδε λέγει.[146] Fifty-three, then, remain to be examined. Having analyzed these verses, we can observe that the verb λέγω, when it introduces direct speech, appears in two different constructions:

---

[143] Blass and Debrunner, *Grammar*, § 318.

[144] Rev 1.10–11; 4.1; 5.11–12, 13; 6.1, 3, 5, 6, 7; 8.13; 9.13–14; 10.4, 8; 11.12; 12.10; 14.13a; 16.1, 5, 7; 18.4; 19.1, 6; 21.3.

[145] This figure excludes the following 18 references: a) the sections in indirect speech (Rev 6.11; 9.4; 10.9a; 13.14); b) the formula used to close the letters, τί τὸ πνεῦμα λέγει ταῖς ἐκκλησίαις (Rev 2.7, 11, 17, 29; 3.6, 13, 22); c) λέγω used in the sense of 'to name, to call oneself' (Rev 2.2, 9, 20, 24b; 3.9; 8.11) or 'to explain' (Rev 17.7b).

[146] Rev 2.1, 8, 12, 18; 3.1, 7, 14.

1. A participle depending on a principal verb (30).[147] This is most often a *verbum dicendi*, but may also be one of movement.[148] An example of this would be:

    ἔκραξαν φωνῇ μεγάλῃ λέγοντες· ἕως πότε, ὁ δεσπότης ὁ ἅγιος ... (Rev 6.10)

    They cried out in a loud voice, saying: How long, Sovereign Lord ...

2. A personal form (23). Although other verb forms (8) may be found,[149] a clear preference is shown for the use of the present indicative (15),[150] as in the following example:

    καὶ λέγει μοι· Λάβε καὶ κατάφαγε αὐτό ... (Rev 10.9)

    And he says to me: 'Take it and eat it ... '

The continued allusion in the narrative to auditory perception through ἤκουσα and λέγω shows another facet of John as witness: his having heard the word of God and the testimony of Jesus Christ (Rev 1.2a).

In the story itself, however, there is no predominance of seeing over hearing, as both are interwoven in the narration. Auditory perception, ἤκουσα, appears first (Rev 1.10), followed by visual perception, εἶδον. John contemplates the son of man and pauses to describe what has appeared before his eyes (Rev 1.12–16). After this, Christ speaks directly, λέγων, to John, our protagonist (Rev 1.17b), revealing his identity (Rev 1.18), giving him the command to write what he sees (Rev 1.19), offering him some keys for interpreting what he sees (Rev 1.20), and, finally, dictating a series of messages addressed to the seven churches (Rev 2.3).

---

[147] Rev 1.17; 4.8, 10; 5.9; 6.10; 7.3, 10, 12, 13; 11.1, 15, 17; 13.4; 14.7, 8, 9, 18; 15.3; 16.17; 17.1; 18.2, 16, 18, 19, 21; 19.4, 5, 17; 21.9. Also included is Rev 18.10, although the principal verb is another participle: ἑστηκότες.

[148] This is often κράζω, 'to shout, cry out' (Rev 6.10; 7.2–3, 10; 18.2, 18, 19; 19.17), although other verbs appear as well: ᾄδω, 'to sing' (Rev 5.9; 15.3); ἀποκρίνομαι, 'to address' (Rev 7.13); φωνέω, 'to speak with a loud voice' (Rev 14.18); λαλέω, 'to speak' (Rev 17.1; 21.9). Other verb types used include: βάλλω, 'to cast' (Rev 4.10); ἐξέρχομαι, 'to leave, to go out' (Rev 16.17); προσκυνέω, 'to fall down and worship' (Rev 7.11–12; 11.16–17; 13.4; 19.4); etc.

[149] Aorist: Rev 7.14b; 17.7a; 21.5, 6; 22.6; perfect: Rev 7.14a; 19.3; imperfect: Rev 5.1.

[150] Rev 2.24a; 3.17; 5.5; 6.16; 10.9b, 11; 14.13b; 17.15; 18.7; 19.9(2), 10; 21.5; 22.9b, 10.

In this first section (Rev 1.10–3.22), hearing does in fact predominate over vision. In the two following chapters (Rev 4.5), however, this is reversed, and it is vision that takes precedence. Indeed, this new section opens with μετὰ ταῦτα εἶδον, 'after these things, I saw' (Rev 4.1a), and, after a brief interruption in which the son of man speaks (Rev 4.1b), John has a vision of God in all his glory upon his throne (Rev 4.2). This continues into the succeeding verses (Rev 4.2–11), in the middle of which John hears the songs praising God (Rev 4.8–11). Next comes the contemplation – καὶ εἶδον, 'and I saw' – of the scroll of the seven seals (Rev 5.1–12). The scroll can only be opened by the Lamb, who is seen on the throne itself (Rev 5.6–8). This section does not conclude with a new vision, but rather with what John hears: the singing of the living beings (Rev 5.13–14); the clamour of the angels (Rev 5.11–12) and the beasts (Rev 5.13–14). And so the narrator announces directly, καὶ εἶδον, καὶ ἤκουσα, 'and I saw and heard' (Rev 5.11–12), then immediately repeats the verb form ἤκουσα, this time followed by the present participle λέγοντας (Rev 5.13) and concludes with ἔλεγον (Rev 5.14).

Chapter 6 begins with καὶ εἶδον, 'and I saw' (Rev 6.1), which frames the progressive opening of the seals. While in the two preceding chapters what is seen predominates over what is heard, now and over the course of the next three chapters, there will be a clear alternation between the two types of perception, giving a sense of completion to both.

The auditory element is the focus in verses 6.1b, 3, 5a, 6, 7, 10, 16–17, while the visual predominates in the alternating verses 6.1a, 2, 4, 5b, 8, 9, 11, 12–15. The content of what John hears serves three different functions within the text: it introduces the vision of the horses and their riders (Rev 6.1b, 2, 5b); it reveals the mission given to the third rider (Rev 6.6); and, finally, it describes the cries of the slain (Rev 6.10) and those fleeing the wrath of the Lamb (Rev 6.16–17). The visual element is used to complete the auditory, except in the final section, when the sixth seal is opened (Rev 6.12–15). In that section, the visual aspect of the scene is presented to the reader in great detail, while the auditory – the shouts of the kings and the wealthy (Rev 6.16–17) – completes the vision of the earthquake.

In Chapter 7, before the opening of the seventh seal, there is a short parenthesis (Rev 7.1–17) in which the multitude of the saved appears. This begins with what John sees, for which expressions such as μετὰ τοῦτο εἶδον, 'after this I saw' (Rev 7.1), and καὶ εἶδον, 'and I saw', are used. What is heard is presented next, introduced by ἔκραζεν ... λέγων, 'he cried out ... saying' (Rev 7.2–3), and by ἤκουσα, 'I heard' (Rev 7.4–8), opening the way for the vision of the multitude, μετὰ ταῦτα εἶδον (Rev 7.9). Once again, the seen is completed by the heard, as John then listens to the dialogue between the saved and the angels (Rev 7.10–12). Finally, there is a conversation between John and one of elders, in which the identity of the saved is revealed: they are those who have washed their robes in the blood of the Lamb (Rev 7.13).

After this digression comes the opening of the seventh seal (Rev 8.1–5). Up to this moment, the narrative has been using the verb forms εἶδον or ἤκουσα, followed or preceded by the temporal clause ὅτε ἤνοιξεν τὴν σφραγῖδα, 'when he opened the seal'. In addition to this, the text now specifies καὶ ὅταν ἐγένετο σιγή, 'there was silence'[151] (Rev 8.1b). That is to say, there is shift in focalization – away from John or any other character – with regard to how the action is framed. Now there is only silence, through which the narrator is able to create an atmosphere of suspense, preparing the listener/reader for the next vision – καὶ εἶδον – in which seven angels appear blowing trumpets (Rev 8.2-5a). This vision, together with the final allusion to the auditory, καὶ ἐγένοντο βρονταί, 'there was thunder' (Rev 8.5b), in turn sets the stage for the sounding of the trumpets.[152]

The section devoted to the first six trumpets presents a homogeneous structure with a thematic progression, in which there is an alternation between what John hears (the trumpets, ἐσάλπισεν: Rev 8.7a, 8a, 10a, 12a; 9.1a; 13–14) and what he sees (the events that occur: Rev 8.7b, 8b–9, 10b–11, 12b; 9.1b–11, 15–21). And so, after the first four trumpets are sounded, we see, successively, the scorching of the land (Rev 8.7c), the boiling of the seas (Rev 8.8b–9), and the contamination of the water (Rev 8.10b–11), while in the sky the celestial bodies are likewise damaged (Rev 8.12b). These events concluded, there is a short interim in which a singular occurrence takes place that John sees and hears simultaneously: a flying eagle announcing the three woes that those living on earth will suffer (Rev 8.13). The fifth and sixth trumpets are then sounded

---

[151] The syntactic value of ὅταν is exactly the same as that of ὅτε, as pointed out in *BDAG*, s.v. ὅταν. The change of conjunction may be a device of the writer's, whose purpose is to call the attention of the listener/reader.

[152] This type of foreshadowing also occurs later, with the description of the seven bowls (Rev 15.5–8).

(Rev 9.1, 13), and the sense of auditory perception is completed with a detailed vision of the plague of locusts (Rev 9.1b-11) and the invasion of a mounted army (Rev 9.15–21).

The sounding of the seventh trumpet does not occur immediately after this, however. Instead, there is another parenthesis dedicated to the second 'woe', which includes the episode in which John is given a book and told to eat it (Rev 10.8–11), and that of the two witnesses (Rev 11.1–14). In Rev 10.1–11, although it opens with καὶ εἶδον (Rev 10.1), the formula of visual perception, it is the auditory that predominates: various spoken discourses are heard (Rev 10.3), with the reappearance of the verb form ἤκουσα at several points (Rev 10.4, 8), as well as λέγω (Rev 10.9[2], 11) and ὤμοσεν (Rev 10.6), which, being a *verbum dicendi*, may be considered a variant of λέγω. This predominance of auditory perception is maintained in the story of the two witnesses by means of direct speech, introduced by λέγων (Rev 11.1–10), and followed by ἤκουσαν ... λεγούσης (Rev 11.12) and the description of their mission. The section closes with a passage spoken by the narrator to the listener/ reader, presenting the end of the second 'woe' and introducing the third (Rev 11.14).[153]

After the scene of the witnesses, we move on to the sounding of the seventh and final trumpet (Rev 11.15a), and here there is a new shift in focalization that helps to enlarge the story. And so, when we hear φωναὶ μεγάλαι ἐν τῷ οὐρανῷ, 'loud voices in heaven' (Rev 11.15a–18), the auditory again becomes prominent. What is seen (ὤφθη) – the temple of God and the ark of the covenant (Rev 11.19) – will come at the end of this section, in preparation for the next (Rev 12), in which visual perception predominates. The same verb form (ὤφθη instead of εἶδον) is even maintained in both.

From Rev 12.1 to Rev 14.20, the visual prevails: the sign of the woman (Rev 12.1–2), the sign of the dragon in the struggle between Michael and Satan (Rev 12.3–18); the visions of the two beasts – one from the sea and the other from the earth – (Rev 13.1–8; 13.11–17), although now with the more usual focalization, i.e., from John's perspective; and, lastly, the vision of the Lamb on Mt Sinai (Rev 14.1–5). The only sections in which the auditory takes precedence are Rev 13.9–10, 18, where John speaks directly to the listener/reader, and Rev 14.6–13, in which the judgment is announced through the three angels.

---

[153] The vision of the second 'woe' has now been completed. That of the third is imminent; see Beale, *Revelation*, p. 609.

Following this, there is a transitional segment that alternates between vision and hearing (Rev 14.14–17, 18), with the latter gradually gaining in priority. Thus, the section on the reaping and harvesting begins with what John sees – καὶ εἶδον, καὶ ἰδού – (Rev 14.14), and continues with what he hears (Rev 14.15), so as to follow this pattern of seeing, hearing, and seeing (Rev 14.16–18b, 19–20).[154] After this section and before the songs of the saved are heard (Rev 15.3–4), there is a reference to John's visual perception, καὶ εἶδον (Rev 15.1–2). When the singing has ended, John sees (μετὰ ταῦτα εἶδον) the seven angels leaving the temple, carrying with them the seven plagues (Rev 15.5–8). There is then an alternation between seeing the actions of the angels (Rev 16.2–4, 8–12, 13–14, 16–17a) and what John hears (Rev 16.1, 5–6, 7, 15, 17b), concluding with the consequences of pouring out the seventh bowl (Rev 16.18–21). After the description of the plagues comes the passage devoted to the great whore and the beast (Rev 17). It opens with what John hears spoken by one of the angels bearing the seven bowls (Rev 17.1–2); he then goes on to contemplate the great whore (Rev 17.3–6). If on earlier occasions the auditory element is completed by the visual, here this is reversed: the seen is placed in relief by the heard, as the angel explains to John the significance of the woman he has just seen (Rev 17.7–18). We then come to a section dominated by the sense of hearing (Rev 18.1–19.10): the announcement of the fall of Babylon (Rev 18.1–24) and the triumphant songs of the saved (Rev 19.1–10).

The focus on the visual now reappears. For this, the narrator returns frequently to the verb form εἶδον (Rev 19.11, 17, 19; 20.1, 4, 11, 12). Then comes a new series of events: the fall of the beast (Rev 19.20–21), the defeat of the dragon (Rev 20.1–5, 9–10), the universal judgment (Rev 20.11–15), and the vision of the New Jerusalem (Rev 21.1–2). The auditory element reappears in a commentary by the narrator (Rev 20.6–8), and then, in Chapter 21, the alternation of hearing (Rev 21.3–9, 24–27; 22.3–5)[155] and seeing (Rev 21.1–2, 10–23; 22.1–2) begins again. Once more, auditory perception is used to complete the visual. Thus, in Rev 21.3–9 it is affirmed that the New Jerusalem is the tent of God among men, ἡ σκηνὴ τοῦ θεοῦ μετὰ τῶν ἀνθρώπων, and later

---

[154] In this case, seeing is understood implicitly, as it is the continuation of καὶ εἶδον, καὶ ἰδού (Rev 14.14).

[155] Neither in Rev 21.24–27 nor in Rev 22.3–5 is it stated expressly who is speaking. As will be shown in Chapter 2, these verses constitute the spoken expression of John's thoughts.

the city itself is described in detail (Rev 21.10–23; 22.1–2). After the vision of the New Jerusalem, the descriptions of what John sees disappear completely; instead, a dialogue is heard taking place between the angel, John, and Jesus (Rev 22.6–16), and it is stressed that the narration is in fact an account of what John has heard and seen, ἤκουσα καὶ ἔβλεψα.

It can be concluded, then, that 'seeing and hearing' alternate and complement each other throughout Rev 1.9–22.16, enabling the recounting of the chain of events that occur in the narrative, to the point that it may be said that John does not see without hearing, nor hear without seeing. This feature imbues the content of the revelation with a heightened sense of realism and verisimilitude.

Both εἶδον and ἤκουσα, however, have their own particular functions. The verb form εἶδον frames the scenes that John contemplates and illustrates the events that occur. On the other hand, ἤκουσα transmits the discourses that interpret these visions, giving them a new perspective,[156] and, on occasion, testifying to what has been seen, as John not only sees, but hears what is said. In synthesis, εἶδον and ἤκουσα are the pillars upon which the narrative in Rev 1.9–22.16 is built, and underscore the role of the narrator as visual and auditory witness.

1.3.3   The Use of Numerical Adjectives

Numerical adjectives, unlike the other adjectives that appear in the book of Revelation, are not used to provide information about the setting or context to which the characters belong. Thus, for example, the celebrated number ἑπτά, 'seven', does not by itself indicate whether it belongs to either the heavenly or the evil context, as the number appears in all manner of contexts: the horns and eyes of the Lamb are each seven in number (Rev 5.6, heavenly context); the dragon and the beast each have seven heads (Rev 12.3; 13.1, evil context); seven plagues are sent to afflict humanity (Rev 15.1, context of the cataclysms). The same is true of τρεῖς, 'three': the gates of Jerusalem are grouped in threes (Rev 21.13), while the spirits that emerge from the enemies of the Lamb are three in number (Rev 16.13). Nonetheless, numerical adjectives such as these do serve a specific function within the narrative.

---

[156] Resseguie, *Revelation Unsealed*, p. 33.

Studies of the symbolic value of numbers in the book of Revelation are well known,[157] and these affirm that such significances are undoubtedly present in nearly all of the numbers that appear.[158] Without rejecting such proposals, it must be said that there is one aspect that has been over-looked, and this is the fact that numerical adjectives are a device for showing what is seen with exactitude and rigour, and thus endow the story with enhanced realism. This rigour asumes a wide variety of forms: numbering what is seen, detailing precisely the object of vision, relating the damage wrought by the cataclysms, and so on. For example, John usually tells us the number of objects that are presented to his eyes: the seven menorahs amidst which the son of man appears (Rev 1.12); the twenty-four thrones and seven torches that surround the throne of God (Rev 4.4–5); the seven seals of the book that the Lamb will open (Rev 5.1); the four winds of the earth (Rev 7.1); the three spirits that issue from the mouths of the dragon, the beast, and the false prophet (Rev 16.13); and the twelve fruits of the tree of life (Rev 22.2).

At other times, numerical adjectives provide a useful tool for detailing the elements of a given character. Thus, Jesus is beheld with seven stars in his hand and a double-edged sword (Rev 1.16); the four living beings each have six wings (Rev 4.8); the Lamb has seven horns and seven eyes (Rev 5.6); the woman clothed in sunlight appears surrounded by twelve stars (Rev 12.1) and later is provided with two wings (Rev 12.14); the dragon has seven heads, ten horns, and seven diadems (Rev 12.3), while the beast appears with seven heads, ten horns, and ten diadems (Rev 13.1); the New Jerusalem has twelve pillars (Rev 21.14), adorned with twelve different gemstones (Rev 21.19–20), and twelve gates distributed in threes, with twelve angels at their cardinal points (Rev 21.12–13). In this way, John manages to infuse his account with realism, as the objects of his vision are not a confusion of ill-defined figures, but rather characters and objects in sharp focus that can be visualized with great clarity.

---

[157] Among others, G. Biguzzi, 'I numeri e il suo linguaggio', in *L'Apocalisse e suoi enigmi* (Brescia: Paideia, 2004), pp. 127–52; Aune, 'Excursus 1E: The Number Seven', 'Excursus 4A: The Twenty-four Elders', *Revelation 1*, pp. 114–16; 291–2 and 'Excursus 13C: 666 and Gematria', in *Revelation 6–16* (Nashville, TN: T. Nelson, 1998), pp. 771–2; A. Yarbro Collins, 'Numerical Symbolism in Jewish and Early Christian Apocalyptic Literature', *ANRW*, II.21.2 (Berlin – New York: De Gruyter, 1984), 1222–87; Vanni, 'Il simbolismo nell'Apocalisse', *Greg* 61 (1980), 489–92.

[158] C. J. Hemer, 'Number. s.v. ἀριθμός. NT', *NIDNTT 2*, 685.

As if he were writing a historical chronicle, John reports to the listener/ reader the details of the cataclysms that occur. After the successive blasts of the first four trumpets, he gives a progressive account of the damage done: a third of the earth, with all its trees and vegetation, is scorched (Rev 8.7); a third of the sea is turned to blood, killing a third of its fish and destroying a third of its ships (Rev 8.9); and, finally, a third of the sun, the moon, and the stars are damaged (Rev 8.12). He does much the same after the account of the earthquake that follows the ascension of the prophets to heaven, when he announces that a tenth of the city is destroyed and seven thousand people killed (Rev 11.13), or when he describes the devastation caused by the tail of the dragon, which destroys a third of the stars (Rev 12.4).

Numerical adjectives also enable the duration of certain events to be reported exactly. In these cases, they appear together with nouns that reflect specific units of time, such as: ὥρα, 'hour'; ἡμέρα, 'day'; μήν, 'month'; and ἐνιαυτός, 'year'. And so it is stated that the tribulation suffered by the church of Smyrna will continue for ten days (Rev 2.10), that the plague of locusts will afflict the earth for five months (Rev 9.5, 10), that the two prophets will continue their ministry for 1,260 days (Rev 11.3), and that later they will be killed and their bodies put on public display for three and half days (Rev 11.9), after which they will be resurrected and ascend to heaven (Rev 11.11). In the same way, the woman will remain in the desert for a period of 1,260 days (Rev 12.6), the duration of the prophets' ministry, and the nations will tread upon the holy city for forty-two months (Rev 11.2), the same duration as the reign of the beast (Rev 13.5). Meanwhile, the fall of Babylon will take place in a single hour (Rev 18.10, 17, 19) and the dragon will be confined to the abyss for a thousand years, bringing about the reign of Christ (Rev 20.2, 3, 4, 5, 6, 7).

Finally, numerical adjectives are used to indicate the dimensions of a city or the extension of a certain phenomenon. The blood that spews forth from the winepress, for example, spreads across 1,600 *stadia* (Rev 14.20). Later, John, when viewing the New Jerusalem, will provide us with its exact measurements, 12,000 *stadia* (Rev 21.16), as well as those of its wall: 144 cubits (Rev 21.17).

Thus, the functions that numerical adjectives serve within the narrative are: giving a sense of exactness to the visions; providing details of the damage done by the catastrophes; indicating the duration of some events; and specifying dimensions. All of these functions are designed to make the narrative clear and precise, and to allow the narrator to present his story as a truthful account.

1.4   Conclusion and Open Questions

By this point, the reader will be aware that the various literary forms that we find the book of Revelation are designed to provide unity to the whole, as each form has a specific function within the totality of the work. Thus, the opening statement and makarism (Rev 1.1–3) tell the listener/reader how the text should be read; the liturgical dialogues that open (Rev 1.4–8) and close (Rev 22.17–21) the work, with their epistolary structure, indicate that the book is read to an assembled community; and, lastly, the content of the revelation itself is transmitted in the form of a story (Rev 1.9–22.16).

The analogy between the book of Revelation and the short story, however, remains at this point an open question. Although there are many similarities, further study is needed to determine whether the descriptive and dialogical techniques employed do in fact conform to this literary genre.

2

JOHN, EYEWITNESS AND HERALD OF THE VISIONS

Beginning with the prologue, the reader is made aware that the book of Revelation has been put into writing as a means of transmitting its content to the first Christian communities (Rev 1.1) – a point which is reiterated in two other places in the narrative. At the beginning of the first vision, Jesus commands John to write what he sees: ὃ βλέπεις γράψον εἰς βιβλίον καὶ πέμψον ταῖς ἑπτὰ ἐκκλησίαις, 'what you see, write it in a roll and send it to the seven churches' (Rev 1.11a); later, in the epilogue – that is, at the end of narrative – the angel insists that the revelation has taken place so that it may be communicated to 'his servants' (Rev 22.6). John is thus presented as seer and hearer, and at the same time as the herald of what is seen and heard. This is particularly important in the book of Revelation, inasmuch as 'making the listener/reader hear and see' will become the narrator's imperatives.

2.1   Introduction: *Ante Oculos Ponere*

Generally speaking, when a narrative text aims to give eyes to the reader, this is done largely through description.[1] Although it may slow the pace of the narrative, it serves to illustrate particular elements so that these may be considered simultaneously.[2] The use of description for this purpose was not new in literature; Cicero had already described it as creating the effect of *ante oculos ponere*, 'placing before the eyes', so that *qui audit, uidere*, 'he who hears, sees', as if personally witnessing the scene described.[3] This is perhaps the reason that John, the narrator of the

---

[1] Garrido Domínguez, *El texto narrativo*, p. 237.

[2] G. Genette, 'Frontières du récit', in *Figures II* (Paris: Seuil 1969), pp. 49–69, later published as G. Genette, 'Fronteras del relato', in R. Barthes, *et al., Análisis estructural del relato*, trans. B. Dorriots (U. Eco's text) and A. N. Vaisse (dossier) (Mexico: Coyoacán, 1996, rep. 1998), p. 59.

[3] Cicero, *Inv.* 1.55.107.

book of Revelation, uses it so frequently. Description enables οἱ ἀκούοντες, 'those who hear' (Rev 1.3), to visualize what John has seen at Patmos.

However, if we examine the narrative carefully, we find that the descriptive technique employed is not always the same, as the narrator places his visions before the eyes of the listener/reader in a variety of ways. Up to seven different types of descriptions may be identified, which I classify as follows:

1. The Vision *in Actu* (καὶ Εἶδον) Descriptions
2. The Audio-Vision (Ἤκουσα καὶ Εἶδον) Descriptions
3. The Vision-Speech (Εἶδον-Λέγων) Descriptions
4. The Anaphoric (τὰ Προλεγόμενα) Descriptions
5. The Angel Vision (καὶ Εἶδον Ἄγγελον) Descriptions
6. The Topography (Τόποι) Descriptions
7. The Integrated (ἐν τῇ Διηγήσει) Descriptions

Before proceeding, I will briefly outline the theoretical proposals upon which I have based the analysis of these descriptions. It is well known that there have been few studies on this particular topic.[4] The most important contributions have come from the French scholar Philippe Hamon, who developed his theory through an analysis of the realist novels of Zola.[5] Realism, by attempting to make the text a faithful reflection of reality, also enables a series of descriptive guidelines to be defined. Although the book of Revelation, given its literary genre and historical context, is somewhat removed from the descriptive models he proposes, the guidelines that Hamon has established are so specific and so closely related to the linguistic and literary character of a given work that they provide a useful tool for the study of description in the present apocalyptic text.

---

[4] For example, Genette, 'Frontières du récit', pp. 49–69, in the course of the five books he has dedicated to the study of the narrative under the title *Figures I–V*, examines description over only 14 pages, in *Figures II*. Similarly, of the 498 pages in García Landa's work *Acción, Relato, Discurso*, only six are dedicated to the topic of description; see J. Á. García Landa, *Acción, Relato, Discurso: Estructura de la ficción narrativa* (Salamanca: Ediciones Universidad de Salamanca, 1998), pp. 184, 359–63.

[5] His principal studies are: P. Hamon, 'Qu'est-ce qu'une description?', *Poétique* 12 (1972), 465–85; 'Pour un statut sémiologique du personnage', in R. Barthes, *et al.* (eds.), *Poétique du récit* (Paris: Seuil, 1977), pp. 115–80 (previously published in *Littérature* 6 [1972], 86–110); *Introduction à l'analyse du descriptif* (Paris: Hachette, 1981); *Le personnel du roman* (Geneva: Droz, 1983); *La description littéraire: De l'Antiquité à Roland Barthes. Une anthologie* (Paris: Macula, 1998). Hamon's influence can be felt in the description theory of narratologist Mieke Bal (*Teoría*, pp. 138–40).

Hamon maintains that description is comprised of two elements: demarcation signs and constitutive elements. Demarcation signs are those elements which establish the boundary between a story's narrative and descriptive aspects, and which serve both to initiate and conclude descriptions. Those which initiate are called 'introductory signs' and those which conclude are called 'concluding signs'. Introductory signs are not difficult to identify. They correspond to 'obligatory themes': recurring circumstances such as transparent contexts (windows, open doors, light, the sun, etc.), stereotyped scenes (looking out of a window, resting, surprises), and psychological motivation (distraction, pedantry, curiosity, and fascination). Concluding signs are closely connected with introductory signs. Thus, if a description begins with the opening of a door or window, it will end with its closing; or, if the starting point is one of light, at the end that light will go out.[6]

As for what are referred to as constitutive elements, the periods of description consist of 'denomination' (or *pantonyme*) and 'expansion'. Their presence, however, is optional. Denomination corresponds to the object described, which may be represented by a proper name, a noun, a syntagma, or a key word. Expansion, on the other hand, outlines the object's characteristics. This expansion may consist of a group of words juxtaposed in the form of a list, or linked by means of coordination and subordination, which correspond to what Philippe Hamon terms 'nomenclature' and the 'predicate group'. He uses the term 'nomenclature' to refer to terms that are employed to designate the reality described. By contrast, a 'predicate group' is comprised of terms that determine the qualities of the *pantonyme*. Recipes or descriptions of the components of a particular medicine, with their lists of ingredients or proper names, are models of descriptions based on nomenclature,[7] while the opening of *Platero y yo* ('Platero is little, hairy, soft ... ')[8] is a good example of a description that, in its expansion, is reduced to predicates. A few lines of a poem by Rabelais, which Hamon quotes, may serve as a paradigm for description, as its expansion includes both nomenclature and a predicate group: '*Les pieds, comme une guinterne. / Les talons, comme une massue. / La plante, comme un creziou ... ' .*[9]

[6] Hamon, 'Qu'est-ce ... ', 473–5.
[7] Hamon, *Introduction*, pp. 140–53.
[8] J. R. Jiménez, *Platero y yo* (Madrid: Biblioteca Nueva, 1997), p. 101.
[9] Hamon, *Introduction*, p. 147. 'Feet like a guitar / Heels like a mace / The sole of the foot, like a crucible ... ' (Rabelais, *Le quart livre*, Chapter 31).

Lastly, description is structured by a group of 'obligatory indicators', i.e., characteristic morphological and syntactic signs, which include:

a)   The use of specific verb tenses, such as the 'present of attestation' (Patmos is an island . . .), the imperfect or preterite, or even other durative verb forms like the gerund or the present participle.

b)   A specific lexis that, while including a wide variety of terms, allows a certain lexical predictability in which inclusion and similarity play important roles.

c)   The use of specific rhetorical figures: metaphors, metonymies, and synecdoches.

In most cases, these elements provide internal cohesion by structuring the description as a whole, or by centring it around one specific term.[10]

2.2   The Vision *in Actu* (καὶ Εἶδον) Descriptions

The vision *in actu* descriptions (the καὶ εἶδον descriptions) are the first to appear in the narration. They have been given this name because they are introduced by the formula καὶ εἶδον. They tend to burst into the text *ex abrupto*, and their function is to present a character whom John sees for the first time and who will be featured again later in the text. Indeed, once such characters have been described, when they appear again, John will simply refer to them by name without adding any further details. The Lamb, for example, when seen for the first time in Rev 5.6, is described in great detail. When he appears again, however, he is simply referred to as τὸ ἀρνίον, 'the Lamb' (Rev 14.1).

The following descriptions belong to this group:

1.   The resurrected Jesus (Rev 1.12b–16)
2.   The One seated upon the throne (Rev 4.2–3)
3.   The twenty-four elders (Rev 4.4)
4.   The four living beings (Rev 4.6-8a)
5.   The Lamb (Rev 5.6)
6.   The woman (Rev 12.1)
7.   The red dragon (Rev 12.3)
8.   The beast that rises from the sea (Rev 13.1–2a)
9.   The one seated on the cloud (Rev 14.14)
10.   The rider (Rev 19.11–16)

---

[10] Hamon, 'Qu'est-ce . . . ', 484; *Introduction*, pp. 57, 66–7, 150.

The καὶ εἶδον descriptions represent in words not only the object of the vision, but also the narrator's own visual action. Seeing, especially when it occurs suddenly, implies a visual perception that is gradual, so that the eye captures reality little by little. Thus, in these descriptions, the object of the vision is first situated in a place (introductory sign of space), and then identified (denomination or *pantonyme*); finally, this object is described in such a way that its most characteristic, or at least most striking, features are revealed (nomenclature and predicate group). In this way, the narrator enables the listener/reader to contemplate with him both what he is seeing and how he is seeing it, thereby endowing his description with a great sense of realism. It may be said that, in this type of description, the narrator manages to capture on paper what today the camera does in cinema, with its shifts from long to medium to close-up shots.[11] The vision *in actu* descriptions (the καὶ εἶδον descriptions) are similar, then, to the transcription of a vision at the moment that it occurs.

2.2.1   Demarcation Signs

In the καὶ εἶδον descriptions, the demarcation signs used are reduced to the introductory, as they lack concluding signals. The description ends because the narrative period is resumed, as in Rev 13.2b.

Introductory signals are always comprised of two elements: an expression of visual perception, and the spatial context in which the object of the vision is encountered.

The expression of visual perception is used to initiate the description. The usual form that this expression takes, as has just been mentioned, is καὶ εἶδον (Rev 1.12b; 5.6; 13.1; 14.14; 19.11), although some variants are also found, such as καὶ ἰδού, 'and behold' (Rev 4.2), or καὶ ὤφθη, 'and then was seen' (Rev 12.1, 3). The use of these variants is not casual, but contributes a meaningful nuance to these descriptions.

The locution καὶ ἰδού is followed by a nominative, in this case θρόνος. This strange construction is no less than the echo of a Semitic construction, used with the demonstrative particle הִנֵּה or the expression וְהִנֵּה. It is employed in biblical texts to highlight certain elements and to make the narration more vivid, among other purposes,[12] and it is usually preceded

---

[11] This is an image that forms the basis for the theory of focalization. Focalization is understood as the relationship that exists in the narrative between the vision, the agent who sees, and what he sees; see Bal, *Teoría*, p. 110.

[12] *BDB*, s.v. הִנֵּה.

by verbs that express visual perception or discovery.[13] Both of these possibilities are found in the book of Revelation, as καὶ ἰδού appears alone (Rev 4.2) as well as preceded by the verb 'to see' in the phrase καὶ εἶδον, or μετὰ ταῦτα εἶδον (Rev 4.1; 6.2, 5, 8; 7.9; 12.3; 14.1, 14; 19.11). The use of the expression καὶ ἰδού is thus not accidental, but designed to give added emphasis to the vision. In Rev 4.2, as well as doing this, it also grants greater realism to one of John's grandest visions: that of God in his glory. At the same time, the inarguable deictic value of the expression speaks directly to the interlocutor, as we will see in Chapter 3.

As for καὶ ὤφθη, the use of this variant is dependent on the type of vision being presented. Following the scene of the ark of the covenant in the firmament (Rev 11.19), two new characters, the woman and the dragon, appear in heaven and enact a new story, i.e., the dragon's attack on the woman and her newborn child. John uses the form καὶ ὤφθη, on the one hand, to create continuity and connect this vision to that of the ark, and, on the other, because the passive form of the verb ὁράω is typically used to introduce theophanies and similar visions.[14] The term thus underscores the idea that whatever appears is not the result of the seer's own initiative, but rather of what is manifested objectively; John continues to be the eyewitness of events, even though it is not directly stated that he saw them. What is more, with the use of the passive, the point of view shifts towards the object being contemplated and gives it greater emphasis.

The formula of visual perception καὶ εἶδον is generally interjected into the narration without warning, except in Rev 1.12 and 4.2, where we are prepared for the vision by the expression ἐγενόμην ἐν πνεύματι, 'I fell into ecstasy' (Rev 4.2), or when this expression is reinforced by creating a type of climax, as occurs in the first vision. There, after the ecstasy (Rev 1.10), John hears a voice and turns to see who is speaking to him (ἐπέστρεψα βλέπειν ...). It is when he turns (ἐπιστρέψας) that he sees (καὶ εἶδον) (Rev 1.12). Here, the act of visual perception pervades the text completely. John does nothing more than see, face-to-face, and thus communicates directly what it is that he sees. In these types of descriptions, John has the double function of eyewitness and transmitter; that is, he describes what is presented to his eyes at the same time that he involves the listener/reader in what he describes. Through the suspension

---

[13] Examples of this include: Gen 8.13; 18.9; 24.51, 63; Jdg 11.34; 1 Sam 9.17.
[14] Aune, *Revelation 2*, p. 679.

of the action in time, the listener/reader shares John's vision and in effect also becomes a spectator of these events.

After the formula of visual perception, John goes on to mention the spatial context in which the object contemplated is presented.[15] Thus, in the first vision, he says: εἶδον ἑπτὰ λυχνίας χρυσᾶς, 'I saw seven golden menorahs' (Rev 1.12b). Later, in Chapter 4, when he has the vision of God the Father, the first element he mentions is a throne: καὶ ἰδοὺ θρόνος ἔκειτο ἐν τῷ οὐρανῷ, 'and behold, a throne was situated in heaven' (Rev 4.2b). It is in the space surrounding this throne that he will discover the twenty-four elders, καὶ κυκλόθεν τοῦ θρόνου θρόνους εἴκοσι τέσσαρες, καὶ ἐπὶ τοὺς θρόνους εἴκοσι τέσσαρας πρεσβυτέρους, 'and around the throne, twenty-four thrones, and on these, twenty-four elders' (Rev 4.4a), and the four living beings, καὶ ἐν μέσῳ τοῦ θρόνου καὶ κύκλῳ τοῦ θρόνου τέσσαρα ζῷα, 'and around the throne in the centre, four living beings' (Rev 4.6c). Then, after weeping at not being able to open the book, he sees the Lamb amidst the throne, the living beings, and the circle of elders: καὶ εἶδον ἐν μέσῳ τοῦ θρόνου καὶ τῶν τεσσάρων ζῴων καὶ ἐν μέσῳ τῶν πρεσβυτέρων ἀρνίον (Rev 5.6a). Further on, after narrating the events that occur with the sounding of the trumpets, he mentions heaven, ἐν τῷ οὐρανῷ, which is where he sees the woman (Rev 12.1) and the dragon (12.3). After these great signs, John sees a beast rising from the sea (Rev 13.1a), and it is precisely here that the narrator's intention to establish the space before anything else is made clear, as he alters the usual order of the sentence by placing the separative genitive before the direct object: καὶ εἶδον ἐκ τῆς θαλάσσης θηρίον ἀναβαῖνον, 'And I saw from the sea a beast rising'. Later, he finds someone seated on a white cloud, καὶ εἶδον, καὶ ἰδοὺ νεφέλη λευκή, καὶ ἐπὶ τὴν νεφέλην καθήμενον, 'and I saw, and behold, a white cloud, and upon the cloud someone seated' (Rev 14.14). Finally, in heaven John sees a rider mounted on a white horse: καὶ εἶδον τὸν οὐρανὸν ἠνεῳγμένον, καὶ ἰδοὺ ἵππος λευκός καὶ ὁ καθήμενος ἐπ' αὐτὸν, 'and I saw heaven open, and behold, a white horse and the one mounted upon it' (Rev 19.11).

The spatial context, then, is in the καὶ εἶδον descriptions – the stage upon which each vision takes place – so much so that, on occasion, the same place is repeated without adding any new details or variations (Rev 4.2;

---

[15] According to David E. Aune, *Revelation 3*, p. 1100, it is the style of the author of the book of Revelation to mention the place where someone is seated before naming the person who occupies this place. As will be shown later on, this tendency is not limited to seated characters.

14.14). The use of this type of space as an introductory sign does not merely serve an aesthetic purpose, but rather corresponds to John's intention to give realism to his visions, as it is precisely this localization of an object in a specific place that is one of the first operations (if not the very first) performed by the sense of vision when perceiving an object: identifying it as something seen in a place.[16] However, John almost never describes what these places are like. The only exception is the throne of God. This description is given not when John contemplates it for the first time (Rev 4.2), but somewhat later on, following the description of the twenty-four elders and before that of the four living beings (Rev 4.5–6). In any case, John's eyes do not linger on the throne itself (perhaps because the splendour emanating from it prevents this), but rather on what surrounds it: an atmosphere characterized by ἀστραπαὶ καὶ φωναὶ καὶ βρονταί, 'flashes of lightning and rumblings of thunder' and ἑπτὰ λαμπάδες πυρός, 'seven torches of fire', and ὡς θάλασσα ὑαλίνη ὁμοία κρυστάλλῳ, 'like a sea transparent as glass'. Thus, John mixes visual and auditory perception, enabling the listener/reader not only to contemplate the place where God is found, but to perceive the surrounding atmosphere acoustically.

2.2.2   Constitutive Elements

Constitutive elements appear according to an established order; first, denomination or *pantonyme,* and second, expansion, composed of nomenclature and predicate groups.

a)   *Denomination or* Pantonyme

Denomination is usually formed by a syntagma: ὅμοιον υἱὸν ἀνθρώπου, 'like a son of man' (Rev 1.13a); ἐπὶ τὸν θρόνον καθήμενος, 'upon the throne, someone seated' (Rev 4.2b); εἴκοσι τέσσαρας πρεσβυτέρους, 'twenty-four elders' (Rev 4.4a); τέσσαρα ζῷα, 'four living beings' (Rev 4.6b); σημεῖον μέγα, 'great sign' (Rev 1.21); ἄλλο σημεῖον,

---

[16] In studies of apocalyptic literature, there is a tendency to identify visions with dreams; see for example J. Meyer Everts, 'Dreams in the NT and Greco-Roman Literature', *ABD 2,* 231–2. In the book of Revelation, however, this identification is not fully possible, as there are several differences between dreaming and the act of seeing. In dreams, in most cases, the space itself is not relevant to the story, and objects or characters may be perceived without the necessity of specifying where they are; on the other hand, when someone sees something in waking life, the perception of place is a key factor in framing that sight.

'another sign' (Rev 12.3); θηρίον ἀναβαῖνον, 'a beast rising' (Rev 13.1a); ἐπὶ τὴν νεφέλην καθήμενον, 'upon the cloud, someone seated' (Rev 14.14b); ὁ καθήμενος ἐπ' αὐτόν, 'the one mounted upon it' (Rev 19.11b). It is only on occasion, e.g., when he contemplates the Lamb (Rev 5.6a), that John employs an unqualified noun: ἀρνίον. Nor is it insignificant that the denomination of the Lamb – ἀρνίον – is different from the rest, as this is yet another way of emphasizing this particular figure's role within the work as a whole.[17]

Denomination plays a fundamental role in these types of descriptions, as it identifies the object of the vision. This function is fulfilled first of all by the strategic place in which the *pantonyme* is placed, after the space itself has been described. And so, through denomination, verisimilitude is again given to the narrative, as, indeed, when one sees something and it is situated in a specific place, it is perceived with clarity and identified, giving rise to statements like 'in the street, I saw a man', 'in the park, I saw a woman', and so on. On the other hand, when the object is not seen clearly or is too surprising, identification is more vague, and other expressions are heard, such as 'I seemed to see . . . ', 'I saw someone who seemed . . . ', 'I saw someone seated . . . ', etc. This is what happens in the καὶ εἶδον descriptions. At times, John perceives the object clearly and is able to identify it, for example: εἴκοσι τέσσαρες πρεσβυτέροι, 'twenty-four elders' (Rev 4.4a); τέσσαρα ζῷα, 'four living beings' (Rev 4.6b); ἀρνίον, 'a Lamb' (Rev 5.6a); and θηρίον, 'a beast' (Rev 13.1a).

At other times, he does not know exactly what it is that he is seeing, as in Rev 1.13, and so he resorts to a simile that has its roots in biblical literature: ὅμοιον υἱὸν ἀνθρώπου, 'like a son of man'. The same occurs in Rev 14.14, although on that occasion it is preceded by a description of the figure's posture: καθήμενον ὅμοιον υἱὸν ἀνθρώπου, 'someone seated, like a son of man'. This type of allusion to bodily position without clear identification of the figure being seen is also found in Rev 4.2b, ἐπὶ τὸν θρόνον καθήμενος, 'upon the throne, someone seated', and in Rev 19.11b, ὁ καθήμενος ἐπ' αὐτόν, 'the one mounted upon it', although

---

[17]   The centrality of the Lamb in the narrative section of the book of Revelation is undeniable. Indeed, numerous studies have been devoted to this figure, among them: J. D. D'Souza, *The Lamb of God in the Johannine Writings* (Allahabad: St Paul Publications, 1968); L. Johns, *The Lamb Christology of the Apocalypse of John: An Investigation into Its Origins and Rhetorical Force* (Tübingen: Mohr Siebeck, 2004); M. R. Hoffmann, *The Destroyer and the Lamb: The Relation Between Angelomorphic and Lamb Christology in the Book of Revelation* (Tübingen: Mohr Siebeck, 2005); S. Stanislas, 'The Slaughtered and Standing Lamb in the Book of Revelation', *IndTheolStud* 43 (2006), 471–94.

the rider in that verse is then immediately identified: πιστὸς [καλούμενος] καὶ ἀληθινός, '[he is called] faithful and true'. Nevertheless, this particular pericope confirms the technique employed in such descriptions: i.e., to reproduce in writing the dynamics of visual perception, so that first a horse is seen to arrive, καὶ ἰδοὺ ἵππος λευκός, then its rider is perceived, ὁ καθήμενος ἐπ' αὐτόν, and finally the rider's identity is established, πιστὸς [καλούμενος] καὶ ἀληθινός.

One small detail that should not be overlooked is that, when John sees God for the first time, he refers to him as ἐπὶ τὸν θρόνον καθήμενος, 'upon the throne, someone seated', logically without an article. From that moment on, whenever he mentions God, he makes a slight change in this expression by introducing the article, used anaphorically and with the usual syntax. Thus, in the rest of the narrative, whether spoken by John (Rev 4.9, 10; 5.1, 7; 19.4; 21.5) or by the chorus of voices that praise God or participate in the narration (Rev 5.13; 6.16; 7.10, 15), we find the expression ὁ καθήμενος ἐπὶ τοῦ θρόνου, 'the One seated upon the throne'. This usage only confirms that the καὶ εἶδον descriptions are an attempt to reproduce the manner in which John perceives the object of his vision.

Lastly, when the seer uses the formula ὤφθη, the denomination has two parts. The first expresses John's judgment about the nature of what he sees, σημεῖον μέγα, 'a great sign' (Rev 12.1), and σημεῖον ἄλλο, 'another sign' (Rev 12.3),[18] as a way of foreshadowing what he is going to relate next and thus preparing the listener/reader for it; in the second part, the object itself is identified: γυνή, 'woman' (Rev 12.1), and δράκων, 'dragon' (Rev 12.3).

Although proper names are absent in the denomination of characters, there are some that do appear over the course of the narrative, making the identification of those characters clearer still. Sometimes it is the narrator himself who provides these names; for example, the dragon that fights with the woman is called Διάβολος καὶ ὁ Σατανᾶς, 'Devil and Satan' (Rev 12.9). It is also John who gives the name of the rider in Rev 19.11. Other times, names are given by the characters themselves, as when the twenty-four elders address the one described initially as ἐπὶ τὸν θρόνον καθήμενος, 'upon the throne, someone seated', as ὁ κύριος καὶ ὁ θεὸς

---

[18] Σημεῖον has a variety of meanings; see Aune, *Revelation 2*, p. 678. I am here following the proposal of THAYER, 4757, s.v. σημεῖον, who suggests a sememe very appropriate to the context of the book of Revelation: 'prodigy, portent'. Along the same lines is *BDAG*, 6634, s.v. σημεῖον.

ἡμῶν, 'Our Lord and God' (Rev 4.11). On still other occasions, a character will identify himself by name, as when he who is described as ὅμοιον υἱὸν ἀνθρώπου, 'like a son of man', introduces himself through a series of titles (Rev 1.17–18) that make it clear both to John and to the listener/reader that it is in fact Christ who is speaking.

There is one character, however, who lacks explicit identification. This is the character whose *pantonyme* is ἐπὶ τὴν νεφέλην καθήμενον, 'upon the cloud, someone seated' (Rev 14.14b). Scholars debate whether this is Jesus or a being of an angelic nature.[19] Taking the description itself as a frame of reference, we find here a key element of identification in the expression ὅμοιον υἱὸν ἀνθρώπου, 'like a son of man', an anomalous formula that also appears in Rev 1.13, where it is clearly applied to Christ. The anomaly resides in the fact that ὅμοιος does not take an accusative but a dative, both in the book of Revelation (18 times)[20] and in the other books of the NT (24 times).[21] Nor, as will be seen in the next chapter, is it characteristic of the author to use a single formula to describe different characters – quite the contrary. The fact that ὅμοιον υἱὸν ἀνθρώπου is repeated for the character in Rev 14.14 is a way of informing the listener/reader that this is Christ in a new appearance.

At the same time, the expression υἱὸς ἀνθρώπου, 'son of man', is frequent in both the Old Testament (113 times)[22] and the New Testament;[23] its meaning, however, is different in each. In the OT, it is used to designate a given being,[24] while in the NT it refers specifically to Jesus, with the meaning that, being divine, he has achieved the height of human existence.[25] In the book of Revelation, the formula υἱὸς ἀνθρώπου carries more the OT sense of 'human person', as John sees an individual but does not know exactly who this person is. He has the aspect of a man, however, and so there is an undeniable parallel with

---

[19] In favour of the angelic being interpretation: Aune, *Revelation 2*, p. 841; M. Kiddle, *The Revelation of St John*, 7th edn (London: Hodder and Stoughton, 1963), pp. 276–7. In favour of the identification with Christ: Vanni, *Apocalisse*, p. 125 and Beale, *Revelation*, pp. 770–1.

[20] Rev 1.15; 2.18; 4.3(2), 6, 7(3); 9.7(2); 10.19; 11.1; 13.2, 4, 11; 18.18; 21.11, 18.

[21] These include: Matt 11.16; Luke 6.47, 48, 49; John 8.55; Heb 17.29; Gal 5.21; 1 John 3.2; Jude 7.

[22] These include: Num 23.19; Job 25.6; Ps 79.18; Ezek 2.1, 3; Dan 7.13.

[23] This is the case, for example, in Matt 8.20; Mark 2.10; Luke 5.24; John 1.51; Acts 7.56; Heb 2.6.

[24] G. W. E. Nickelsburg, 'Son of Man', *ABD* 6, 137–50.

[25] J. Mateos and F. Camacho, *El Hijo del Hombre: Hacia la plenitud humana* (Córdoba: El Almendro, 1995), p. 34.

Daniel (Dan 7.13).[26] John, in any case, seems mindful of the messianic interpretation of the NT expression, given that, when he relates his encounter with the resurrected Christ at the beginning of the book, the first thing he says when describing him is ὅμοιον υἱὸν ἀνθρώπου, 'like a son of man' (Rev 1.13), just before Christ himself reveals his identity.

b) Expansion

The narrator treats the expansion of the vision *in actu* descriptions (the καὶ εἶδον descriptions) differently according to whether a given description refers to God, people (both male and female characters) or animals. Nevertheless, all of these have a common characteristic; namely, that they describe features that are purely external and, therefore, perceptible through the sense of vision. References to qualities, defects, or ways of being that cannot be grasped in a simple glance, therefore, are absent.

The expansion of 'the One seated upon the throne' lacks nomenclature, in contrast to what occurs with other characters. John's gaze is focalized on a single aspect; i.e., the splendour that emanates from the figure. It is as if John, dazzled and blinded by this light, is unable to describe anything beyond its brightness. The predicate groups are thus reduced to the semantic field of elements which have a certain radiance, such as precious stones – ὅμοιος ὁράσει λίθῳ ἰάσπιδι καὶ σαρδίῳ, 'like jasper and carnelian' (Rev 4.3a); ὅμοιος ὁράσει σμαραγδίνῳ, 'like an emerald in appearance' (Rev 4.3b)[27] – and the rainbow that surrounds the throne.[28]

This kind of description is not exceptional in biblical literature, as Ezekiel uses the same technique to describe his own vision of God (Ezek 1.26–8; 10.1; 28.13). And so, it would seem that John's imprecision in this description is not a matter of chance, but completely intentional. The

---

[26] Beale, *Revelation*, p. 771; Prigent, *Commentary*, p. 450; Thomas, *Revelation 8–22*, p. 218; S. S. Smalley, *The Revelation to John: A Commentary on the Greek Text of the Apocalypse* (London: SPCK Publishing, 2005), p. 371.

[27] Although there is some disagreement over the exact referent for each term, a certain consensus has been reached regarding their colours: ἴασπις refers to green, σάρδιον to red, and σμάραγδος to emerald green; see LOUW and NIDA, 2.23, s.v. λίθος; 2.29, s.v. τίμιος; 2.30, s.v. ἴασπις; 2.36, s.v. σάρδιον; 2.33, s.v. σμάραγδος.

[28] I am more inclined to follow the traditional translation of 'rainbow' for the term ἶρις, rather than 'halo', as proposed by Juan Mateos (*NBE*), because it preserves an echo of the Old Testament tradition according to which the rainbow was an external manifestation of the eternal covenant established by God with men (Gen 9.8–17).

seer stands before God and, unable to contemplate his face directly, describes his glory by using a terminology already established in similar contexts. By this extremely simple method, John also reveals who it is that is seated on the throne: YHWH.

Something completely different occurs in the expansion of descriptions of male characters. Here, John describes in detail what he sees,[29] despite the radiance with which some of these figures are accompanied. The nomenclature here is centred principally on their external appearance, and so the semantic fields are reduced to two:

a)   Clothing, in a broad sense, referring to objects that cover the body and not strictly apparel. Thus, we have: ποδήρης, 'robe'; ζώνη, 'sash'; ἱμάτιον, 'robe'; and στέφανος, 'crown'.[30]

b)   Corporality: μαστοί, 'chest'; κεφαλή, 'head'; τρίχες, 'hair'; ὀφθαλμοί, 'eyes'; στόμα, 'mouth'; ὄψις, 'face'; δεξιὰ χείρ, 'right hand'; χείρ, 'hand'; μηρός, 'thigh'; and πόδες, 'feet'.

These two semantic fields have a primary function: the first, because clothing itself qualifies a person and places him in relation to the one who witnesses;[31] and the second, corporality, because this is the aspect of a person that gives him or her visibility. Once again, John shows us that the people he sees are, above all, flesh-and-blood individuals, despite their peculiarities.

Expansion is effected in accordance with the natural movement of the eyes. First, one's attention focuses on those elements of a figure that are the most striking when seen for the first time, such as clothing or the head, especially if this is covered with a crown or other headgear. Thus, in the descriptions of Christ (Rev 1.13b) and the twenty-four elders (Rev 4.4c), the first element that John refers to is their attire: Christ is dressed in a ποδήρης, 'robe', cinched with a ζώνη χρύσα, 'golden sash'; the twenty-four elders, ἐν ἱματίοις λευκοῖς, 'in white robes'. The second element that draws attention to a particular figure is the head (Rev 1.14; 4.4d; 14.14c), as this is the part of the body that allows identification; what is more,

---

[29]   In the description of Christ, the narrator includes an auditory element: ἡ φωνή, 'the voice' (Rev 1.15). For methodological reasons, this will be addressed in greater detail in Chapter 3.

[30]   A certain degree of lexical restriction can be observed where clothing is concerned, as the term ἱμάτιον is used on various occasions, in allusion to the twenty-four elders (Rev 4.4) or to the rider (Rev 19.13).

[31]   Vanni, *Apocalisse*, p. 126.

being always covered with a στέφανος, 'crown', or a διάδημα, 'diadem', it towers above all other elements. There is only one exception to this, and that is Rev 1.14, in which the head of the resurrected Christ is free of all adornment, save for his τρίχες λευκαί, 'white hair'.

Although this is the general tendency in these descriptions, some variations exist, as in the case of the other two visions that John has of Christ; i.e., seated on a cloud (Rev 14.14), and mounted on a horse (Rev 19.11). In Rev 14.14, John focuses first of all on the head, rather than the clothing, of the seated figure, who wears a στέφανον 'crown'; later, his gaze fixes upon the δρέπανον ὀξύ, 'sharp sickle', that Christ holds in his hand. In Rev 19.11, however, John's gaze is arrested by ὀφθαλμοὶ αὐτοῦ, 'his eyes' (Rev 19.12). The reason for this seems clear: the seer is once again focusing his attention on what is to him most striking. In the case of the figure seated on the cloud, it is the στέφανον, 'crown', and δρέπανον ὀξύ, 'sharp sickle'; for the other figure, it is his ὀφθαλμοί, 'eyes', as these have already been remarked upon in John's first vision (Rev 1.14) with the same simile: ὡς φλὸξ πυρός, 'like a flame of fire'. The initial allusion to Christ's eyes, then, may be a manifestation of the surprise John feels upon recognizing in the rider the gaze of Christ, which he contemplated in the earlier vision.

Where the predicate groups attached to male characters are concerned, radiance is the key element that reveals John's intention to transmit his own sensory perception to the listener/reader. To do this, he draws on the resources of language not only to make this reality visible, but to imbue it with light and glory. These include:

1.　　The repetition of the colour λευκός, 'white', whether by use of this adjective or through similes such as ὡς ἔριον λευκόν, 'like white wool' or ὡς χιών, 'like snow' (Rev 1.14a).

2.　　Expressions that transmit the idea of radiance, such as: the adjectival lexeme χρυσοῦς, 'golden', for the crowns of the elders (Rev 4.4d) and the one seated on the cloud (Rev 14.14), and for Christ's sash (Rev 1.13); the mention of objects whose sharpness, noted by forms of the adjective ὀξύς, also suggests their brightness, as in ῥομφαία δίστομος ὀξεῖα, 'sharp, double-edged sword' (Rev 1.16), δρέπανον ὀξύ, 'sharp sickle' (Rev 14.14), ῥομφαία ὀξεῖα, 'sharp sword' (Rev 19.15); and similes that express brightness, such as ὡς φλὸξ πυρός, 'like a flame of fire' (Rev 1.14c; 19.12), ὅμοιοι χαλκολιβάνῳ ὡς ἐν καμίνῳ πεπυρωμένης, 'like precious metal in a hot furnace' (Rev

1.15a), ὡς ὁ ἥλιος φαίνει ἐν τῇ δυνάμει αὐτοῦ,[32] 'like the sun shining with all its strength' (Rev 1.16).

On occasion, this radiance is reinforced by other elements, such as sound or the colour red. Sound appears in the first of John's visions, when he refers to the voice of Christ through a simile rooted in the Old Testament: ὡς φωνὴ ὑδάτων πολλῶν, 'like the roar of vast waters' (Rev 1.15). Thus, the listener/reader perceives the grandeur of the vision not only by what he sees, but also by what he hears.

The colour red appears in the description of the rider in Rev 19.11–16, not through the adjectival lexemes that denote colour – κόκκινος, πορφυροῦς, πύρινος, πυρρός – and which are used for the context of evil, but rather by means of two nouns for real substances that are red in colour: the blood in which the horseman's robe is soaked, ἱμάτιον βεβαμμένον αἵματι, 'robe stained with blood' (Rev 19.13);[33] and the wine of God's wrath, τὴν ληνὸν τοῦ οἴνου τοῦ θυμοῦ τῆς ὀργῆς τοῦ θεοῦ, 'the winepress of the fury of God's wrath' (Rev 19.15). The radiance of the mounted figure is thus presented to the listener/reader intermingled with the red of blood and wine.

Unlike earlier descriptions, the description of the rider (Rev 19.11–16) shows some features that are in fact unusual in predicate groups. The most significant of these is a shift in focalization. Up to this point, the καὶ εἶδον descriptions have been made according to the ocular movement of the witness – John – through external focalization.[34] However, in the description of the rider this emphasis changes to zero focalization.[35] For this reason, the various names by which the rider is known, πιστὸς καὶ

---

[32] The form πεπυρωμένης is a grammatical anomaly. It is, nevertheless, found in the *Codex Alexandrinus* and in the *Ephraemi Parisiensis*. In the *Codex Sinaiticus*, however, as well as in the translations offered in the *Vulgate* and by Irenaeus, we find πεπυρωμένῳ, which would be concordant with χαλκολιβάνῳ. This seems to be the form that John would have used, with the form πεπυρωμένης corresponding to a later revision of the text; see Charles, *Commentary 1*, p. 29; Smalley, *Revelation*, p. 45.

[33] I here follow the proposals of Charles, *Commentary 2*, pp. 133–4, and Vanni, *Apocalisse*, p. 323, note 38, which maintain that the meaning of βάπτω is 'soak, immerse' without modifying this to conform with Isa 63.3, in which the expression 'sprinkled upon my garments' appears; cf. Aune, *Revelation 3*, p. 1048; Beale, *Revelation*, p. 957.

[34] Marguerat and Bourquin, *Per leggere*, p. 80, following Genette, define external focalization as the mode of narration that coincides with what might be the perspective of the reader.

[35] Zero focalization is understood as the narrative point of view that transmits more information than is known by the characters of a story, and so transgresses the limits of time and space in a given scene; *ibid.*

ἀληθινός, 'faithful and true' (Rev 19.11), and ὁ λόγος τοῦ θεοῦ, 'the word of God' (Rev 19.13),[36] are provided, as is the purpose of the sharp sword that emerges from the horseman's mouth (Rev 19.15). John also offers brief comments about Christ's future task as well as the one at hand, i.e., treading on the winepress.[37] Thus, for the first time in a καὶ εἶδον description, John inserts, along with the visual aspects of the object being described, other elements that serve to complete the vision.

Finally, it should be noted that the predominant tone in the syntactic structures of this type of expansion is one of simplicity and brevity.[38] Expansion is thus constructed through the use of participles or clauses with the verb ἔχω (Rev 1.16; 14.14; 19.16), as well as simple clauses in which the verb εἰμί is implicit, linked sometimes to a coordinate (Rev 4.3). The similes used are remarkable both for their simplicity of structure (consisting of vehicle and tenor alone)[39] and for the semantic foundation upon which they are built; that is, elements of nature that are universally familiar: ὡς ἔριον λευκόν, 'like white wool'; ὡς χιών, 'like snow' (Rev 1.14a); ὡς φλὸξ πυρός, 'like a flame of fire' (Rev 1.14b; 19.12); etc.

The woman (Rev 12.1) is described in a somewhat different way from that in which the male characters are portrayed. Rather than describing her attire in detail (only the στέφανος, 'crown', she is wearing is mentioned), John fixes his attention on those elements in the firmament that highlight this particular female figure, obliging the listener/reader to focus on them as well: first, the sun;[40] then, the moon; and finally, the stars. The effect that this expansion produces in the listener/reader is one of wonder and astonishment. This is fully consistent with the technique

---

[36] The presence here of these two explicit nouns may be interpreted as a way of revealing the unknown name on the rider's diadem (Rev 19.12) – see Beale, *Revelation*, p. 957 – as opposed to later additions to the text, as proposed by Charles, *Commentary 2*, p. 132.

[37] John here introduces a present indicative, πατεῖ, according to Robertson, *Comentario*, p. 758, and Boring, *Revelation*, p. 196, which confers immediacy on the rider's mission. The future form would be πατήσω; see THAYER, 4090, s.v. πατέω.

[38] This is a common feature of all these descriptions, and so it is an aspect that will not be dealt with explicitly in the following pages.

[39] The vehicle is the carrier of the image, while the tenor is the term that pertains to real communicative discourse; see I. A. Richards, *The Philosophy of Rhetoric* (New York, NY: Oxford University Press, 1967), p. 118.

[40] On the meaning of περιβεβλημένη τὸν ἥλιον: L. García Ureña, 'El rigor del método: Una ayuda para el exegeta y traductor', in L. Roig Lanzillotta and I. Muñoz Gallarte, *Liber amicorum en honor del profesor Jesús Peláez del Rosal* (Córdoba: El Almendro, 2013), pp. 53–63.

used in the καὶ εἶδον descriptions: John describes what he sees, giving priority to that which he finds most striking.

At the same time, the semantic field of these celestial elements does connote radiance, as with the male characters. The difference is that the radiance that emanates from the woman comes not from her, but from the celestial elements that envelop her so completely. If we consider the biblical tradition, this is an audacious sort of expansion, as the sun, the moon, and the stars are the three celestial beings that bowed down before Joseph in one of his dreams (Gen 37.9), and whose worship God would later forbid (Deut 4.19), punishing those who disobeyed (Jer 8.2). On the other hand, in the book of Psalms these same elements are used to support the speaker's praise of God (Ps 148.3).[41] Therefore, the woman whom John contemplates here is presented as having a certain eminence.

Lastly, there is the expansion of animal descriptions. Nomenclature here is reduced to the semantic field of corporality, in this case, the corporality of animals: ὀφθαλμοί, 'eyes' (Rev 4.6; 5.6); πρόσωπον, 'face' (Rev 4.7); πτέρυγες, 'wings' (Rev 4.8); κέρατα, 'horns' (Rev 5.6; 12.3; 13.1); κεφαλή, 'head' (Rev 12.3; 13.1); πόδες, 'feet'; and στόμα, 'jaws' (Rev 13.2).

However, these expansions lack a common nomenclature, as there is little repetition, except in the case of κέρατα, 'horns', but none of the four living beings are explicitly described as having horns. This diversity is not surprising, as the seer's attention is not centred on the animal in itself (head, body, extremities), but on its monstrous appearance. Still more, it is this very monstrosity which explains why John chooses to focus on this aspect and make it the foundation for the construction of predicates, resorting frequently to similes, as these animals transcend established canons: ὅμοιον λέοντι, 'like a lion'; ὅμοιον μόσχῳ, 'similar to a calf' (Rev 4.7); ὡς ἐσφαγμένον, 'as though it had been slain' (Rev 5.6); etc.

Despite the extravagance of the descriptions, the listener/reader may recognize traces of other descriptions of monstrous animals in the OT, such as: the four living creatures in the first vision of Ezekiel (Ezek

---

[41] Charles, *Commentary 1*, p. 316, observes that a parallel can be found with the Testaments of the Twelve Patriachs 5.3–4. Unlike the situation in the book of Revelation, however, in which the woman embodies the celestial triad, Levi is presented as being like the sun and Judah like the moon, whose twelve rays seem to suggest the twelve stars.

Table 4 Nomenclature

CORPORALITY	REVELATION	DANIEL	EZEKIEL
ὀφθαλμοί / eyes	Rev 4.6, 8; 5.6	Dan 7.8	Ezek 10.12
κέρατα / horns	Rev 5.6; 12.3; 13.1	Dan 7.7, 8	–
κεφαλή / head	Rev 12.3; 13.1	Dan 7.6	–
πόδες / feet	Rev 13.2	Dan 7.4	Ezek 1.7
στόμα / mouth	Rev 13.2	Dan 7.5, 8	–
πτέρυγες / wings	Rev 4.8	Dan 7.4, 6: πτερά	Ezek 1.6, 8, 11; 10.5, 8, 12

Table 5 Predicate groups

REVELATION	DANIEL	EZEKIEL
Rev 4.7: ὅμοιον λέοντι' like a lion'	Dan 7.4: כְּאַרְיֵה OG-Th: ὡσεὶ λέαινα*	Ezek 1.10: וּפְנֵי אַרְיֵה LXX: πρόσωπον λέοντος Ezek 10.14: פְּנֵי אַרְיֵה
Rev 4.7: τὸ πρόσωπον ὡς ἀνθρώπου 'a face like a man's'	Dan 7.4: וְעַל־רַגְלַיִן כֶּאֱנָשׁ 'standing on two feet like a man' OG: ἐπὶ ποδῶν ἀνθρωπίνων, 'on human feet' Th: ἐπὶ ποδῶν ἀνθρώπου, 'on the feet of a man'	Ezek 1.10: פְּנֵי אָדָם LXX: πρόσωπον ἀνθρώπου Ezek 10.14: פְּנֵי אָדָם
Rev 4.7: ὅμοιον ἀετῷ 'like an eagle'	Dan 7.4: דִּי־נְשַׁר OG-Th: ὡσεὶ ἀετοῦ	Ezek 1.10: וּפְנֵי־נָשֶׁר LXX: πρόσωπον ἀετοῦ Ezek 10.14: פְּנֵי־נָשֶׁר
Rev 13.2: ὅμοιον παρδάλει 'like a leopard'	Dan 7.6: כִּנְמַר OG: ὡσεὶ πάρδαλιν Th: ὡσεὶ πάρδαλις	–

* Surprisingly, in both the OG and Th, this term is translated not as 'lion', but as 'lioness', in variance with the Hebrew text.

1.4–24), the four cherubim (Ezek 10.14), and the four beasts of Daniel (Dan 7.2–8), to the point that it is possible to draw a common nomenclature from them, as shown in Tables 4 and 5.[42]

[42] Table 5 shows these texts according to their existing variants. As is well known, there are two different Greek versions of the book of Daniel: that of the LXX and that of Theodotion; see N. Fernández Marcos, *Introducción a las versiones griegas de la Biblia* (Madrid: CSIC, 1998), pp. 100–3. In the present work, these variants are referred to

2.3   The Audio-Vision (Ἤκουσα καὶ Εἶδον) Descriptions

The audio-vision descriptions (the ἤκουσα καὶ εἶδον descriptions) are those that are based on both vision and hearing. They consist of a brief narrative section, a dialogue, and the description itself. Belonging to this group are the descriptions of the great whore (Rev 17.1–6)[43] and the New Jerusalem (Rev 21.9b–22.5). Their function is to give the listener/reader an image of two cities: Babylon, presented as a woman; and the New Jerusalem.

If we consider only the objects of these two descriptions (i.e., the great whore and the New Jerusalem), they can be seen to coincide with a type of description known as ecphrasis. Ecphrasis is the literary description of a work of pictorial or sculptural art,[44] or of a natural scene such as a landscape. Its function is to inform the recipient and to move them emotionally.[45] The classic example is that of Achilles' shield in the *Iliad* (18.478–606).

Examined in detail, these two descriptions in the book of Revelation share the characteristic features of ecphrasis. The great whore, according to D. E. Aune, recalls an image stamped on a *sestertius* from the time of Vespasian, which portrays the goddess Rome seated on the seven hills;[46] the New Jerusalem, meanwhile, is presented as a city.[47] Both descriptions have an informative function, as they tell us what their objects are like, but an emotional one as well, for John, upon concluding his description of the

---

respectively as OG (Old Greek, ancient Septuagint) and Th (Theodotion). When neither is specified, it is because both versions have the same reading.

[43] Rev 17.7–18 is excluded, as it is the interpretation of a vision; that is to say, it is a narrative, rather than a descriptive section. Although David E. Aune, *Revelation 3*, pp. 919, 924, considers that all of Chapter 17 is descriptive, I disagree with this, as the situation of a character explaining what John sees is not exclusive to Rev 17, but similar to that of John's first vision. On seeing Christ, the seer is overwhelmed, and it is Christ himself who comes to his aid, explaining to him the significance of part of what he has seen (Rev 1.20).

[44] L. Spitzer, 'The "Ode on a Grecian Urn"', or Content vs. Metagrammar', in A. Hatcher (ed.), *Essays on English and American Literature* (Princeton, NJ: Princeton University Press, 1962), p. 72.

[45] V. Pineda, 'La invención de la écfrasis', in C. Pérez Romero (ed.), *Homenaje a la profesora Carmen Pérez Romero* (Cáceres: Universidad de Extremadura, Servicio de Publicaciones, 2000), pp. 251–62.

[46] Aune, *Revelation 3*, pp. 919–23.

[47] David E. Aune argues that the description of the New Jerusalem does not constitute ecphrasis, as it contains movement (*ibid.*, p. 919). However, this does not seem to me a sufficient reason for excluding it from this category, as the ecphrasis of the shield of Achilles also features movement in its depictions of dancing, the building of cities, and various agrarian labours (Homer, *Il.* 18.478–606).

great whore, says that ἐθαύμασα ἰδὼν αὐτὴν θαῦμα μέγα, 'when I saw her, I was astonished, in great awe ... ' (Rev 17.6de). Meanwhile, in his description of the New Jerusalem, the seer is so impressed that he is led to predict the destiny of the holy city (Rev 21.24–27), as we will see later on.

In terms of technique, the ecphrasis maintains a certain structure and order within the expansion. In the case of the great whore, John chooses to describe her external aspects from bottom to top. Thus, he refers first to the beast on which she is seated (Rev 17.3), and then goes on to describe how she is dressed (Rev 17.4a), after which he focuses on the cup she holds in her hand (Rev 17.4b), and then the name written on her forehead (Rev 17.5a). The description closes with an allusion to the state she is seen to be in (μεθύουσαν, 'drunken', Rev 17.6). When he later describes the New Jerusalem, John begins with an outer view of the city (Rev 21.10–21a) and then goes on to explore its interior (Rev 21.21b–22.5).

2.3.1   Demarcation Signs

In the audio-vision descriptions (the ἤκουσα καὶ εἶδον descriptions), the introductory sign is a circumstance; i.e., John's encounter with an angel, the *angelus interpres*.[48] This may be broken down into three parts:

a)   The angel's arrival and meeting with John (Rev 17.1a; 21.9a). This is effected through a verb of movement, ἦλθεν, and a lexical group of *verba dicendi*: ἐλάλησεν ... λέγων.

b)   The invitation of the angel (Rev 17.1b; 21.9b). This consists of the invitation itself (δεῦρο, δείξω σοι, 'come, I will show you') and the object that John is invited to view (τὸ κρίμα τῆς πόρνης τῆς μεγάλης, 'the judgment of the great whore'); τὴν νύμφην τὴν γυναῖκα τοῦ ἀρνίου, 'the bride, the wife of the Lamb').

c)   The relocation to the place indicated by the angel (Rev 17.3a; 21.10a). In the case of the great whore, this is the ἔρημον, 'desert', and for the New Jerusalem, ὄρος μέγα καὶ ὑψηλόν, 'a great and high mountain'. Both locations, in perfect contrast,

---

[48] The angel has been given the name *angelus interpres* as he interprets and so clarifies the vision; see J. Kovacs and C. Rowland, *Revelation: The Apocalypse of Jesus Christ* (Malden, MA: Blackwell, 2004), p. 3. Precedents may be found both in the OT (Ezek 40–48; Zech 1–6; Dan 7–12) and in Jewish apocalyptic literature (1 Enoch 21.5–10; 22.1–14; 4 Ezra 4.1–5.13); see Aune, *Revelation 1*, pp. 15–16.

also serve to frame the vision in a specific place, by which method John once again manages to give verisimilitude to his story.

Furthermore, after this encounter, there appears the formula of visual perception, which for the whore is καὶ εἶδον (Rev 17.3b) and for the New Jerusalem is καὶ ἔδειξέν μοι (Rev 21.10b). The description of the whore thus underscores the active nature of the seer's own role, while this is more passive in his vision of the New Jerusalem; that is to say, in the second case, John sees by means of the angel's mediation. The focalization does not change, however, as the description of the New Jerusalem is given from John's point of view. He will later return to the formula of visual perception, but this time to comment on what he did not see: καὶ ναὸν οὐκ εἶδον, 'and I saw no temple at all' (Rev 21.22).

Once again, the descriptions lack specific concluding signs. The listener/reader knows that the descriptive section has concluded when the angel is heard to speak, through the expression καὶ εἶπέν μοι, 'and he said to me' (Rev 17.7a; 22.6). In any case, in the description of the whore, with the statement καὶ ἐθαύμασα ἰδὼν αὐτὴν θαῦμα μέγα, 'and when I saw her, I was astonished, in great awe . . . ' (Rev 17.6de),[49] the listener/reader is given a hint that the description is about to end, if it has not already ended, as it expresses John's perplexity on experiencing this vision.[50]

2.3.2   Constitutive Elements

a)   Denomination or Pantonyme

After the formula of visual perception comes the denomination that identifies what John sees: a woman and a city.[51] The first is indicated by a common noun, γυνή, 'woman' (Rev 17.3), while a syntagma is used to designate the second, τὴν πόλιν τὴν ἁγίαν Ἰερουσαλήμ, 'the holy city, Jerusalem' (Rev 21.10b). These denominations are in contrast to the presentations of these same elements by the angel. The angel does not mention the woman directly, but refers to τὸ κρίμα τῆς πόρνης τῆς

---

[49] Beale, *Revelation*, p. 863, holds that, to the feeling of awe expressed by the verb θαυμάζω, the context adds the elements of fear, perplexity, and admiration.

[50] Something similar occurs in Rev 1.17. The difference lies in the fact that the narrative section in that pericope has already opened by means of a time clause: καὶ ὅτε εἶδον αὐτόν, 'and on seeing this'.

[51] J. E. Bruns, 'The Contrasted Women of Apocalypse 12 and 17', *CBQ* 26 (1964), 459.

μεγάλης, 'the judgment of the great whore' and, according to Gregory K. Beale, goes on to state the motives for this judgment: μεθ' ἧς ἐπόρνευσαν οἱ βασιλεῖς τῆς γῆς καὶ ἐμεθύσθησαν οἱ κατοικοῦντες τὴν γῆν ἐκ τοῦ οἴνου τῆς πορνείας αὐτῆς, 'with whom the kings of the earth have fornicated, and the inhabitants of the earth have become drunk with the wine of her prostitution' (Rev 17.2). Nevertheless, what John sees at this moment is not the execution of the sentence, but the whore herself. For the definitive identification of this woman, we must wait for the expansion. It is then that we are told her name, as it is inscribed on her forehead: Βαβυλὼν ἡ μεγάλη, 'Babylon the great' (Rev 17.5a).

As for the holy city, the angel's presentation of it is a peculiar one, as he does not tell John that he is about to see the New Jerusalem, but rather τὴν νύμφην τὴν γυναῖκα τοῦ ἀρνίου, 'the bride, the wife of the Lamb' (Rev 21.9b).[52] To understand the apparent leap from alluding to the bride of the Lamb to the holy city, two earlier passages should be kept in mind: Rev 19.7–9 and 21.2. The first includes part of the triumphant song of the saved, announcing the marriage of the Lamb to a bride who has been adorned but not named. The second refers to the moment at which John, after seeing a new heaven and a new earth, watches as the New Jerusalem descends from heaven, ἡτοιμασμένην ὡς νύμφην, 'dressed as a bride'.[53]

Again, John tells us what he sees and how it appears to him: the New Jerusalem seems like (ὡς) a bride, because of the way it is 'dressed', although at no time does he identify it with the bride of the Lamb. It is when the angel speaks (Rev 21.9b) that the New Jerusalem is confirmed to be τὴν νύμφην τὴν γυναῖκα τοῦ ἀρνίου, 'the bride, the wife of the Lamb'.[54] In his description, John does not say καὶ εἶδον, 'and I saw', but rather ἔδειξέν μοι τὴν πόλιν τὴν ἁγίαν Ἰερουσαλήμ, 'he . . . showed me the holy city, Jerusalem' (Rev 21.10b), as he not only discovers the city,

---

[52] The identification of Jerusalem with the bride stems from an Old Testament tradition with its origins, principally, in the prophetic writings, in which the relationship of God with his people is frequently expressed in nuptial terms (Isa 54.5–6; 61.10).

[53] Although, for a period of time, exegesis maintained that Rev 21.2 was in fact a later addition – see Charles, *Commentary 2*, pp. 144–54 – it is now considered to be part of a single literary unit; see Aune, *Revelation 3*, pp. 1113, 1120. In the body of the text itself there is evidence that supports this idea: Rev 21.2 corresponds to the moment when John discovers the New Jerusalem, while Rev 21.9a focuses on the identification of the New Jerusalem with the bride of the Lamb and provides a detailed description of the same.

[54] This interpretation is also maintained by R. Zimmermann, 'Nuptial Imagery in the Revelation of John', *Bib* 84 (2003), 170.

but is given the information that was lacking; i.e., that Jerusalem and the bride of the Lamb are one and the same.[55]

b)   *Expansion*

In the audio-vision descriptions (the ἤκουσα καὶ εἶδον descriptions), expansion is built upon longer clauses, linked by coordination or juxta-position, and upon enumerations (Rev 17.4; 21.19–20). Nomenclature and predicate groups alternate constantly, and so it is difficult to establish the limits between them. For this reason, they will be examined here simultaneously, unless it is relevant to do otherwise. As the descriptions of the great whore and the New Jerusalem have different expansions, I consider it appropriate to address each one separately.

b.1)   *The Great Whore*   The expansion of the description of the great whore (Rev 17.1–6) also includes that of the θηρίον, 'beast', on which she is seated (Rev 17.3bc). The beast is described first, and the expansion here has much in common with the description of the dragon in Rev 12.3. Each has seven heads and ten horns. The difference is in their colour and in the expression ὀνόματα βλασφημίας, 'blasphemous names'.[56] As opposed to πυρρός, 'bright red', there appears κόκκινος, 'scarlet', the same colour worn by the whore, and one that connotes the sin of lust.[57] Therefore, the use of κόκκινος in a sense reinforces ὀνόματα βλασφεμίας by making reference to a moral dimension: i.e., the presence of sin.

Expansion in the case of the great whore is achieved through five participial forms used in succession to show her external features: her posture, καθημένη (Rev 17.3b); how she is dressed, περιβεβλημένη, and adorned, κεχρυσωμένη (Rev 17.4a); what she holds in her hands, ἔχουσα (Rev 17.4b); and, lastly, her state of drunkenness, μεθύουσα (Rev 17.6). Three dominant semantic fields are used for this expansion:

---

[55] Based on what is presented in the body of the text, the hypothesis put forward by Aune, *Revelation* 3, p. 928, that the use of the verb δείκνυμι pertains to a final compositional stage of the book of Revelation, does not seem to be supported.

[56] This is an example of Hebrew genitives of quality; see G. Mussies, *The Morphology of Koine Greek, As Used in the Apocalypse of St. John: A Study in Bilingualism* (Leiden: Brill, 1971), p. 96. The interpretation given by Aune, *Revelation* 2, p. 734, seems accurate; he maintains that these names or titles may be κύριος, 'lord'; σωτήρ, 'saviour'; and *divi filius*, 'son of God', which the Roman emperors applied to themselves.

[57] O. Michel, 'κόκκος, κόκκινος', *TDNT* 3, 810–14.

a) The colour red: κόκκινος, 'scarlet'; πορφυροῦς, 'purple'; αἷμα,
    'blood' (Rev 17.4a, 6a).

b) Jewels: χρυσίον, 'gold'; λίθος τίμιος, 'precious stone'; μαργαρίτης,
    'pearl'; ποτήριον χρυσοῦν, 'golden cup' (Rev 17.4ab).

c) Sin: βδέλυγμα, 'abominations'; ἀκάθαρτα, 'filthiness'; πορνεία,
    'fornication'; πόρναι, 'prostitutes' (Rev 17.4b, 5b).

This nomenclature, however, will project a meaning that transcends
the literal sense of these terms. The reason for such a double significance
is that, unlike the characters featured in the καὶ εἶδον descriptions, the
woman is not so much a woman as merely, as mentioned before, a visual
image of the city of Babylon.[58] By extension, through the semantic fields
employed, a new sense is projected: that of her power and her lust.

One manifestation of this power is the woman's posture, καθημένην
ἐπὶ θηρίον, 'seated on a beast' (Rev 17.3b), because in antiquity kings
were usually portrayed seated to show their sovereignty.[59] Additionally,
it underscores her domination of the beast. Later on, her power is
reaffirmed by her being dressed in πορφυροῦς, 'purple' (Rev 17.4a),
a colour reserved exclusively for monarchs,[60] and adorned with a variety
of jewels; even the cup she holds is made of gold (Rev 17.4b). It is
a description that recalls representations of the *Magna Mater*, whose
iconography is the same as that of the goddess Cybele: enthroned upon
a podium, wearing a tower-shaped crown, holding a libation bowl and
a tympanum or sceptre, accompanied by lions or in a carriage drawn by
them.[61]

The sin of lust is also underscored by these three semantic fields, which
succeed each other in a crescendo. The colour red frames the pericope by
means of a circular structure: first, scarlet and purple (κόκκινος and
πορφυροῦς, Rev 17.4a) are introduced through the woman's garments;
later, red reappears in the αἷμα τῶν ἁγίων, 'blood of the saints', adding
a dramatic tone which is further reinforced by the repetition of the
syntagma ἐκ τοῦ αἵματος τῶν μαρτύρων Ἰησοῦ, 'of the blood of the

---

[58] The representation of a city as a woman is frequent in prophetic writings and, as Adela
Yarbro Collins points out in *Apocalypse*, p. 118, this was also true among the peoples of the
Ancient Near East.

[59] C. Schneider, '† κάθημαι, † καθίζω, † καθέζομαι', *TDNT 3*, 440–4.

[60] F. W. Danker, 'Purple', *ABD 5*, 557–660.

[61] F. R. Walton and J. Scheid, 'Cybele', in S. Hornblower and A. Spawforth (eds.), *The
Oxford Classical Dictionary* (Oxford: Clarendon Press, 1996), p. 416; T. Vega, 'Cibeles',
in J. Alvar Ezquerra (ed.), *Diccionario Espasa Mitología Universal* (Madrid: Espasa-
Calpe, 2000), pp. 189–90.

martyrs of Jesus' (Rev 17.6). The description is thus imbued with red and, as the beast is described as having the same colouring (Rev 17.3b), it can be said that the scene is doubly tinged with red: the red of lust and the red of the martyrs' blood.

The jewels that are here enumerated, aside from their sumptuousness, also have a connotation of seduction and lust, as such adornments were used by prostitutes to enhance their attractiveness (Jer 4.30; Isa 3.23). The circular structure used for this enumeration adds further emphasis, opening with a noun, χρυσίον, 'gold' (Rev 17.4) and closing with its adjectival form, χρυσοῦς, 'golden' (Rev 17.4b).

Finally, lust is made present through the semantic field of sin. The description begins with βδέλυγμα (Rev 17.4b) and concludes by alluding to the woman's drunkenness, μεθύουσα (Rev 17.6a). Later comes a series of repetitions that emphasize the presence of sin through idolatry – βδελύγματα, 'abominations' (Rev 17.4b, 5b)[62] – and lust itself – τὰ ἀκάθαρτα τῆς πορνείας αὐτῆς, 'the filthiness of her fornication' (Rev 17.4b); ἡ μήτηρ τῶν πορνῶν, 'the mother of prostitutes' (Rev 17.5b).

b.2)   The New Jerusalem   The expansion of the description of the New Jerusalem is the broadest in the book of Revelation. The narrator describes the city at three different moments: when John contemplates it for the first time (Rev 21.10b–14); when the angel describes its dimensions (Rev 21.15–27); and after the angel's final speech (Rev 22.1–5).

While the angel facilitates the movement from one descriptive section to the next, making it possible to determine clearly the beginning of each expansion, the same cannot be said for their conclusions; more specifically, it is not clear where the descriptive sections contained in Rev 21.15–27 and 22.1–5 end, as here there is also a temporal shift. In Rev 21.24–27 and 22.3.5, the present tense, which has been maintained in the description up to now, is abandoned in favour of the future (περιπατήσουσιν, ἔσται, ὄψονται, etc.), which seems inconsistent with the description as a whole, as John is describing the city as he sees it at the moment, with no reference to future time. What is more, in both texts there is a shift in perspective with respect to the principal line followed in the description. The seer does not centre his discourse exclusively on the city itself, but focuses mainly on its inhabitants. More properly, Rev 21.24–27 and 22.3–5 constitute a commentary by the narrator, in which

---

[62] THAYER, 987, s.v. βδέλυγμα.

John, elated by his contemplation of the New Jerusalem and realizing that the revelation is about to conclude, abandons his role of narrator–witness and once again adopts a zero focalization, so that he looks towards the future, showing the listener/reader what will take place when the New Jerusalem is not merely a vision, but a reality. For this reason, the structure that I propose for the description of the New Jerusalem is as follows:

1.   Rev 21.10b–14: introductory vision
2.   Rev 21.15–23: outer description of the city
3.   Rev 22.1–2: inner description.

Despite this division, there are elements that help to confer a sense of unity on the description as a whole. These include its circular structure and the repetition of specific semantic fields and lexemes.

With respect to its circularity, if we examine this descriptive period closely, we can observe that the first section (Rev 21.10b–14) and the last (Rev 22.1–2) share the same structure. Rev 21.10b–14 is comprised of a main clause, headed by the formula of visual perception καὶ ἔδειξέν μοι (Rev 21.10b) and followed by a series of juxtaposed participles:[63] καταβαίνουσαν (Rev 21.10); ἔχουσαν (Rev 21.11); ἔχουσα (Rev 21.12 [2]); and ἔχων (Rev 21.14). Rev 22.1–2 concludes in the same manner: the formula of visual perception, καὶ ἔδειξέν μοι; and then the participles ἐκπορευόμενον (Rev 22.1b), ποιοῦν, and ἀποδιδοῦν (Rev 22.2b). In the central section is the description of the outer city (Rev 21.15–23), in which the use of participles is replaced primarily by simple or nominal clauses, linked by juxtaposition or coordination, except for the participial construction κεκοσμημένοι, 'they were adorned' (Rev 21.19a), with the verb used in a personal form.

---

[63] Once again, there is an irregular use of participles. First, agreement in case is abandoned, with ἔχουσαν used instead of ἔχουσα. Then, in terms of gender, the masculine form ἔχων is used, rather than the expected neuter, in agreement with τὸ τεῖχος. Two explanations have been given for this anomaly: a) it is a solecism; see N. Turner, *Syntax*, vol. 3 of J. H. Moulton and N. Turner, *A Grammar of New Testament Greek* (Edinburgh: T & T Clark, 1963), p. 315; Blass and Debrunner, *Grammar*, § 136.136.4; or b) it is a case of confusion, as in the LXX an interchange of o/ω is observed; see Aune, *Revelation 3*, p. 1138. As for the function of these participles, there is today a tendency to believe that they are being used in a personal form; see S. E. Porter, *Verbal Aspect in the Greek of the New Testament with Reference to Tense and Mood* (New York, NY: P. Lang, 1989, rep. 2003), p. 376. Thus, in the case of ἔχουσα, the seer changes his point of view: Jerusalem ceases to be the object of the vision, and becomes its subject. The same occurs with ἔχων, as it is the wall that now becomes the focus of attention; see Beale, *Revelation*, p. 1068.

The semantic fields employed are seven in number: the constitutive elements of the city, characters, numbers, radiance, precious stones, measurements, and compass points. Not all of these appear in all three sections, however. The fact that three of the semantic fields – the constitutive elements of the city, characters, and numbers – are repeated throughout the description intensifies their unity, which might otherwise have been affected by the presence of the two non-descriptive pericopes (Rev 21.24–27; 22.3–5).

This sense of unity is further reinforced by the repetition of ὁ θεός, 'God' (Rev 21.10, 11, 22; 22.1), ἀρνίον, 'Lamb' (Rev 21.14, 22; 22.1), and δώδεκα, 'twelve' (Rev 21.12[3], 14[3], 16, 21[2]; 22.2), endowing the description with additional significance.

God and the Lamb appear separately in the first descriptive section, while in the second and third they are mentioned together, first God and then the Lamb (Rev 21.22; 22.1). With this alternation the narrator shows not only that the city comes from God, and that the Lamb is inherent within it, but also that between God and the Lamb there is an intimate communion. Meanwhile, the repeated use of the number δώδεκα, even within the same context – the city has twelve gates, with twelve angels whose names are those of the twelve tribes of Israel (Rev 21.12) – illustrates the importance of this number in the New Jerusalem, to the point that δώδεκα may be seen as the principal number of the holy city.

The first two times that John uses δώδεκα he is referring to the city's gates and pillars. Each has a name: the gates are αἱ δώδεκα φυλαὶ υἱῶν Ἰσραήλ, 'the twelve tribes of Israel', and the pillars are οἱ δώδεκα ἀπόστολοι τοῦ ἀρνίου, 'the twelve Apostles of the Lamb'. In this way, the New Jerusalem embodies in the 'today' of the vision what are in fact two realities: the past (the people of Israel) and the present (the Apostles of the Lamb), which are anything but exclusive of each other, as both combine to make up the holy city. The 'twelve' of the gates and the pillars will be repeated in the second part of the description, but in reverse order: first the twelve stones of the pillars (Rev 21.19–20) and then the twelve pearls of the gates (Rev 21.21), evoking the presence of the twelve Apostles and of Israel. There is, then, a certain intention on the part of the narrator to show that the New Jerusalem embodies in some way both Israel and the twelve Apostles, and thus comprises a unity, a single people.

The number twelve is also made present through its multiples,[64] when the angel measures the dimensions of the city: ἐμέτρησεν τὴν πόλιν τῷ

---

[64] Following this idea of multiples, others might be included here as well, such as the ἑκατὸν τεσσαράκοντα τεσσάρων πηχῶν, 'one hundred and forty-four thousand cubits', of

καλάμῳ ἐπὶ σταδίων δώδεκα χιλιάδων, 'he measured the city with the measuring rod at twelve thousand *stadia*' (Rev 21.16). The twelve thousand *stadia* refer to its totality (length, width, and height). It is logical here to wonder what δώδεκα refers to: the tribes of Israel, or the Apostles. Given the place where the phrase 'twelve thousand' appears in the description – i.e., after the mention of the two δώδεκα – it may be said that δώδεκα χιλιάδων encompasses both, while up to this point (and later in Rev 21.19–21) each time that δώδεκα is mentioned it refers to one of the two realities and not to both. Not indicating one or the other precisely here suggests that it refers both to the tribes of Israel and to the twelve Apostles, as together they form a unity. This is a way of placing in relief the inclusion of all God's people in the New Jerusalem.[65] Much the same occurs at the end of the description, with the mention of the καρποί δώδεκα, 'twelve fruits', of the tree of life (Rev 22.2).

As a result, in the description of the New Jerusalem, δώδεκα acquires a new meaning: the historical reality of the chosen people, beginning with the tribes of Israel and concluding with the twelve Apostles. The holy city appears as the city of these chosen people, from Israel to the Apostles.

The expansion of the introductory vision (Rev 21.10b–14) is achieved through what John is able to see of the city 'in motion', καταβαίνουσαν ἐκ τοῦ οὐρανοῦ, 'descending from heaven' (Rev 21.10b). The semantic fields here are focused mainly on the outer aspect of the city, on its radiance (ἡ δόξα, 'the glory'; ὁ φωστήρ, 'the light'; λίθος τιμιώτατος, 'precious stone'; λίθος ἴασπις κρυσταλλίζων, 'jasper stone clear as crystal', Rev 21.11), and on its constitutive elements (τεῖχος, 'wall'; πυλῶνες, 'gates'; θεμέλιοι, 'pillars', Rev 21.12, 14), although characters also appear (ὁ θεός, 'God'; ἄγγελοι, 'angels'; φυλαὶ υἱῶν Ἰσραήλ, 'tribes of the sons of Israel'; ἀπόστολοι τοῦ ἀρνίου, 'Apostles of the Lamb', Rev 21.10, 11, 12, 14), as well as the compass points (ἀνατολή, 'east'; βορρᾶς, 'north'; νότος, 'south'; δυσμή, 'west', Rev 21.13) and various numbers (τρεῖς, 'three'; δώδεκα, 'twelve', Rev 21.12[3], 13[4], 14[3]), all of which add qualitative features of the city.

The expansion of the description of the outer city (Rev 21.15–23) takes place unhurriedly, perhaps because the city has come to rest in a place of

the wall, whose dimensions are 12 x 12; see Biguzzi, *Apocalisse*, p. 136. However, given that this analysis of the text is focused on the lexeme δώδεκα, I have decided not to examine these here.

[65] Beale, *Revelation*, p. 1073.

stability. Its semantic fields take in not only the various elements that comprise the city and its characters, but also its dimensions and the materials of which it is built. The semantic field of the city's constitutive elements includes a wide variety of lexemes, as these deal with aspects of the city that are both outer (τεῖχος, 'wall'; θεμέλιοι, 'pillars'; πυλῶνες, 'gates', Rev 21.15, 17, 18, 19, 21) and inner (ἐνδώμησις, 'material'; πλατεῖα, 'square'; ναός, 'temple', Rev 21.18, 21, 22). Thus, the way is paved for the third and final expansion (Rev 22.1–2).

The semantic field of the measurements is concentrated at the beginning of the expansion and coincides with that used in the Septuagint (Ezek 40–42):[66] τετράγωνος, 'squared'; μῆκος, 'length'; πλάτος, 'width'; κάλαμος, '(measuring) rod'; στάδια, *stadia*; ὕψος, 'height'; πήχεις, 'cubits'; μέτρον, 'measurement' (Rev 21.16–17). The measurements are linked to the movements of the angel, who first measures the city, and then its wall.[67] Despite the logical perplexity of the listener/ reader at the surprising dimensions,[68] John strives to give objectivity to what he is communicating, as the city has these measurements not because the seer says it does, but because he is transmitting what the angel has told him in units of human measurement (Rev 21.17). The exactness of these measurements in turn obliges the listener/reader to contemplate the city just as John himself sees it.

In any case, the most striking element here is the lexical richness of the nomenclature used for the materials. The city is erected upon a foundation of gold, pearls, and precious stones – luxurious materials unthinkable for the construction of an earthly city. The nomenclature thus highlights an idea that John points out from the beginning of the description: i.e., that the New Jerusalem is in fact a heavenly city. To focus the reader's attention, the narrator employs the list effect,[69] by a series of syntactically similar structures dominated by nominal clauses.

---

[66] The description of the New Jerusalem is also found in the Qumran mss., as well as in a composition entitled *The Description of the New Jerusalem*. These texts have a certain similarity to the book of Revelation, as it is an angel who measures the city and provides its dimensions. The fundamental difference is that, in the Qumran texts, all of the elements of the city are measured: its blocks (2Q24 Fr. 1.3–4; 4Q549 Fr. 1 col. 2.14–15), the distance between gates (4Q549 Fr. 1 cols. 1–2), its streets (4Q549 Fr. 1 col. 2.16–22; 5Q Fr. col. 1.3–6), houses (4Q550 Fr. 1.1–12), and so on.

[67] The syntactic structure (καὶ + ἐμέτρησεν + direct object) is repeated each time a new measurement is made (Rev 21.16b, 17).

[68] The dimensions are thus on a grand scale: 12,000 *stadia* equals 1,500 miles/2,000 km; see Smalley, *Revelation*, p. 551. The walls, however, are relatively low.

[69] Hamon, *Introduction*, p. 67.

The participle κεκοσμημένοι, which was used earlier, also reappears: ὡς νύμφην κεκοσμημένην τῷ ἀνδρὶ αὐτῆς, 'like a bride adorned for her husband' (Rev 21.2);[70] its repetition may indicate that these bridal adornments are precious stones.

The detailed enumeration of the stones allows us not only to contemplate the stones themselves, but to envision something of their radiance and the colours with which they adorn the city: the white of ἴασπις, 'jasper' (Rev 21.18, 19);[71] the blue of σάπφιρος, 'sapphire' (Rev 21.19);[72] the green of χαλκηδών, 'chalcedony';[73] the emerald green of σμάραγδος, 'emerald' (Rev 21.19b); the dark brown of σαρδόνυξ, 'onyx'; the reddish tone of σάρδιον, 'carnelian'; the yellow of χρυσόλιθος, 'chrysolite'; the sea green or dark blue of βήρυλλος, 'beryl'; the bright yellow of τοπάζιον, 'topaz'; the apple green of χρυσόπρασος, 'chrysoprase';[74] the dark blue of ὑάκινθος, 'jacinth';[75] and, finally, the violet of ἀμέθυστος, 'amethyst' (Rev 21.20).[76] John, and with him the listener/reader, views the New Jerusalem as being immersed in an amalgam of colours, a genuine rainbow.[77] All of this is further intensified in the verses that follow, as, after this listing of precious stones, their colours are still present in the μαργαρῖται, 'pearls', of the gates (Rev 21.21a) and the χρυσίον, 'gold', of the πλατεῖα, 'square' (Rev

---

[70] Beale, *Revelation*, p. 1080.

[71] According to *BDAG*, 3646, s.v. ἴασπις, jasper may possess a variety of hues: reddish, green, brown, blue, yellow. Josephine Massyngberde, quoting Spencer, notes that it was at the time a common stone; hence, one is inclined to believe that the stone referred to in Rev 21.19 is a highly coveted variety of jasper that was white in colour; see J. Massyngberde Ford, *Revelation: Introduction: Translation and Commentary* (New York, NY: Doubleday, 1975), p. 335. This would be consistent with the contexts in which it appears in the book of Revelation (Rev 4.3; 21.11) and for this reason I have considered it here to be white.

[72] This would be an intense blue, especially if we remember that in antiquity it was identified with lapis lazuli; see *BDAG*, 6580, s.v. σάπφιρος.

[73] Robertson, *Comentario*, p. 763, basing his ideas on *Historia Natural*, suggests that this was a copper silicate of chalcedony that was green in colour.

[74] LOUW and NIDA, 2.40, s.v. χρυσόπρασος.

[75] *BDAG* and Massyngberde hold that the colour blue is here only probable; see *BDAG*, 7492, s.v. ὑάκινθος; Massyngberde Ford, *Revelation*, p. 336. THAYER, 5389, s.v. ὑάκινθος, however, supports this idea, as Homer and other poets mention a flower of the same colour.

[76] In *BDAG*, 388, s.v. ἀμέθυστος, it is said to have had the colour of wine mixed with water.

[77] For this reason, it might be thought that the hypothesis on colours given in Chapter 1 is invalidated, but this is not the case. The New Jerusalem is not built on earth, but on a new earth with a new heaven; as this is a new creation, colours such as red or green have lost their negative connotations.

21.21b). This is also true for the idea of radiance, with gold modified by καθαρός, 'pure', and the simile ὡς ὕαλος διαυγής, 'like shining crystal', both of which act to underscore the city's resplendent aspect.[78]

John is so impressed by this wealth of colour and radiance that he then feels obliged to explain that the brilliance of the New Jerusalem comes not from any celestial body, as in the new heaven these no longer exist, but from the glory of God and the Lamb, who have their dwelling there (Rev 21.22). The New Jerusalem is, by its very name, the City of God. What is more, its description harks back to its earlier announcement in Tob 13.16–17 and Isa 54.11–12. However, what in Tobit and Isaiah was merely promised is in the book of Revelation a reality: a city built of precious stones.

The expansion of the description of the city's interior (Rev 22.1–2) begins with a discourse by the angel: καὶ ἔδειξέν μοι. It is as if John needed the angel's help to continue viewing the city. And so, after first referring to the angel, the seer goes on to describe what he sees in the great square,[79] which he has just mentioned (Rev 21.21).

As in Rev 21.10–14, the expansion here alternates between nomenclature and predicate groups. In any case, nomenclature continues to be the usual style of John's descriptions; i.e., he shows what he sees. Thus, in Rev 22.1–2, the listener/reader takes, along with John, a brief tour of the city's main square, in the centre of which (ἐν μέσῳ τῆς πλατείας), along with a flowing river (καὶ τοῦ ποταμοῦ), we find the tree of life occupying a central place within the square itself.

The lexical reduction of the nomenclature – ποταμός ὕδατος ζωῆς, 'river of the water of life' (Rev 22.1); ξύλον ζωῆς, 'tree of life' (Rev 22.2) – is striking, if one considers the general tone of the previous descriptive sections. Both of these elements appear in other biblical settings as well: the Garden of Eden, as described in Genesis (Gen

---

[78] Beale, *Revelation*, p. 1089.

[79] The term πλατεῖα is not found in Rev 22.1. However, that verse comes between Rev 21.21 and 22.2 and, as it is not expressly stated that there has been a change of location, it is logical to think that John and the angel are still in the main square of the New Jerusalem. The lexeme πλατεῖα is, in any case, somewhat difficult to translate. I'm inclined towards 'the main square of the city', because this would explain the subsequent mention of the temple, which would logically be located in the centre of a city. In addition, after the parenthesis (Rev 21.23–24), John resumes his description by showing us what there is in this square.

2.9–10); and the future temple, glimpsed by Ezekiel in one of his visions (Ezek 47.1–12).

In Genesis, the expression ξύλον ζωῆς, 'tree of life' (Gen 2.9; 3.22, 24), is used directly and in the singular, as in Rev 22.2. The fruit of this tree gave one immortality. There is, then, a certain similarity between the fruits of the New Jerusalem and those of Eden, as the tree of the New Jerusalem produces its fruits constantly and, through them, 'heals the nations'; that is to say, it gives life continually, as did the tree in the Garden of Eden. Furthermore, when he alludes explicitly to the ξύλον ζωῆς, John is revealing something else as well, as, in the last part of the letter to the church of Ephesus (Rev 2.7), Christ says that the tree of life is found in paradise. When it reappears planted in the New Jerusalem, he is therefore indicating that the holy city is in fact that same paradise.

In Ezekiel (Ezek 47.12), it is not a single tree that is mentioned, but several – πᾶν ξύλον – and their qualifier is not ζωῆς, 'of life', as in Rev 22.2, but rather βρώσιμον, 'edible'.[80] The similarity, however, is undeniable, and constitutes a clear example of intertextuality. That which is edible provides, to a certain extent, life to the individual; therefore, the curative properties of these trees are similar to those in the book of Revelation. The syntax employed in Greek is also similar, and the form ἔνθεν καὶ ἔνθεν in Ezek 47.12 even corresponds to ἐντεῦθεν καὶ ἐκεῖθεν in Rev 22.2. In any case, ἐντεῦθεν καὶ ἐκεῖθεν is problematic when it comes to translation, especially if one tries to visualize what is being described. It is difficult to explain how the tree of life could be found in the centre of the square and on both sides of the river at the same time. One is led to think that the river, in this part of the square, becomes divided into two,[81] recalling the division of a river into tributaries in Gen 2.10 ('a river was born in Eden … and from there it divided into four branches') and in written testimonies that describe the channelling of the great Persian rivers in the ancient world.[82]

The exclusive presence, then, of ποταμός ὕδατος ζωῆς and ξύλον ζωῆς is not casual. The New Jerusalem is presented as the paradise announced by Ezekiel, which has become a reality in John's vision. This paradise is

---

[80] THAYER, 1561, s.v. βρώσιμος.

[81] Given the difficulty of translating ἐντεῦθεν καὶ ἐκεῖθεν and the absence of an article in the expression ξύλον ζωῆς, some authors consider that it is not a singular, but rather a singular collective noun; see Swete, *Apocalypse*, p. 295; Charles, *Commentary 2*, p. 176; Aune, *Revelation 3*, p. 1177. In spite of this, David E. Aune, in his commentary on Rev 22.2c, feels obliged to recognize its singular value; see *Revelation 3*, p. 1178.

[82] Ammianus Marcellinus 23.6.25; 24.2.7.

not new, but connects perfectly with that of Genesis. What is more, it is John himself who identifies it as such.

As for the predicate groups used here, their function is to describe the elements of nomenclature, i.e., the river of life and the tree of life. The first is notable for its radiance, λαμπρὸν ὡς κρύσταλλον, 'as bright as crystal', which is not surprising, considering its origin: ἐκ τοῦ θρόνου τοῦ θεοῦ καὶ τοῦ ἀρνίου, 'from the throne of God and of the Lamb' (Rev 22.1). With respect to the tree of life, the predicate groups are focused on two completely different aspects: its fecundity (ποιοῦν καρποὺς δώδεκα, κατὰ μῆνα ἕκαστον ἀποδιδοῦν τὸν καρπὸν αὐτοῦ, 'produces fruit twelve times a year, once every month') and its curative properties (εἰς θεραπείαν τῶν ἐθνῶν, 'to heal the nations'). Two aspects are especially interesting here: a) John is describing characteristics that he does not actually see (that the tree produces fruit once a month, and that it has healing properties); and b) although it is customary to do so in descriptions of cities, this is the first time that he mentions its inhabitants.[83] Perhaps the reason for this change is that the narrator himself, who once again abandons the role of witness and its external focalization, has assumed a position of zero focalization. John, dazzled by what he sees, decides to add more information that he knows about the city.

2.4   The Vision-Speech (Εἶδον-Λέγων) Descriptions

The vision-speech descriptions (λέγων καὶ εἶδον descriptions) receive this name because their demarcation signs are the formula of visual perception καὶ εἶδον and a reporting verb, generally λέγω, which appears in its participial form. It is thus possible to move from the visual to the auditory very naturally, without the narration losing continuity. On the contrary, it reinforces the ability to identify the voices that transmit relevant messages. Descriptions of this type are a clear example of the interrelation that exists between visual and auditory perception.

The εἶδον-λέγων descriptions are quick sketches of characters or groups of characters who, generally speaking, will transmit a particular message. They include:

1.   Descriptions of angels:
    a)   The 'mighty' angel (Rev 5.2)
    b)   The angel who rises from the east (Rev 7.2)

---

[83] Swete, *Apocalypse*, p. 296.

    c)   The angel who flies through heaven (Rev 14.6–7a)

    d)   The angel who descends from heaven (Rev 18.1–2a)

    e)   The angel standing on the sun (Rev 19.17ab).

2.   Descriptions of groups of characters belonging to the heavenly context:

    a)   The multitude (Rev 7.9–10a)

    b)   The conquerors (Rev 15.2–3b).

2.4.1 Demarcation Signs

Once again, it is the formula of visual perception καὶ εἶδον that constitutes the introductory sign (Rev 5.2; 7.2; 14.6; 15.2; 19.17). It is used as a means of introducing the description, endowing it with realism, and reaffirming its verisimilitude: what is described is true, because John, the narrator–eyewitness, has seen and heard it.

In these descriptions, the introductory sign alternates between two variants:

μετὰ ταῦτα εἶδον, καὶ ἰδού, 'after these things I saw, and behold' (Rev 7.9), and μετὰ ταῦτα εἶδον 'after these things I saw' (Rev 18.1). Both introduce a pause, facilitating the entry of the descriptive section and indicating the temporal order of John's visions.[84] As in the καὶ εἶδον descriptions, the formula καὶ ἰδού, 'and behold', followed by the nominative ὄχλος, makes what is described more vivid, creating a greater sense of involvement for the listener/reader.

As for the concluding signs, these usually consist of a *verbum dicendi*, the expression φωνῇ μεγάλῃ, 'in a loud voice' (Rev 5.2; 7.2, 10a; 14.7a; 19.17b), or ἰσχυρᾷ φωνῇ, 'in a strong voice' (Rev 18.2a),[85] and the participle of λέγω. Their function is to introduce the message in direct speech; for example:

καὶ ἔκραξεν [ἐν] φωνῇ μεγάλῃ λέγων . . . (Rev 19.17b)

and cried in a loud voice, saying . . .

---

[84] Beale, *Revelation*, p. 892; Smalley, *Revelation*, p. 443.

[85] The locution ἰσχυρᾷ φωνή seems to be a variant, employed because μέγας has just been used to qualify a characteristic of the angel (Rev 18.1), to avoid redundancy. The expression ἰσχυρὰ φωνή, however, is not original to the book of Revelation, but also appears in the book of Daniel (Dan Th 6.21). A similar function seems to be perfomed by the internal accusative τὴν ᾠδὴν Μωϋσέως, 'the song of Moses' (Rev 15.3), for the verb ᾄδω, 'to sing', although in this case the atmosphere it creates is entirely musical.

The *verba dicendi* are κηρύσσω (Rev 5.2), κράζω (Rev 7.2, 10a; 18.2a; 19.17b), λέγω (Rev 14.7a), and ᾄδω (Rev 15.3b). Of these, κηρύσσω and κράζω have particular connotations. Κηρύσσω means 'to transmit an official announcement through a herald or someone who serves this function'.[86] The herald, in antiquity, was marked by his wisdom and prudence, as well as blessed with a strong voice.[87] Thus, κηρύσσω expresses not only an action, but also qualifies its subject and endows the content of the message with importance and solemnity. Meanwhile, κράζω means 'to shout'; that is to say, 'to communicate something in a loud voice'.[88] Its presence in the text creates a certain tension through the fact that the message is being transmitted at a loud volume.

These descriptions, concluded as they are by hearing, serve to create an atmosphere that then becomes part of the narrative. It may be one of tension or solemnity, or, as in the case of the heavenly songs (Rev 15.3), one of peace.

2.4.2   Constitutive Elements

a)   Denomination or Pantonyme

After the introductory sign, John identifies what he sees and tells us expressly what it is: 'I saw' … ἄγγελον, 'an angel' (Rev 5.2); ἄλλον ἄγγελον, 'another angel' (Rev 7.2; 14.6; 18.1); ὄχλος, 'a multitude' (Rev 7.9); τοὺς νικῶντας ἐκ τοῦ θηρίου καὶ ἐκ τῆς εἰκόνος αὐτοῦ καὶ ἐκ τοῦ ἀριθμοῦ τοῦ ὀνόματος, 'the conquerors of the beast, its image, and the number of its name' (Rev 15.2) and ἕνα ἄγγελον, 'an angel' (Rev 19.17).

In the case of Rev 15.2, it is logical to wonder if John is once again stepping out of his role as witness, as in this denomination he claims to behold τοὺς νικῶντας ἐκ τοῦ θηρίου, 'the conquerors of the beast', an observation which, at first glance, could not result from visual perception, but only from the seer's own knowledge. The answer is provided by the narrative itself in Chapter 13, with the apparition of the beast from the sea, which has the power to defeat the saints (Rev 13.7), as does its statue (Rev 13.15). John is therefore observing characters, τοὺς νικῶντας, that he has seen before (Rev 13.7, 15), although now in a completely different context: ὡς θάλασσαν, 'something like a sea' (15.2). This is perhaps the

---

[86]   *BDAG*, 4232, s.v. κηρύσσω; LOUW and NIDA, 33.206, s.v. κηρύσσω.
[87]   G. Friedrich, 'κῆρυξ (ἱεροκῆρυξ), κηρύσσω, κήρυγμα, προκηρύσσω', *TDNT 3*, 683–718.
[88]   *BDAG*, 4381, s.v. κράζω; THAYER, 3068, s.v. κράζω.

reason that Rev 15.2 is the only εἶδον-λέγων description that alludes first to space, because here it is necessary to indicate where the conquerors are at the moment.

To this is added another peculiarity, i.e., the use of the preposition ἐκ, dependent on the verb νικάω. This is a strange grammatical construction, unique to the book of Revelation, and one that has given rise to diverse interpretations.[89] Ultimately, it seems to be a way for John to direct the attention of the listener/reader, given that he is identifying characters who are not appearing for the first time in the narrative, but have been presented earlier.

b)   Expansion

Expansion in descriptions like these is characterized by brevity, order, and structural succession, as they are not constructed to be visually arresting, but rather present an intermingling of what John sees with what he knows. They also vary according to whether they describe angels or human beings.

The expansions of descriptions of angels are drawn from three semantic fields: movement, space, and possession. Exceptions to this are Rev 5.2 and 19.17, where expansion is reduced, respectively, to ἰσχυρόν, 'mighty', and ἑστῶτα ἐν τῷ ἡλίῳ, 'standing on the sun'.

The semantic fields of movement and space guide the expansion, infusing it with dynamism, indicating the provenance of the angels and providing a spatial framework. Examples include: ἀναβαίνοντα ἀπὸ ἀνατολῆς ἡλίου, 'rising from the east' (Rev 7.2); πετόμενον ἐν μεσουρανήματι, 'flying in mid-heaven' (Rev 14.6);[90] and καταβαίνοντα ἐκ τοῦ οὐρανοῦ, 'descending from heaven' (Rev 18.1).

As for the semantic field of possession, the angel that rises from the east is the only one that carries a visible object: σφραγῖδα θεοῦ ζῶντος, 'the seal of the living God' (Rev 7.2). According to Henry B. Swete, this seal would seem to be of the type used to validate official documents or to

---

[89] Blass and Debrunner, *Grammar*, § 212, among others, have postulated that this is an ellipsis of a broader expression. Still others, David E. Aune among them, see it as a Latinism (*victoriam ferre ex*) – Aune, 'A Latinism in Revelation 15:2', *JBL* 110 (1991), 691–2 – or even, as in the case of C. C. Torrey, an Aramaism: *Apocalypse*, pp. 108–9, cited by Aune in *Revelation 2*, p. 871.

[90] This is the first and only time in the book of Revelation that the angels are referred to as flying. Πέτομαι is used to refer to the action of the four living beings (Rev 4.7), the eagle (Rev 8.13), the woman (Rev 12.14), and to birds in general (Rev 19.17).

prove the ownership of some object or document.[91] Royal seals – a result of Babylonian or Egyptian influence – are known to have been used in ancient Israel (LXX 1 Kings 20.8), although none have been preserved.[92]

The other two angels possess a εὐαγγέλιον, 'gospel' (Rev 14.6), and ἐξουσίαν μεγάλην, 'great authority' (Rev 18.1), respectively. The εὐαγγέλιον is something that cannot be seen; that is, it reflects what John knows, an external focalization. Here, John's voice seems to merge with his vision, preparing the listener/reader for what the angel is about to say. Besides describing the gospel by the predicate αἰώνιον, 'eternal', its purpose is indicated by the adoption of a new focalization, this time internal:[93] εὐαγγελίσαι ἐπὶ τοὺς καθημένους ἐπὶ τῆς γῆς καὶ ἐπὶ πᾶν ἔθνος καὶ φυλὴν καὶ γλῶσσαν καὶ λαόν, 'to announce to all the inhabitants of the earth, to every nation and tribe and language and people' (Rev 14.6).

The adjective αἰώνιος implies that the aforementioned gospel has no beginning and no end,[94] and connotes that it belongs to God, as in biblical texts αἰώνιος is used as an attribute of God (Isa 26.4), or of realities that in some way refer to God; examples include: διαθήκη αἰώνιος, 'eternal covenant' (Gen 9.16; Exod 31.16; Lev 24.8; etc.); νόμιμον αἰώνιον, 'perpetual law' (Exod 12.14; Lev 6.11; Num 10.8); ζωὴ αἰώνιος, 'eternal life' (Matt 19.16, 29; Mark 10.17, 30; Luke 10.25; etc.); τὸ πῦρ τὸ αἰώνιον, 'eternal fire' (Matt 18.8; 25.41).

In Rev 18.1, the expansion focuses on ἐξουσίαν μεγάλην, 'great authority', and on a particular characteristic of the angel, i.e., his radiance,[95] which is such that ἡ γῆ ἐφωτίσθη, 'the earth was illuminated'.[96] In this case, the predicate groups, rather than revolving around the character described, are used to create a particular effect, by means of which the description's own visual aspect is strengthened. To this effect, John

[91] Swete, *Apocalypse*, p. 94.

[92] G. Fitzer, 'σφραγίς, † σφραγίζω, † κατασφραγίζω', *TDNT* 7, 939–53.

[93] Internal focalization is understood as that in which the narrator familiarizes the reader with the inner nature of a given character; see Marguerat and Bourquin, *Per leggere*, p. 80.

[94] THAYER, 172, s.v. αἰώνιος; LOUW and NIDA, 67.96, s.v. αἰώνιος.

[95] This is the only time in the book of Revelation that the term δόξα is attributed to an angel, rather than to God.

[96] This corresponds to Ezek 43.2, in which it is affirmed that: וְהָאָרֶץ הֵאִירָה מִכְּבֹדוֹ, 'the earth shone with his glory'. The translation in the LXX is somewhat different in this case: ἡ γῆ ἐξέλαμπεν ὡς φέγγος ἀπὸ τῆς δόξης κυκλόθεν, 'the earth shone with a splendour from the glory all around'.

watches as an angel passes through heaven and lights up the world, and the setting in which the message will be transmitted is thus created.

The expansions of the descriptions of characters belonging to the heavenly context share the same semantic fields:

1. Bodily position and space: ἑστῶτες ἐνώπιον τοῦ θρόνου καὶ ἐνώπιον τοῦ ἀρνίου, 'standing before the throne and before the Lamb' (Rev 7.9); ἑστῶτας ἐπὶ τὴν θάλασσαν τὴν ὑαλίνην, 'standing on a sea of glass' (Rev 15.2).

2. Objects: φοίνικες, 'palms' (Rev 7.9); κιθάραι τοῦ θεοῦ, 'kitharas of God'[97] (Rev 15.2).

In these expansions, John holds fast to the principle of describing what he sees. In addition, the lexemes used in the various semantic fields portray the heavenly context in a victorious mood, as these characters are shown in relation to God and the Lamb (whether before the throne or before the sea of glass), and in a bodily position (standing) that denotes an active attitude, as well as holding objects that to some extent symbolize victory: φοίνικες, 'palms',[98] and κιθάραι, 'kitharas'.

Each of these expansions of descriptions of people has its own peculiarity. I will take as an example the expansion of the description of the multitude (Rev 7.9), which describes them as πολύ and specifies the clothing that they are wearing. John, however, does not leave the meaning of πολύ to the listener/reader's interpretation, but, to some extent, provides the correct interpretation himself: ὃν ἀριθμῆσαι αὐτὸν οὐδεὶς ἐδύνατο, 'whose number no one could count' (Rev 7.9a). Therefore, πολύ is here not merely generic ('much/big'), but has the more precise meaning of 'innumerable'. This sense is further heightened by the *amplificatio* that follows: ἐκ παντὸς ἔθνους καὶ φυλῶν καὶ λαῶν καὶ γλωσσῶν, 'of all nations, tribes, peoples, and languages' (Rev 7.9b). The singular is here alternated with the plural, calling the attention of the listener/reader to the universal character of the multitude. This type of expansion would undoubtedly recall to the listener/reader the promises that God made to Abraham in Genesis, which employ similar language.

---

[97] There is a certain ambiguity in this expression, as it may be a possessive or objective genitive, or even a Hebraic periphrasis used to express the superlative; see Aune, *Revelation 2*, p. 852. Considering the context and the fact that a similar expression is found in 1 Chron 16.42, I feel, like Smalley, *Revelation*, p. 385, that it is an objective genitive.

[98] Aune, *Revelation 2*, pp. 468–9, presents an exhaustive study of how palms symbolized victory in the ancient Mediterranean world.

As for their clothing, περιβεβλημένους στολὰς λευκάς, 'dressed in white robes' (Rev 7.9), the participle is used in the accusative, introducing a shift in the grammatical form that has been maintained up to now (the nominative), with the form ἰδού preceding it and the expansion concluded by φοίνικες.[99] The use of the accusative is therefore curious here; it presupposes that the author is thinking of the verbal lexeme εἶδον as a verb used with the direct object περιβεβλημένους.[100] For this reason, Pierre Prigent considers it to be a manifestation of the oral character of John's language.[101] Without dismissing this possibility, it may also be a stylistic innovation by the author, who is quick to distort grammar in order to draw the attention of the listener/reader to certain aspects of his story.[102] In this case, the use of the accusative περιβεβλημένους would be a way of calling attention to a particular aspect of the expansion, i.e., the nomenclature of clothing.

The term στολή[103] appears in the book of Revelation five times (Rev 6.11; 7.9, 13, 14; 22.14). In Rev 6.11, the narrator informs the listener/reader that στολὴ λευκή is the clothing given to the martyrs. And so, in describing how the multitude is dressed (Rev 7.9), John is identifying its members as ὄχλος, meaning that they are not just any multitude, but a multitude of martyrs. It is perhaps for this reason that he chooses to alter the grammar here, so that, jarred by this anomaly, the listener/reader will give closer attention as the author describes and identifies the multitude.

Lastly, στολή has its own predicate in λευκή, 'white', which indicates not only colour, but the context to which the multitude belongs, i.e., the heavenly. Curiously, the only biblical text that uses the same expression is Mark 16.5, where the women come to the tomb and, finding it open, discover a young man inside 'dressed in a white robe' (περιβεβλημένον στολὴν λευκήν). By this we understand that the angel likewise belongs to the heavenly context.[104]

---

[99]   The form περιβεβλημένοι is found in: ℵ² P 1854. 2053. 2329. 2344. 2351 𝔐ᴬ.

[100]   Smalley, *Revelation*, p. 176.

[101]   Prigent, *Commentary*, p. 288.

[102]   A. D. Callahan, 'The Language of Apocalypse', *HTR* 88 (1995), 464–5; Beckwith, *Apocalypse*, p. 544; G. K. Beale, 'Revelation', in D. A. Carson and H. G. M. Williamson, *It is Written: Scripture Citing Scripture. Essays in Honour of Barnabas Lindars, S.S.F.* (Cambridge: Cambridge University Press, 1988), p. 332.

[103]   THAYER, 4916, s.v. στολή, defines this as a loose outer garment worn by men, that extended to the feet.

[104]   E. P. Gould, *The Gospel According to St Mark* (Edinburgh: T & T Clark, 1948), p. 300; C. S. Mann, *Mark: A New Translation, with Introduction and Commentary* (New York, NY: Doubleday, 1986), p. 666.

2.5   The Anaphoric (τὰ Προλεγόμενα) Descriptions

The anaphoric descriptions (τὰ προλεγόμενα descriptions) are those that describe collectives mentioned earlier in the narrative. The descriptions examined so far have generally been of individual characters, or those who, although they appear in a group, are presented as having a common identity defined by a number, as in the case of the twenty-four elders (Rev 4.4), or who share some common feature, such as the conquerors of the beast (Rev 15.2). However, there are other descriptions of collectives whose number is not precise, such as the army of locusts (Rev 9.7–11), or, if mentioned, is so large that what is described is in effect a multitude; this is the case for the mounted armies that ravage humanity at the sounding of the sixth trumpet (Rev 9.17–19) or the 144,000 followers of the Lamb (Rev 14.1).

Expansion in descriptions of this type is based, above all, on visual images. Through these, the description gains in realism and the listener/reader is able to visualize easily what John sees.

2.5.1   Demarcation Signs

Introductory signs in the τὰ προλεγόμενα descriptions are comprised of the formula of visual perception in its form καὶ εἶδον, καὶ ἰδοὺ, 'and I saw, and behold' (Rev 14.1), or its variant καὶ οὕτως εἶδον, 'and so I saw' (Rev 9.17). The presence of the adverb οὕτως is explained by the fact that the object to be described has just been mentioned (Rev 9.16), while οὕτως carries with it a powerful referential impact, precisely through this allusion to something already named.[105]

The description of the locusts (Rev 9.7–11) is an exception to this, as it lacks an introductory sign, properly speaking. They make their appearance for the first time in Rev 9.3, after the fifth trumpet is sounded. It is then that the listener/reader would expect their description. However, the narration instead goes on to tell of the powers that the locusts receive (Rev 9.3b, 4, 5) and how human beings will react to them (Rev 9.6). It is only after this that the description actually begins, with the expression καὶ τὰ ὁμοιώματα τῶν ἀκρίδων, 'and the appearance of the locusts' (Rev 9.7). By inserting it here, at the end, John manages to slow the narration in such a way that the listener/reader is doubly shocked at their visual aspect, which is almost more

---

[105] THAYER, 3896, s.v. οὕτω.

terrifying than the damage they cause. What is more, as there is no introductory sign, the listener/reader's attention to the narrative is not diminished, but intensified.

These descriptions also lack concluding signs. Once again, the listener/reader knows that the description has ended when a new narrative section begins.

2.5.2   Constitutive Elements

a)   Denomination or Pantonyme

As usual, immediately after the introductory formula, John identifies the object of the description in terms that are quite direct: 'locusts' (Rev 9.7), 'horses' (Rev 9.17), and 'one hundred and forty-four thousand' (Rev 14.1).

It should be noted that the denomination of his description of the cavalry is limited exclusively to the horses. Their riders are named later, as part of the expansion, since what is most striking about these troops is the horses themselves (Rev 9.17–19).

b)   Expansion

Given the diversity of expansions in this type of description, they will be examined here individually.

To examine the expansion of the description of the locusts in all its depth, it will be useful to summarize briefly what this insect is like in reality. Relatively large in size compared to most insects, they have a chewing mouth structure, antennae of varying length, and compound eyes. They are also capable of emitting and receiving sounds. In their adult phase they have wings and three pairs of legs, the third pair being especially strong, to enable jumping. They migrate in cloud-like swarms, devastating wide tracts of land, in effect devouring the earth,[106] as described in Exodus (Exod 10.12–14).

The expansion of the description of the locusts is based on nomenclature as well as predicates. The nomenclature focuses on the parts of their bodies that John finds worthy of description. He begins with the front:

---

[106] L. Ryken, *et al.* (eds.), *Dictionary of Biblical Imagery: An Encyclopedic Exploration of the Images, Symbols, Motifs, Metaphors, Figures of Speech and Literary Patterns of the Bible* (Downers Grove, IL: InterVarsity, 1998), s.v. *locust*; E. Firmage, 'Locust', *ABD 6*, 1119–51.

κεφαλαί, 'heads'; πρόσωπα, 'faces'; τρίχες, 'hair'; ὀδόντες, 'teeth' (Rev 9.7–8); he then continues with the body: θώρακες, 'breastplates'; φωνὴ τῶν πτερύγων, 'noise of their wings' (Rev 9.9); and concludes with the rear section: οὐραί, 'tails'; κέντρα, 'stingers' (Rev 9.10).

Obviously, this nomenclature is a departure from what we know of actual locusts, specifically as it mentions τρίχες, 'hair'; ὀδόντες, 'teeth'; θώρακες, 'breastplates'; οὐραί, 'tails'; and κέντρα, 'stingers'. Thus, the majority of scholars consider that John, in this part of the description, is transposing terms, so that τρίχες does not literally refer to 'hair' but to the antennae of the locust; just as ὀδόντες, 'teeth', is an allusion to their voracity – Wis 16.9 speaks of the locust's bite – and the θώρακες, 'breastplates', to the hardest part of the insect's body.[107]

It is, however, difficult to find a transposition of terms for οὐραί and κέντρα, as locusts have neither tails nor stingers. Their presence in the description is perhaps due to the fact that, when these creatures first appear in the text, we are told that they have received a power similar to that of the scorpion: καὶ ἐδόθη αὐτοῖς ἐξουσία ὡς ἔχουσιν ἐξουσίαν οἱ σκορπίοι τῆς γῆς, 'and they were given a power like that of the scorpions of the earth' (Rev 9.3), and so they are here described as having tails and stingers. Another explanation for the appearance of tails may lie in the initial simile, which compares the locusts to horses, ὅμοιοι ἵπποις, and it is precisely here that the destructive power of their tails is mentioned (Rev 9.19). From all of this, more than simply affirming that the nomenclature used is based on imagery, it may be said that the seer is again describing what he sees, as he did in the καὶ εἶδον descriptions. In this case, it is an army of locusts with strange, monstrous features.

The predicate groups are here comprised of a series of similes headed by ὡς and ὅμοιος. Their repetition reveals the difficulty that John encounters in putting the locust's horrifying aspect into words. The only exception comes at the end of this part of the expansion, where he describes their power (Rev 9.10b). Here he does not use the language of comparison, but makes a categorical affirmation: ἡ ἐξουσία αὐτῶν ἀδικῆσαι τοὺς ἀνθρώπους μῆνας πέντε, 'the power to harm people for five months'.

While the nomenclature follows a certain order of presentation – i.e., in accordance with the bodily structure of the locust – the predicates seem, at first glance, to lack this; indeed, the similes offer comparisons to animals (horses, Rev 9.7a; lions, Rev 9.8b; scorpions, Rev 9.10a), to

---

[107] Beckwith, *Apocalypse*, pp. 562–3; Robertson, *Comentario*, p. 740.

objects (crowns, Rev 9.7b; chariots, Rev 9.9b) and to human beings (men, Rev 9.7b; women, Rev 9.8a). This mixing of elements, especially the theriomorphic with the anthropomorphic, and the deliberate repetition of lexemes (τὰ πρόσωπα αὐτῶν ὡς πρόσωπα, Rev 9.7b; τρίχας ὡς τρίχας, Rev 9.8a, etc.) presents a terrifying vision of these locusts that transmits to the listener/reader the same dread that the seer feels on witnessing them at first hand.

This is only a seeming disorder, however; the description expands its predicates over a background theme that is latent in all these similes, however diverse they may be. The locusts are said to be ὅμοιοι ἵπποις ἡτοιμασμένοις εἰς πόλεμον, 'like horses prepared for battle' (Rev 9.7a).[108] Therefore, the locusts have the appearance of horses in formation, fitted with battle gear and exhibiting the tension felt by both men and animals before going into combat.[109]

In the description of the locusts, there is also an alternation in focalization and a change in viewpoints. It opens with a panoramic view, ὅμοιοι ἵπποις ἡτοιμασμένοις εἰς πόλεμον (Rev 9.7a), followed by a series of closer views. Thus, John's eyes come to rest on the heads of the locusts (a close-up image), which have on them ὡς στέφανοι ὅμοιοι χρυσῷ, 'something like gold crowns' (Rev 9.7b). He is perhaps referring to the protruding outer structure of the locust's head that, given its antennae, may resemble a crown, although he could also be referring to the helmets of the hoplites, the crests of which took the form of an aureole.[110] He goes on to describe their faces (Rev 9.7a), which are seemingly human, adding to the listener/reader's terror, not only because the locusts have human faces, but because these are more expressive than those of animals and reflect the tension of battle to a greater extent. This feeling of terror rises in a crescendo with the description of their 'hair': ὡς τρίχας γυναικῶν 'like the hair of women' (Rev 9.8a); that is to say, long and black, like that of the women of

---

[108] By contrast, in the OT we find this simile inverted: the horses are said to be like locusts (LXX Jer 28.27).

[109] Although the OT does not offer any data as to the number of soldiers and horses that made up the cavalry regiments of Israel, it is known, for example, that the Roman army assigned 300 horses to each of its legions and that in the battle of Cannae (216 BC), it included as many as 6,000; see Y. Le Bohec, 'Armies. III. Rome. A. The Era of the Republic', *BNP* 2, 10–11.

[110] An example of this is the bronze helmet (seventh century BC) found in a tomb in Argos; see. S. Hornblower and A. Spawforth (eds.), *The Oxford Companion to Classical Civilization* (Oxford: Oxford University Press, 1998), p. 77.

first-century Palestine.[111] Their teeth are then described as ὡς λεόντων, 'like those of lions' (Rev 9.8b), again underscoring their voracity, but also suggesting that their teeth and jaws have the same exclusively vertical movement as a lion's.

After describing the heads of the locust-soldiers, John turns his gaze to the insects' θώρακες, 'breastplates' (Rev 9.9a). These are ὡς θώρακας σιδηροῦς; that is to say, like iron. Although θώραξ is the name for the breastplates worn by soldiers, it seems to refer here to the *flanchard*, an element of equine armour known to have been used in antiquity.[112] This may have been made of chain mail, composed of interlinked metallic rings, and would thus bear a great resemblance to the scaly backs and sides of the locust.[113]

After this, the sound of their wings is described as ὡς φωνὴ ἁρμάτων ἵππων πολλῶν τρεχόντων εἰς πόλεμον, 'like the noise of chariots with many horses rushing into battle' (Rev 9.9b). This aspect is concordant with one real characteristic of the locust, and this is its ability to emit sounds. At this point, John leaves off describing what he sees and turns to what he hears, revealing himself to be both the visual and auditory witness of these events. He is thus able to transmit the vision in all its vividness, as no real manifestation of such insects could be silent, given their number and their ability to make sounds. A more detailed study of this aspect will be presented in Chapter 3.

After describing the sound of their wings, John's attention turns to their tails and stingers (Rev 9.10). In one of the predicates, the scorpion simile is maintained, while in the other it is not. The simile ὁμοίας σκορπίοις echoes Rev 9.3, although, considering the predominant image of a warhorse ready for battle, another explanation also comes to mind. The tails may be a reference to one of the war machines that were used in battle during this period. One such machine that the Roman army possessed for launching lances and arrows was in fact known as a *scorpio*,[114] while κέντρον, 'stinger', may refer to the projectiles it shot, as the term was also a name for the goads used for herding oxen (Prov 26.3; Heb 26.14).[115]

---

[111] Smalley, *Revelation*, p. 231.

[112] J. B. Campbell, 'κατάφρακτοι', *BNP* 7, 32–3.

[113] Robertson, *Comentario*, p. 740.

[114] Vitruvius (first century BC) catalogued various war machines in his work *De Architectura*. Among them is the *scorpio*, described as a small ballista that shot arrows by means of a two-armed torsion system (Vitr. 10.10.1). It is also mentioned in 1 Mac 6.51.

[115] Robertson, *Comentario*, p. 740.

Finally, the expansion undergoes a change of tone. John no longer tells us what he sees, but what he knows; i.e., the power of the locusts (Rev 9.10b) and the name of their king (Rev 9.11). Unlike the book of Proverbs, which states that the locusts have no king (Prov 30.27), the book of Revelation not only presents this king but informs the listener/reader very clearly of both his origin (he is the king of the abyss) and his name, giving it in both Hebrew and Greek. The meaning of the two names, Ἀβαδδών, 'destruction', and Ἀπολλύων,[116] 'he who destroys', after the horrific description of the locusts, helps to intensify the climax still more, and leaves the listener/reader with a feeling of total desolation. This reference to the king of the locusts, then, serves to close the description.

Shortly after this comes the description of a cavalry squadron (Rev 9.17–19). The expansion here is brief and orderly, its nomenclature and predicate groups based only on visual perception. The nomenclature refers to those elements that any observer would perceive if such a squadron were advancing towards him: καθήμενοι ἐπ' αὐτῶν, 'riders'; θώρακες, 'breastplates' (Rev 9.17a); κεφαλαί, 'heads' (Rev 9.17b); στομάτα, 'mouths' (Rev 9.17c).

Predicates complete the nomenclature and are drawn from three semantic fields:

1.   Colours: πύρινος, 'fiery red'; ὑακίνθινος, 'sapphire blue';[117] θειώδης, 'sulphurous yellow' (Rev 9.17a).

2.   Animals: ὡς κεφαλαὶ λεόντων, 'like the heads of lions' (Rev 9.17b).

3.   Elements of nature: πῦρ, 'fire'; καπνός, 'smoke'; θεῖον, 'sulphur' (Rev 9.17c).

The vivid colours of their breastplates show that this is a powerful, formidable army. Indeed, this cavalry will be responsible for a great slaughter throughout the world (Rev 9.18).

The horses' heads are compared to those of lions – the first time that a simile is used in the description. In the ancient world, the lion was famed for its fierceness; the Israelites, especially, thought of it as a ruthless hunter with no mercy for its prey, and this is how it is portrayed

---

[116]   Prigent, *Commentary*, pp. 316–17.

[117]   L. García Ureña, 'Colour Adjectives in the New Testament', *NTS* 61 (2015), 234, note 63.

in the OT.[118] Comparing the heads of the horses to those of lions, with their great size and thick manes, transmits to the former something of the lion's ferocity, destructive power, and unstoppable force.

The elements of nature (Rev 9.17c) that we see coming out of the horses' mouths add further to their terrifying aspect, and the listener/reader's emotions are stirred even more. The description brings to mind God's punishment of Sodom and Gomorrah with a rain of sulphur and fire – θεῖον καὶ πῦρ (Gen 19.24)[119] – as well as the monster Leviathan in the book of Job, from whose mouth came billows of fire and smoke (Job 41.11–13). Πῦρ καὶ καπνὸς καὶ θεῖον, 'fire and smoke and sulphur', also increase the chromatic sensation produced by the θώρακες, 'armour', as there is a perfect correspondence between the colour of what emerges from the mouths of the horses and the colours of the riders' breastplates: πῦρ, 'fire', corresponding to πύρινος, 'fiery red'; καπνός, 'smoke', to ὑακινθίνους, 'blue'; and θεῖον, 'sulphur', to θειώδης, 'sulphurous yellow'.

Lastly, a bit later on, there is the expansion of the description of the horses' tails and the damage that they cause (Rev 9.18–19).[120] It is stated expressly that αἱ γὰρ οὐραὶ αὐτῶν ὅμοιαι ὄφεσιν, ἔχουσαι κεφαλάς, καὶ ἐν αὐταῖς ἀδικοῦσιν, 'their tails, like those of snakes, have heads, and with these they do harm'. The expansion establishes a similarity to snakes by claiming that their tails have heads. Described like this, the horses recall the chimaera, a mythological animal with the head of a lion and a snake for a tail.[121] The vision of these creatures, then, is again a terrifying one.

It now remains to examine the expansion of the description of the 144,000 (Rev 14.1). This is brief and highlights only a single aspect of visual perception, i.e., τὸ ὄνομα, 'the name', which is in fact repeated, and refers to what is inscribed ἐπὶ τῶν μετώπων αὐτῶν, 'on their foreheads'. This sign distinguishes them from the followers of the beast, who also carry a χάραγμα, 'mark', on their foreheads. In the case of the 144,000, these are the names of the Lamb and his Father, by which it is implicitly stated that they are the citizens of the New Jerusalem, as, when the city descends from heaven and its inhabitants are identified, we are told that

---

[118] Ryken, *et al.*, *Dictionary*, s.v. *lion*.

[119] Swete, *Apocalypse*, p. 121; Prigent, *Commentary*, p. 321.

[120] This is yet another example of an integrated description. It is included in this section for methodological reasons.

[121] F. Graf, 'Chimaera', *BNP* 3, 228–9; Beckwith, *Apocalypse*, p. 569; Aune, *Revelation 2*, pp. 539–40.

the name of God will be written on their foreheads: τὸ ὄνομα αὐτοῦ ἐπὶ τῶν μετώπων αὐτῶν (Rev 22.4).

2.6   The Angel Vision (καὶ Εἶδον Ἄγγελον) Descriptions

Given the number of angels who participate in the narration without names to identify them,[122] the angel vision description (the καὶ εἶδον ἄγγελον descriptions) are essential because they allow both John and the listener/reader to individualize each one of these angelic beings and to identify them easily if they should appear again in some other part of the story. In the book of Revelation, the angels not described are those who do not have a specific role of their own, whether this is because they form part of a choir to praise God (Rev 7.11), or because they belong to the retinue of some other angel or devil (Rev 12.7, 9), or because one appears right after another, and their origin is indicated in that way (Rev 14.15, 17, 18).

2.6.1   Demarcation Signs

As is the usual practice in the book of Revelation, the introductory sign in these cases is again the formula of visual perception καὶ εἶδον (Rev 8.2; 10.1; 15.1; 20.1). In Rev 7.1, however, a variant on this is used: μετὰ τοῦτο, 'after this', which establishes a brief pause between what has been narrated before and the description itself. Concluding signs are absent in this type of description.

2.6.2   Constitutive Elements

a)   Denomination or Pantonyme

After the formula of visual perception, the object contemplated is identified: τέσσαρες ἄγγελοι, 'four angels' (Rev 7.1); οἱ ἑπτὰ ἄγγελοι, 'the seven angels' (Rev 8.2); ἄλλος ἄγγελος, 'another angel' (Rev 10.1); ἄγγελος, 'an angel' (Rev 20.1). The only exception is found in Rev 15.1, where the listener/reader is made ready for the vision before the *pantonyme* is named, creating a feeling of suspense: ἄλλο σημεῖον ... μέγα καὶ θαυμαστόν, ἀγγέλους ἑπτά, 'another sign ... great and admirable, seven angels' (Rev 15.1). What is more, the order of the denomination is altered, the more

---

[122] In the book of Revelation, only Michael (Rev 12.7) and the angels of the seven churches (Rev 2.1, 8, 12, 18; 3.1, 7, 14) have proper names.

usual practice being to place the numerical adjective before the term itself. This alteration may be explained as a way of highlighting this group of angels, the description of whom continues in Rev 15.6. One might also consider ἑπτά to be not an attribute, but a predicate, due to the ambiguity of its grammatical position. In that case, ἑπτά, instead of belonging to the denomination, would form part of the expansion and add realism to the description.

The denomination of the angels is usually comprised of two elements: a numerical or indefinite adjective and the noun ἄγγελος, except in Rev 8.2, which has in addition the article ὁ. Its presence has sparked a certain amount of discussion among scholars about the identity of this group of angels.[123] In my opinion, the article is used here because John is referring to 'the seven angels' mentioned in the biblical tradition (Tob 12.15), in the Pseudepigrapha (1 Enoch 20.1–7), and even in the Dead Sea Scrolls.[124] They were, therefore, angels that John's audience would have been very familiar with.

The denomination of the descriptions reveals that there is no hierarchy of angels in the book of Revelation, in contrast to the NT and, above all, to pseudepigraphal literature, which make mention of ἀρχάγγελοι, 'arch-angels' (1 Thess 4.16; Jdg 9; 1 Enoch 9.4; 20.7; etc.); θρόνοι, 'thrones'; and ἐξουσίαι, 'dominions' (Eph 6.12; Col 1.16; Levi 3.8), etc.

b) Expansion

Once again, John does not give a complete description of each angel, but only of what grabs his attention, and this method allows him to highlight specific aspects of each one. The expansion is thus rich and unique to each angel, based, above all, on visual perception, in this case so clear that there is no need for simile.

The reference to space, however, which also indicates the movement or bodily position of these angels, is common to all and constitutes the first element of expansion: ἑστῶτας ἐπὶ τὰς τέσσαρας γωνίας τῆς γῆς, 'standing at the four corners of the earth' (Rev 7.1); οἳ ἐνώπιον τοῦ θεοῦ ἑστήκασιν, 'who stand before God' (Rev 8.2); ἰσχυρὸν καταβαίνοντα ἐκ

---

[123] Aune, *Revelation 2*, p. 509, and Beale, *Revelation*, p. 454, believe that this refers to the seven angels of the seven churches, who appear first in a group (Rev 1.20) and later individually (Rev 2.1, 8, 12, 18; 3.1, 7, 14).

[124] The *4Q Songs of the Sabbath* texts use the expressions רוש נשׂאי or ראשׁי נשׂיאים, 'the seven main princes'; according to David E. Aune, *Revelation 2*, p. 509, these should be identified as the seven archangels mentioned in the Qumran texts.

τοῦ οὐρανοῦ, 'mighty ... descending from heaven' (Rev 10.1); ἐν τῷ οὐρανῷ, 'in heaven' (Rev 15.1); καταβαίνοντα ἐκ τοῦ οὐρανοῦ, 'descending from heaven' (Rev 20.1). With this type of expansion, each character becomes situated in a given place and further realism is added to the vision.

The expression ἑστῶτας ἐπὶ τὰς τέσσαρας γωνίας τῆς γῆς, 'standing at the four corners of the earth', repeated later in Rev 20.8, is a reference to a new space within the narrative: the four regions into which the earth is divided. This is an echo of Old Testament cosmology (Isa 11.12; Ezek 7.2; Job 38.13), which is found in other literary texts and inscriptions of the Ancient Near East.[125]

After this spatial reference, the expansion continues. That of the four angels standing on the four compass points (Rev 7.1) concentrates only on this aspect, showing the dominion they have over τοὺς τέσσαρας ἀνέμους τῆς γῆς, 'the four winds of the earth', which, through the use of the article, refers to the four principal winds: of the north, the south, the east, and the west. The power of these angels is thus made clear to the listener/reader; this also explains the presence of the merism μὴ ... ἐπὶ τῆς γῆς μήτε ἐπὶ τῆς θαλάσσης, 'neither on the earth nor on the sea', completed by the expression μήτε ἐπὶ πᾶν δένδρον 'nor on any tree', which emphasizes still more the power of the angels, as not even the leaves on the trees would be moved by the breeze were it not commanded by them.

The expansions of the descriptions of the seven angels standing before God in Rev 8.2, the seven angels of Rev 15.1, and the angel of Rev 20.1 all coincide and are centred on the idea of possession. The groups of seven angels carry, respectively, seven trumpets and seven plagues, while the single angel holds the key to the abyss and a chain. The objects that they carry will allow us to identify them over the course of the story. Thus, the angels of Rev 8.2 are the angels of the seven trumpets (Rev 8.6); the angels of Rev 15.1 are those of the seven plagues (Rev 15.6), and the angel of Rev 20.1 is that of the key.

However, considering that John usually describes what he sees, the expression ἔχοντας πληγάς is a strange one, as the plagues, unlike the trumpets, are public calamities rather than objects that can be possessed.

---

[125] An example is the inscription of the Babylonian king, Samsuiluna: [l]uga[l KÁ. DINGIR.RA^(KI)]| l lugal ^(an)ub-da [límmu], '(Samsuiluna,) king of Babylonia / king of the four regions', I. Márquez Rowe, 'Inscripciones reales cuneiformes del II y I milenio a. de C.', *Aula Orientalis* 15 (1997), 77.

From the context and the fact that the verb ἔχω followed by a direct object is also used for someone who is responsible for something being done,[126] Isbon T. Beckwith proposes that the meaning of the verbal lexeme ἔχω in Rev 15.1 is 'to be responsible for inflicting plagues',[127] and this does seem a logical explanation. Therefore, this part of the expansion is built not so much upon what John sees, but what he knows, with the consequent change in focalization.

Something similar occurs with the expansion of the description of the angel in Rev 20.1. Here there is an intermingling of what John knows with what he sees; that is, a large key and a chain. The key, however, is presented as an element that is already known, through the use of the article, perhaps because it is the κλεὶς τοῦ φρέατος τῆς ἀβύσσου, 'key to the shaft of the abyss', which has already been mentioned (Rev 9.1), or because it is a key which is familiar both to John and to the listener/reader. In antiquity, the belief that both heaven and the abyss had gates with their own keys was widespread.[128] Indeed, it is a recurring theme in both the book of Revelation, which mentions αἱ κλεῖς τοῦ θανάτου καὶ τοῦ ᾅδου, 'the keys to Death and Hades' (Rev 1.18), and in the rest of the NT: αἱ κλεῖς τῆς βασιλείας τῶν οὐρανῶν, 'the keys to the kingdom of heaven' (Matt 16.19); ἡ κλεὶς τῆς γνώσεως, 'the key of science' (Luke 11.52).

The angels of the seven plagues are described in greater detail in Rev 15.6, in terms of what they are wearing: ἐνδεδυμένοι λίνον καθαρὸν λαμπρόν, 'dressed in pure, radiant linen' (Rev 15.6b); περιεζωσμένοι περὶ τὰ στήθη ζώνας χρυσᾶς, 'girthed with golden sashes at the breast' (Rev 15.6c). This expansion leads the listener/reader to fix his attention on the outer appearance of these angels, who are presented in the same attire – a linen robe with a golden sash – as the heavenly beings in the last visions of Daniel (Dan 10.5; 12.6–7) and Ezekiel (Ezek 9.2, 3, 11).[129] It should be kept in mind, however, that this type of clothing was similar to that worn by priests (Lev 16.4). For this reason, the clothing of the angels presents a double significance: angelical and priestly. The first is obvious, given the fact that they are angels, while the second becomes clearer

---

[126] THAYER, 2330, s.v. ἔχω, 2.k.

[127] Beckwith, *Apocalypse*, p. 673.

[128] J. Jeremias, '† κλεὶς. A. The Different Applications of the Image of the Keys in the NT', *TDNT 3*, 440–4; '† πύλη, † πυλῶν. C. The Gates of Hades in Matt 16:18', *TDNT 6*, 921–8.

[129] However, in the book of Revelation the lexeme λίνον is used (for the first and only time) instead of βύσσινον.

when the angels later assume the role of mediators, pouring out the bowls that cause the plagues and thus fulfilling the divine design (Rev 16.1–17). Of these expansions, the most elaborate is that of the angel in Rev 10.1. It begins with the expression ἄλλον ἄγγελον ἰσχυρόν, 'another mighty angel', and goes on to examine three aspects of this figure: his provenance (Rev 10.1a), his physiognomy (Rev 10.1b–2a), and his action (Rev 10.2b–3).

The locution ἄλλον ἄγγελον ἰσχυρόν, 'another mighty angel', is the author's method of informing the listener/reader that this angel is not the one described with the same qualifier in Rev 5.2, when the closed scroll appears. Although some exegetes believe that this angel may be identified as Christ,[130] the basic features described are in fact similar to those of other male characters as well. As there are not enough reasons to believe that this angel is Christ, it is more likely to be a new angel.

With respect to physiognomy, the angel is described as having human features and, indeed, the nomenclature here is focused on the semantic field of corporality: κεφαλή, 'head' (Rev 10.1b); πρόσωπον, 'face' (Rev 10.1c); πόδες, 'feet' (Rev 10.1c); and χείρ, 'hand' (Rev 10.2a). This may be somewhat surprising to the modern reader, who, influenced by Christian iconography, is used to seeing angels portrayed with wings.[131] This is not the case for this narrator, however, for he never describes angels as having them.[132]

In contrast to the nomenclature, the predicates move away from the features that characterize the human being to focus principally on the semantic field of radiance, based on elements of the firmament such as ἶρις, 'rainbow' (Rev 10.1b), ἥλιος, 'sun', and the so-called στῦλοι πυρός, 'columns of fire'[133] in Rev 10.1c. The description infuses the angel with

---

[130] Beale, *Revelation*, pp. 522–6.

[131] Consider the various representations of angels by artists such as Giotto, Fra Angelico, Raphael, Tiepolo, Zurbarán, and Goya. Even Van Gogh portrays angels as having wings ('Angel', 1889).

[132] This tradition is maintained in the New Testament (Heb 12.7–11). It is in the Pseudepigrapha that angels with wings appear (2 Enoch 16.7; 3 Bar 7.5).

[133] The expression οἱ πόδες αὐτοῦ ὡς στῦλοι πυρός, 'his feet like columns of fire', is unusual. It is difficult to grasp the proportion suggested by the simile: the size of the feet and their horizontal angle do not correspond to the shape of columns, which are vertical structures of great height. The proportion is maintained, however, if πόδες is translated as 'legs' rather than 'feet'. It would be, then, a case of metonymy, as Smalley affirms, *Revelation*, p. 257. This hypothesis is corroborated by the biblical texts themselves, which contain similes comparing the legs of both men and women to columns: στῦλοι μαρμάρινοι (Song 5.15); στῦλοι χρύσεοι (Sir 26.18).

light and colour to the point that, even though he appears enveloped in a cloud, these elements are still visible to John. Indeed, it is precisely this light and colour that indicates his angelic nature.

The predicates are completed by what the angel holds in his hand: βιβλαρίδιον ἠνεῳγμένον, 'an open scroll' (Rev 10.2a). However, this will not be the angel's defining characteristic, which is instead something that he does: i.e., standing with his right foot on the sea and his left on the land. It is this extraordinary act that both characterizes him and provides him with his own individuality. As a result, when he is mentioned again later, he will be referred to as ὁ ἄγγελος, ὃν εἶδον ἑστῶτα ἐπὶ τῆς θαλάσσης καὶ ἐπὶ τῆς γῆς, 'the angel that I saw standing on the sea and on the land' (Rev 10.5).

Finally, the angel's voice is described, with the expression φωνῇ μεγάλῃ ὥσπερ λέων μυκᾶται, 'with a loud voice like a lion roaring'.

2.7   The Topography (Τόποι) Descriptions

The topography (τόποι descriptions), known in classical rhetoric as τοπογραφία,[134] are those that paint an image of what a specific place is like, as in the descriptions of the new heaven and the new earth (Rev 21.1–2), or of a natural physical phenomenon such as an earthquake. Such descriptions are not frequent in the book of Revelation, as there is a certain preference for integrated descriptions, perhaps so as not to slow down the narration. In fact, of the four earthquakes that are mentioned (Rev 6.12–17; 11.13, 19; 16.18), the only one described in detail is that of Rev 6.12–17.

2.7.1   Demarcation Signs

Descriptions of this type have only introductory signs, and lack concluding signs. We know that the description has concluded when another description begins, as marked by its own introductory sign (μετὰ τοῦτο εἶδον ..., 'after this I saw', Rev 7.1), or because the narration has resumed (καὶ ἤκουσα φωνῆς μεγάλης ἐκ τοῦ θρόνου, 'and I heard a loud voice from the throne', Rev 21.3).

The introductory sign is again the formula of visual perception. However, in Rev 6.12, καὶ εἶδον has a function similar to that of καὶ

---

[134] H. Lausberg, *Manual de retórica literaria*, trans. J. Pérez Riesgo, vol. 2 (Madrid: Gredos, 1967), pp. 234–5, § 819.

ἰδού,[135] as it lacks a direct object and is followed by a time clause. After this comes the principal clause, which begins the description:

> Καὶ εἶδον ὅτε ἤνοιξεν τὴν σφραγῖδα τὴν ἕκτην, καὶ σεισμὸς μέγας ἐγένετο . . . (Rev 6.12)

> And behold, when he opened the sixth seal, a great earthquake occurred . . .

This particular use of καὶ εἶδον seems completely intentional and designed to draw the attention of the listener/reader to the fact of visual perception. What will be told next is an account of what John saw.

2.7.2   Constitutive Elements

a)   Denomination or Pantonyme

In Rev 6.12, after the introductory sign, the denomination of the phenomenon described (σεισμός, 'an earthquake') takes place. However, unlike the descriptions examined so far, the denomination in Rev 21.1–2 alternates with the expansion of the description of the object described: οὐρανὸν καινὸν καὶ γῆν καινήν . . . καὶ τὴν πόλιν τὴν ἁγίαν Ἰερουσαλὴμ καινὴν εἶδον, 'a new heaven and a new earth . . . and the holy city, the New Jerusalem, I saw'. Identification here even precedes the formula of visual perception, giving priority to the object being contemplated. The explanation for this apparent anomaly may be found in John's tendency to write as if he were transcribing in the moment; that is, he describes what is presented to his eyes at the same time that he sees it. Thus, when John sees the New Jerusalem for the first time, after beholding the new heaven and the new earth, in astonishment he begins immediately to describe it. Only later does he realize that he needs to include the formula of visual perception.

b)   Expansion

Expansion in these two descriptions is developed quite differently. That of the σεισμός (Rev 6.12–17) is broad and may be divided into two clearly differentiated parts: the effects of the σεισμός (Rev 6.12–14), and the reaction of the inhabitants of the earth (Rev 6.15–17).

---

[135] Although this is found in some manuscripts, it does not seem to be the original form; see Smalley, *Revelation*, p. 145.

The nomenclature employed includes, in order of importance, the elements of the firmament that were known at the time – ἥλιος, 'sun' (Rev 6.12b); σελήνη, 'moon' (Rev 6.12c); ἀστέρες, 'stars' (Rev 6.13); and οὐρανὸς, 'heaven' (Rev 6.14a) – and elements of the earth – ὄρος, 'mountain'; and νῆσος, 'island' (Rev 6.14b). This creates a merism, as there is an allusion to two poles: the surfaces of the earth and of the sea. Moreover, by using the verb of motion κινεῖν, 'to move, to shake', the climate of tension is maintained and it is clear that chaos reigns over the earth. Thus, it is briefly stated that the earth has in fact been profoundly shaken. The same sensation is transmitted by the nomenclature of the celestial vault overhead, reinforced by the use of the adjectival lexeme μέγας. The listener/reader is therefore able to judge of the extent and intensity of the earthquake by its effects.

As for the predicates, John uses a series of images drawn from daily life – sackcloth, blood, a fig tree – introduced by means of the adverb ὡς. In this way, he gives a certain rhythm to the expansion, one that progresses from symmetry, created by parallel structures – καί + subject (article + noun) + verb + simile: καὶ ὁ ἥλιος ἐγένετο μέλας ὡς σάκκος τρίχινος καὶ ἡ σελήνη ὅλη ἐγένετο ὡς αἷμα, 'the sun became as black as sackcloth and all of the moon became like blood' (Rev 6.12bc) – to asymmetry, in the next clauses: καὶ οἱ ἀστέρες τοῦ οὐρανοῦ ἔπεσαν εἰς τὴν γῆν, ὡς συκῆ βάλλει τοὺς ὀλύνθους αὐτῆς ὑπὸ ἀνέμου μεγάλου σειομένη, 'and the stars of the sky fell upon the earth, as a fig tree drops its figs when shaken by a strong wind' (Rev 6.13). He then concludes in the same way that he began: καί + subject (article + noun) + verb + simile (καὶ ὁ οὐρανὸς ἀπεχωρίσθη ὡς βιβλίον ἑλισσόμενον, 'and heaven shrank away like a scroll rolled up', Rev 6.14a).

The predicates also combine two sensations that may be perceived by the eyes: colour and movement, giving a strong dramatic effect to the description and, at the same time, a great sense of realism and visuality.

Colour predominates initially, not only through the presence of the word μέλας, 'black', or the red colour implied by ὡς αἷμα, 'like blood', but through the contrasts that result. Although the sun is normally seen as yellow, it is now μέλας, 'black', and the moon, instead of being white, now has a reddish hue.[136] These two colours have also just been mentioned to describe the horses that brought with them such grave misfortunes: ἵππος πυρρός, 'bright red horse' (Rev 6.4), and ἵππος μέλας, 'black

---

[136] Both expressions are echoes of Joel 3.4; the image of a blackened sun is also found in Joel 2.10 and Isa 50.3.

horse' (Rev 6.5), so that the presence of these colours in the firmament reminds the listener/reader of those same calamities and heightens the drama of the description.

The shift from colour to movement takes place in Rev 6.13 with the simile of the fig tree, which combines both of these perceptions. Although it is not specified directly, the idea of colour is implicit here, as both the tree and its fruit have distinctive colours. The fruit is designated by the lexeme ὄλυνθος, which in the NT is found only in Rev 6.13 and, in the LXX, in Song 2.13. This corresponds to the Hebrew hapax פַּג, and is usually translated as 'fig'.[137] The same is true of ὄλυνθος.[138] This translation, however, is problematic in both the book of Revelation and in the Song of Songs.

In the book of Revelation, it is difficult to explain the similarity between the fall of the fruit and the fall of the stars. The fig is a small, green fruit, which, if it does not reach maturity, will logically survive the autumn and winter without falling from the tree, becoming brebas in the spring;[139] it does not seem very coherent, then, that the fall of the stars should be compared to that of this small fruit.

In the Song of Songs, after mentioning that the winter has passed (Song 2.11), the author goes on to mention the ripening of the fruit of the fig tree and the flowering of the grapevines. This happens precisely in the spring, the season for brebas, and not at the end of summer, when the ripened fruit are still figs. For this reason, translating ὄλυνθος or פַּג as 'figs' would seem to be inaccurate.

In Hebrew, the lexeme used for figs is תְּאֵנָה, which the LXX translates as σῦκον (2 Kings 20.7; Neh 13.15; Jer 8.13; etc.). In contrast, when brebas are referred to, בְּכוּרָה is used (Isa 28.4; Jer 24.2) and is translated in the LXX as πρόδρομος σῦκον or τὰ σῦκα τὰ πρόϊμα. Jesús Luzárraga, based on a profound linguistic study of this topic, holds that, as the perfect form of the Hebrew principal verb חָנַט indicates that the fruit of the fig tree has fully ripened, these could be nothing other than brebas,

---

[137] L. Alonso Schökel, *Diccionario bíblico hebreo-español* (Madrid: Trotta, 1994), p. 601, s.v. פַּג; L. Koehler and W. Baumgartner, *A Bilingual Dictionary of the Hebrew and Aramaic Old Testament, English and German* (Leiden – Cologne – New York, NY: Brill, 1998), p. 750, s.v. פַּג.

[138] J. Lust, *et al.*, *A Greek-English Lexicon of the Septuagint* (Stuttgart: Deutsche Bibelgesellschaft, 2003), p. 435, s.v. ὄλυνθος; LOUW and NIDA, 3.37, s.v. ὄλυνθος; *BDAG*, 5275, s.v. ὄλυνθος.

[139] H. N. Moldenke and A. L. Moldenke, *Plants of the Bible* (Waltham, MA: Chronica Botanica, 1952), p. 104, s.v. *ficus carica*; M. Zohary, *Plants of The Bible* (Cambridge: Cambridge University Press, 1982), p. 58, s.v. *fig*.

which change colour at the beginning of spring and may be harvested at the end of May.[140]

To identify these as brebas, then, would preserve the coherence of the texts (Rev 6.13; Song 2.13). In the case of the book of Revelation, this is because the stars are compared to brebas, a fruit larger than the fig, with a heavy appearance and purplish colour. They tend to fall from the tree easily – an event which, in the Song of Songs, would seem to confirm the arrival of spring (Song 2.11).

The appearance of the fig tree and the brebas, with their dark hues, serves to maintain the chromatic sensation created by the black sun and red moon, as well as to intensify the drama, as the comparison of the stars with the brebas introduces a sharp contrast between the stability of stars and the ease with which brebas fall from the tree. The simile underscores the force and speed with which the stars collide with the earth, and the great damage they cause.

Through the simile ὡς βιβλίον ἑλισσόμενον, 'like a scroll rolled up' (Rev 6.14), the ideas of movement, chromatic change, and contrast are maintained in the expansion. Heaven, which has been depicted up to now as an enormous blue surface that covers the earth, has become no more than a βιβλίον ἑλισσόμενον, 'scroll rolled up'.[141]

What comes next is not a description of the injuries and deaths caused by the earthquake, but of the rebellious reaction of human beings to the catastrophe (Rev 6.15–17). At this point, the style changes completely, and alongside the sense of visual perception, the auditory appears. First, there is a description of what is seen: men hiding themselves to escape death. Here, an *amplificatio* is used (Rev 6.15), as the great men of earth are listed, either according to their position (οἱ βασιλεῖς τῆς γῆς καὶ οἱ μεγιστᾶνες καὶ οἱ χιλίαρχοι, 'the kings of the earth, the magnates, and the generals'), or their power (καὶ οἱ πλούσιοι καὶ οἱ ἰσχυροί, 'and the rich and powerful'), and finally all of humanity is referred to, by means of a merism: καὶ πᾶς δοῦλος καὶ ἐλεύθερος, 'every slave and every free man'. This merism gives a tone of pathos to the *amplificatio*; it is not just one group of individuals who reject God and the Lamb, but all of humanity. There is a contrast, then, between the attitude of the people fleeing from the earthquake and their own wish to die. To express this, John uses direct speech supported by imperatives: πέσετε ἐφ᾽ ἡμᾶς καὶ

---

[140] J. Luzárraga, *Cantar de los Cantares: Sendas del amor* (Estella: Verbo Divino, 2005), pp. 279–80.

[141] An allusion to Isa 34.4.

κρύψατε ἡμᾶς ἀπὸ προσώπου τοῦ καθημένου ἐπὶ τοῦ θρόνου καὶ ἀπὸ τῆς ὀργῆς τοῦ ἀρνίου, 'fall on us and hide us from the presence of the One seated upon the throne and from the wrath of the Lamb' (Rev 6.16).[142] The description concludes with a rhetorical question charged with drama and suspense: ὅτι ἦλθεν ἡ ἡμέρα ἡ μεγάλη τῆς ὀργῆς αὐτῶν, καὶ τίς δύναται σταθῆναι, 'because the great day of their wrath has come, and who is able to withstand it?' (Rev 6.17).

The description of the new heaven, the new earth, and the New Jerusalem (Rev 21.1–2) comes nearly at the end of the narrative. The expansion of the description of heaven and earth is reduced to a minimum of predicates; indeed, the same adjectival lexeme is used to describe both: καινός. The repetition of the term may be due to its deep semantic content. Καινός not only expresses 'that which is new, fresh, recently made', as in classical Greek,[143] but also includes the particular connotations that it acquires in the NT: contrast, continuity, dynamism, and purpose.[144] It may thus be affirmed that, although it is especially emphasized that the new heaven and the new earth are different from the former ones, they have their origins in their earlier counterparts; otherwise, they could not be called such. Moreover, what is new is also dynamic, with the capacity to renew and dominate the old, and from this arises its sense of purpose.

If we consider the dense significance suggested by καινός, it seems logical that John feels the need to explain it to his audience; he therefore adds a brief commentary to the description: ὁ γὰρ πρῶτος οὐρανὸς καὶ ἡ πρώτη γῆ ἀπῆλθαν, καὶ ἡ θάλασσα οὐκ ἔστιν ἔτι, 'as the first heaven and the first earth have passed away, and the sea no longer exists' (Rev 21.1), indicating continuity by the adjective πρῶτος and disappearance by the verbal lexeme of motion ἀπῆλθαν, as well as the absence of the sea.

As for the expansion of the description of the New Jerusalem (Rev 21.2), some elements have already appeared in the discussion of the ecphrasis of the holy city, above, and so I will limit myself here to sketching its outlines. It is divided into two sections: the origin of the New Jerusalem (Rev 21.2a), and its appearance (Rev 21.2b).

The city's origin is described in detail, with reference made to its movement (καταβαίνουσαν, 'descending'), its spatial framework (ἐκ τοῦ οὐρανοῦ, 'from heaven'), and its provenance (ἀπὸ τοῦ θεοῦ, 'from

---

[142] The expression used is very similar to that of the LXX in Hos 10.8.

[143] THAYER, 2676, s.v. καινός; it appears in Aeschylus and Herodotus.

[144] R. A. Harrisville, 'The Concept of Newness in the New Testament', *JBL* 74 (1955), 69.

God'). This last aspect is especially striking here, as, in the descriptions examined so far, once a character has been situated in a particular context, his origin is no longer specified. An example of this is the origin of the angels in Rev 10.1, 18.1, and 20.1, who are all described with the same expression: καταβαίνοντα ἐκ τοῦ οὐρανοῦ. However, John now feels the necessity to say more about the origin of the New Jerusalem. The holy city comes not only ἐκ τοῦ οὐρανοῦ, 'from heaven', but ἀπὸ τοῦ θεοῦ, 'from God'. In this way, John connects the city that he is seeing now in his vision with the New Jerusalem that was announced earlier in the letter to the church of Laodicea: τὸ ὄνομα τῆς πόλεως τοῦ θεοῦ μου, τῆς καινῆς Ἰερουσαλὴμ ἡ καταβαίνουσα ἐκ τοῦ οὐρανοῦ ἀπὸ τοῦ θεοῦ μου, 'the name of the city of my God, the New Jerusalem, which descends from heaven from my God' (Rev 3.12).

To describe the outer aspect of the New Jerusalem, he uses nuptial imagery, comparing it to a bride adorned for her wedding: ἡτοιμασμένην ὡς νύμφην κεκοσμημένην τῷ ἀνδρὶ αὐτῆς, 'dressed like a bride adorned for her husband'. In this suggestive manner, the colour, the elegance, the shining jewels, and the beauty of the bride are implicitly alluded to.

2.8   The Integrated (ἐν τῇ Διηγήσει) Descriptions

The ἐν τῇ διηγήσει descriptions, also referred to as 'integrated descriptions',[145] are those inserted into predominantly narrative sections by means of a single lexeme or syntagma. They enable the listener/reader to visualize what John sees, without losing the thread of the narration. They are also capable of quickly describing some aspect of a character, animal, or event as if in the flash of a camera, hence their brevity.

The structure is a simple one, consisting only of denomination – i.e., a noun – and expansion. The latter is constituted of one or two adjectival lexemes, a simile, or both. Thus, the θρόνον, 'throne', of God is μέγαν λευκὸν, 'great white' (Rev 20.11); the κέρατα, 'horns', of the beast of the earth are ὅμοια ἀρνίῳ, 'like a lamb's' (Rev 13.11); the spirits are ἀκάθαρτα ὡς βάτραχοι, 'unclean like frogs' (Rev 16.13).

---

[145] H. Bonheim, *The Narrative Modes: Technique of the Short Story* (Woodbridge: Brewer, 1982), p. 24.

The predicates are often expanded through the use of two semantic fields in particular: that of size, or rather, enormity (ὡς ὄρος μέγα, 'like a great mountain', Rev 8.8b; μέγας, 'great', Rev 8.10b; μεγάλη ὡς ταλαντιαία, 'weighing about a hundred pounds',[146] Rev 16.21); and that of fire, with the presence, once again, of the colour red (πυρὶ καιόμενον, 'burning with fire', Rev 8.8b; καιόμενος ὡς λαμπάς, 'burning like a torch', Rev 8.10b; ὡς καπνὸς καμίνου, 'like smoke from a furnace', Rev 9.2).

These two semantic fields help to create a feeling of terror and dread in the listener/reader. And so, when a star is said to have fallen (Rev 8.10b), the addition of μέγας, 'great', and καιόμενος ὡς λαμπάς, 'burning like a torch', makes an even greater impression on the listener/reader, who thinks not only of the destruction caused by the impact, but of the fire it brings with it.

The same feeling of terror is achieved in the expansion of the description of the sea that changes to blood (Rev 16.3). This is not just any blood, but αἷμα ὡς νεκροῦ, 'blood as from a corpse'; that is, coagulated, rotting blood,[147] which, far from giving life, has none of its own. Such images serve both to transmit visual perception and to move the listener/reader emotionally.

Integrated descriptions like these, by using images that are well known to the audience, help to grant realism and visual form to the narration, at the same time that they resonate on an emotional level.

2.9   Narration and Description in the Book of Revelation

Without doubt, the book of Revelation has been constructed in a specific and deliberate way. To this end, the narration is frequently interrupted by descriptive passages the aim of which is to place the visions of John of Patmos before the eyes of the listener/reader.

The continual repetition of the formula καὶ εἶδον, 'and I saw' – and its variants, especially καὶ ἰδού, 'and behold' – as the introductory sign in nearly all of these descriptions, reminds the listener/reader constantly that what they are hearing is what John saw, and that this is being transmitted to them through his words. The repeated use of the formula καὶ εἶδον, then, gives John the role of narrator–witness, and makes the

---

[146]   Robertson, *Comentario*, p. 753: in the LXX, a talent is said to weigh between 49 and 59 kilogrammes.

[147]   Mounce, *Revelation*, p. 294.

focalization of his narrative exclusively his own. Even in the ἤκουσα καὶ εἶδον descriptions, in which John sees through the mediation of an angel, the description is given from his own point of view and not the angel's.

Although there is a greater degree of external focalization (what John sees) than of other types of focalization, the point of view from which the focalized object is seen is not constant; John begins the expansion with a panoramic vision of this object, and follows this with a series of closer views. The description is thus expanded through movements that are much like those of a movie camera. Such a style, together with an apparent lack of order and a simplicity and concision of syntax, endows the description with great dynamism and agility, so that the listener/reader, not knowing what is coming next, is given the impression that he is seeing the vision at the same time as John.

The fact that proper names are not used in the denomination helps to underscore the feeling that the seer is telling and writing what he saw, given that the listener/reader is not provided with any advance information as to the identities of the characters.

It could be said that the use of description in the book of Revelation, far from serving as a mere pause in the narration, contributes instead to its development; indeed, the vision (description) of characters, animals, angels, events, etc., is equal in importance to the actual succession of those events. These descriptions, then, are not superfluous, nor are they superimposed over the narrative in such a way as to make them difficult to follow, but rather combine with it to form a single narrative texture. This truly enables the audience to visualize John's experience. Without such descriptions, one of the narrator's principal objectives, i.e., to make known ὅσα εἶδεν, 'all that he saw' (Rev 1.2), could not have been achieved.

It is now the moment to reaffirm the idea that the descriptive technique employed in the book of Revelation does indeed resemble that of the short story. Rev 1.9–22.16 is an example of how, in the world of literature, description and narration are two aspects inherent in the short story form, just as body and soul are two aspects of the human being in the real world.[148]

---

[148] Anderson Imbert, *Teoría y técnica del cuento*, p. 230.

3

JOHN, AUDITORY WITNESS AND HERALD OF THE WORD

Another of the reading guidelines that the listener/reader discovers in the prologue of the book of Revelation (Rev 1.1–3) is that the revelation itself is also transmitted by means of the spoken word. Indeed, the seer is presented as ὃς ἐμαρτύρησεν τὸν λόγον τοῦ θεοῦ καὶ τὴν μαρτυρίαν Ἰησοῦ Χριστοῦ, 'the one who gives testimony to the word of God and to the testimony of Jesus Christ' (Rev 1.2a). Therefore, John is also an auditory witness, as will be reaffirmed in the epilogue: Κἀγὼ Ἰωάννης ὁ ἀκούων ... ταῦτα, 'I, John, am the one who heard ... these things' (Rev 22.8).

Thus, just as the narrator enables the listener/reader to see, he takes equal care to ensure that the words he has heard are made audible, and that they may be perceived in the context in which they are pronounced. The fact that John depicts himself as the herald of the revelation gives a very specific character to the work, and to achieve this effect he employs the stylistic and narrative strategies needed to transmit faithfully what he has heard while maintaining the close attention of his audience.

3.1   What John Hears: Scenes of Dramatization

When reading the book of Revelation, the listener/reader is aware that a message is being transmitted, as they frequently hear the formula of auditory perception, καὶ ἤκουσα, as well as the repeated use of direct speech. This is in fact so frequent that even within one discourse in direct speech there may appear another, spoken by a third voice (Rev 18.7, 10, 16–17, 19). What is more, the listener/reader can observe that indirect speech is relegated to specific contexts: those in which there is either no express desire to indicate the giver of the message, as in the instructions received by the slain souls or the locusts (Rev 6.11; 9.4), or in which the character speaking belongs to the context of evil, as in the case of the earth beast (Rev 13.14).

What characterizes direct speech is the reproduction of characters' words or thoughts in a textual manner, in the exact terms, it is supposed, in which they themselves expressed them.[1] It is therefore the ideal instrument for expressing the words that John has heard.

At the same time, direct speech endows the narrator with a special ability: that of hiding himself momentarily from the narration. This temporary disappearance brings with it certain changes. The voices that John hears and the characters who speak come to the foreground and are in a sense transformed into actors, while their discourses become dramatic dialogue,[2] and the narration is to some extent eclipsed, to make way for 'moments of dramatized narrative';[3] or rather, 'scenes'. More precisely, these scenes allow the discourses to be reproduced just as they are spoken, and in the order that they occur.[4] The narrative, then, moves away from diegesis and comes as close as possible to mimesis, creating an effect of reality – of referential illusion. The climax of the narrative is thus intensified, and the listener/reader gets the impression that they have abandoned their conventional role and become a mere spectator of what is happening.

One emblematic example of this shift from diegesis to mimesis is the vision of the glory of God (Rev 4.1–11). The entire story contained in this passage is built through a combination of narration, description, and direct speech. The narration begins with the first-person singular ἤκουσα, 'I heard' (Rev 4.1), and ἐγενόμην ἐν πνεύματι, 'I fell into ecstasy' (Rev 4.2). Immediately after this come the καὶ εἶδον descriptions (Rev 4.2–3, 4, 6–8a). When these have concluded, the voice of the narrator speaks in the third-person plural (ἐκπορεύονται, Rev 4.5; γέμουσιν/ἔχουσιν, Rev 4.8b; δώσουσιν, πεσοῦνται, etc., Rev 4.9–10), so that the facts to which John is witness are recounted, but are seen from outside. Little by little, the pericope undergoes a gradual transformation, as the seer, in the role of narrator, begins to disappear through this use of the third person. He then uses the opportunity, first of all, to define the space in which the action takes place, as if he were giving stage directions:[5]

---

[1] Villanueva, *Glosario*, s.v. *estilo directo*.

[2] Reis and Lopes, *Diccionario*, p. 62, s.v. *diálogo*. In the theatre, the term 'dialogue' is used to refer to all that is spoken in a dramatic work; cf. J. L. García Barrientos, *Cómo se comenta una obra de teatro: Ensayo de método* (Madrid: Síntesis, 2003), p. 62.

[3] Reis and Lopes, *Diccionario*, p. 79, s.v. *escena*.

[4] *Ibid.*

[5] Bowman, *Drama*, p. 42, sees these spatial elements of the book of Revelation as the stage directions of its 'second act', i.e., the vision of God in heaven.

Καὶ ἐκ τοῦ θρόνου ἐκπορεύονται ἀστραπαὶ καὶ φωναὶ καὶ βρονταί· καὶ ἑπτὰ λαμπάδες πυρὸς καιόμεναι ἐνώπιον τοῦ θρόνου, ἅ εἰσιν τὰ ἑπτὰ πνεύματα τοῦ θεοῦ, [6] καὶ ἐνώπιον τοῦ θρόνου ὡς θάλασσα ὑαλίνη ὁμοία κρυστάλλῳ (Rev 4.5–6a).

And from the throne came flashes of lightning and rumblings of thunder. Seven torches of fire burn before the throne, which are the seven spirits of God. [6] Before the throne, something like a sea transparent as glass.

He then details the movements of the characters, further adding to the composition of the scene:

πεσοῦνται οἱ εἴκοσι τέσσαρες πρεσβύτεροι ἐνώπιον τοῦ καθημένου ἐπὶ τοῦ θρόνου καὶ προσκυνήσουσιν τῷ ζῶντι εἰς τοὺς αἰῶνας τῶν αἰώνων καὶ βαλοῦσιν τοὺς στεφάνους αὐτῶν ἐνώπιον τοῦ θρόνου λέγοντες . . . (Rev 4.10)

the twenty-four elders prostrate themselves before the One seated upon the throne, they worship him who lives for ever and ever and throw down their crowns before the throne, saying . . .

The participle λέγοντες serves as a bridge between what might be called stage direction and, in the foreground, the discourse of the twenty-four elders. It is here that dramatic dialogue takes over the text completely, to the point that the listener/reader momentarily forgets the presence of the narrator and loses themselves in the songs that they hear sung:

ἄξιος εἶ, ὁ κύριος καὶ ὁ θεὸς ἡμῶν, λαβεῖν τὴν δόξαν καὶ τὴν τιμὴν καὶ τὴν δύναμιν, ὅτι σὺ ἔκτισας τὰ πάντα καὶ διὰ τὸ θέλημά σου ἦσαν καὶ ἐκτίσθησαν (Rev 4.11).

Worthy are You, our Lord and God, to receive glory, honour and power, because You created all things and through your will they existed and were created.

Thus, through mimesis, John manages to create such a sense of realism that the listener/reader who hears the seer's message feels that this audition is in fact taking place at the same time that they are reading the text. It may therefore be concluded that, just as description is the medium used to make the listener/reader feel that they are sharing John's visions, direct speech is one of the devices used to create a similar effect of shared hearing.

3.1.1   Dramatization and Drama in Rev 1.9–22.16

The repeated use of direct speech might have been monotonous were it not tempered by several strategies characteristic of Greek drama: dialogue used as deixis and to express movement, the messenger speech, and the chorus. These were elements already in use in the dramatic tradition of John's time,[6] or even earlier,[7] and which create a varied, dynamic mimesis.

At the same time, this presence of dramatic elements in the book of Revelation further underscores the analogy to the short story form, in which borrowings from the theatre are common (the use of dialogued scenes, situating the action in a particular setting, and so on). Some short stories may even be classified formally as either comedy or drama; that is to say, they have the form of a theatrical text.[8]

a)   Dialogue as Deixis

Given the total absence of stage directions in Greco-Roman theatre, gestures or movement may be expressed through the inherently dramatic device of dialogue. It is the words spoken by the actors, through deixis, that indicate the presence of a given character and their gestures or actions. To help achieve this effect, the pronominal and demonstrative lexemes used, and the adverbs 'here', 'there', 'now', and 'then', serve to fix the attention of the audience and to identify contextual elements.[9]

More specifically, the appearance of the personal pronouns ἐγώ, 'I', and σύ, 'you', is a way of presenting characters in the here and now of their discourses, as the deictics in the scene indicate both the speaker (I) and the listener (you, plural or singular).[10] The way in which John opens his account of the vision is here especially significant:

Ἐγὼ Ἰωάννης, ὁ ἀδελφὸς ὑμῶν . . . (Rev 1.9)

I, John, your brother . . .

---

[6] See the study by J. A. A. Brant, *Dialogue and Drama: Elements of Greek Tragedy in the Fourth Gospel* (Peabody, MA: Hendrickson, 2004).

[7] A more detailed analysis of this question may be found in L. García Ureña, 'El diálogo dramático en el Apocalipsis: De Ezequiel, el trágico, a Juan, el vidente de Patmos', *Greg* 92 (2011), 26–54.

[8] Anderson Imbert, *Teoría y técnica del cuento*, pp. 150–1, 188–9.

[9] Brant, *Dialogue and Drama*, p. 79.

[10] K. Elam, *The Semiotics of Theatre and Drama*, 2nd edn (London: Routledge, 2002), p. 128.

The first-person singular pronoun, ἐγώ, opens the discourse, and by this the speaker/listener is able to identify John, who addresses his words to a ὑμεῖς, 'you'.

Something similar occurs in the epilogue, with the peculiarity that the personal pronoun ἐγώ is repeated three times, once by John (Rev 22.8) and twice by Jesus (Rev 22.13, 16). This repetition is the means by which the characters call attention to their presence within the scene: John and Jesus both see and hear each other; they are, in effect, 'there', while the listener/reader is obliged to focus on the here and now of the dramatization.

As for the demonstratives, there is in the book of Revelation a clear preference for οὗτος, αὕτη, τοῦτο, as these express nearness. They are in fact used 49 times in 43 verses, as opposed to ἐκεῖνος, -η, -ov, which appear on only two occasions (Rev 9.6; 11.13).

In such moments of dramatization, the demonstrative pronoun οὗτοι carries all of its deictic power, so that the listener/reader understands that the speaker is in fact performing the gesture of pointing out the characters, identifying them and indicating their settings.[11] In other words, the listener/reader links gesture to object thanks to these deictics.[12] A representative example of this is Rev 7.13–14, in which John, conversing with one of the elders, is asked about the identity of those who are dressed in white robes (οὗτοι). The elder responds to his own question using the lexeme οὗτοι:

οὗτοι οἱ περιβεβλημένοι τὰς στολὰς τὰς λευκὰς τίνες εἰσὶν καὶ πόθεν ἦλθον; [14] (...)
οὗτοί εἰσιν οἱ ἐρχόμενοι ἐκ τῆς θλίψεως τῆς μεγάλης ... (Rev 7.13–14)

These dressed in white robes, who are they and from where have they come? [14] (...)
These are the ones who come from the great tribulation ...

The reiteration of the demonstrative pronoun οὗτοί conveys the elder's gesture of pointing to the multitude, at the same time that it reminds the listener/reader that the multitude is still present, after the hymn of praise to God (Rev 7.12).

---

[11] G. A. Miller, 'Some Problems in the Theory of Demonstrative Reference', in R. J. Jarvella and W. Klein (eds.), *Speech, Place, and Action: Studies of Deixis and Related Topics* (Chichester – New York, NY: Wiley, 1982), p. 62.

[12] Elam, *Semiotics*, p. 65.

Lastly, I will address the use of the adverbs ἄρτι and δεῦρο. Ἄρτι expresses a present time originating at a given moment and projected into the future. It differs from other adverbs of time, such as νῦν or ἤδη, in that it refers strictly to the present ('just now'),[13] with a certain suggestion of the future ('from now on'). Its presence in these scenes of dramatization thus intensifies the sense of an eternal present, that *hic et nunc* which is so characteristic of the book of Revelation. And so, for example, ἄρτι intensifies the dramatic context of the beatitude in Rev 14.13, the 'now' of which is from this specific moment onwards being fulfilled: μακάριοι οἱ νεκροὶ οἱ ἐν κυρίῳ ἀποθνήσκοντες ἀπ' ἄρτι, 'Blessed [are] the dead who die in the Lord from this moment on'.

This deictic power is even greater in Rev 12.10, where the adverb is used to open the dialogue: ἄρτι ἐγένετο ἡ σωτηρία, 'from now on, there is salvation'. Ἄρτι confirms that the victory of Michael and his angels over the devil occurs at a specific moment, but is prolonged in time, unlike the salvation announced in Rev 11.15.[14]

With regard to the adverbial lexeme δεῦρο (or δεῦτε), 'here', this term not only expresses proximity to the speaker, but also indicates movement towards them; indeed, it has often been translated as 'come'.[15] Its function within the text, therefore, is both deictic and indicative of movement, as may be seen in Rev 17.1, 19.17, and 21.9.

Rev 17.1 and 21.9 form part of the introductory signs of the ἤκουσα καὶ εἶδον descriptions. These are the words that the angel addresses to John, bidding him to contemplate the great whore and the New Jerusalem: Δεῦρο, δείξω σοι, 'Come, I will show you'. The deictic power of the adverbial lexeme δεῦρο, as well as showing the proximity of the angel to the seer, seems to carry with it the implicit expression of a gesture inviting John to come nearer.[16] In this way, δεῦρο becomes in turn a dramatic device that indicates to the listener/reader that the seer is moving from one location to another.

The same occurs with the angel's invitation to the supper of God: Δεῦτε συνάχθητε εἰς τὸ δεῖπνον τὸ μέγα τοῦ θεοῦ, 'come, and gather together at the great supper of God' (Rev 19.17). The adverbial lexeme, here in its plural form δεῦτε, becomes a device for showing the gesture that the angel uses to summon together the birds of the air.

---

[13] THAYER, 764, s.v. ἄρτι.
[14] Prigent, *Commentary*, p. 390.
[15] LOUW and NIDA, 84.24, s.v. δεῦρο.
[16] Elam, *Semiotics*, p. 65.

b)   Dialogue as Indicator of Movement

This particular function of dialogue appears in dramatic scenes that are characterized by their brevity and vibrancy, and gives to each scene a great dynamism, as it highlights what is occurring. The opening of the first four seals is a relevant example of this.

After hearing the heavenly songs (Rev 5.9–14), John begins to narrate the opening of the seals, using in each case a time clause and another principal clause headed by καὶ ἤκουσα: Καὶ εἶδον ὅτε ἤνοιξεν τὸ ἀρνίον μίαν ἐκ τῶν ἑπτὰ σφραγίδων, καὶ ἤκουσα ἑνὸς ἐκ τῶν τεσσάρων ζῴων λέγοντος ὡς φωνῇ βροντῆς . . ., 'I saw, when the Lamb opened the first of the seven seals, and I heard the first of the living beings saying, like the rumbling of thunder . . . ' (Rev 6.1). The presence of ἤκουσα . . . λέγοντος compels him to interrupt the narration and introduce a brief dialogue by saying: Ἔρχου, 'Come'. Much the same happens when the last three horses enter the scene; first the narrative section is announced – καὶ ὅτε ἤνοιξεν τὴν σφραγῖδα, 'and when he opened the seal' (Rev 6.3, 5, 7) – and then direct speech is resumed with the verb of movement ἔρχου.

The function of ἔρχου is none other than to indicate to the listener/reader the arrival of the horses. A more dramatic effect is thus achieved, as the listener/reader hears what is being told, perceives the successive arrival of the horses, and visualizes the scene through what John is saying: καὶ εἶδον, καὶ ἰδοὺ ἵππος . . . (Rev 6.2, 5, 8).

This use of dialogue to express movement may be found in other sections of the narrative as well; e.g., Rev 9.14; 10.8–10; 16.1.[17]

c)   The Messenger Speech

The messenger speech is another element proper to Greek tragedy, inherited from Homeric epic. In most cases, it consists of a monologue delivered by a single character, generally anonymous and having the role of messenger, who narrates events that have taken place 'offstage'.[18] It is usually presented in direct speech, which gives a dramatic, realistic character to the events being narrated, so that the messenger may seem to have been an eyewitness of what

---

[17] García Ureña, 'El diálogo dramático', 53–4.
[18] B. Goward, *Telling Tragedy: Narrative Techniques in Aeschylus, Sophocles and Euripides* (London: Duckworth, 1999), p. 26.

he is recounting, while at the same time communicating his own subjective point of view.[19]

Along general lines, this type of speech is found in the three monologues that we hear after the vision of the great whore: that of the angel in Rev 18.2–3, of the voice from heaven in Rev 18.4–20, and of the mighty angel in Rev 18.21–24. The three anonymous speeches announce the same event, which is not typical of the messenger speeches in tragedy. The reason for such an innovation may lie in the fact that, as has already been mentioned, for a testimony to be valid, the presence of at least two witnesses is required; hence the testimonies of three different messengers.

In the first speech, the angel announces, without the slightest preamble, the fall of Babylon, and transmits to the listener/reader his joy at this news. To do so, he makes use of repetition: Ἔπεσεν, ἔπεσεν Βαβυλὼν ἡ μεγάλη, 'Fallen, fallen, is Babylon the great' (Rev 18.2).[20] Immediately afterwards, he describes the resulting state of the city and explains the reasons for the fall: the lust of the nations, the fornication of the kings, and the luxury of Babylon (Rev 18.3). The angel thus focuses on the causes of the fall rather than on how it occurred.

After this monologue, that of the voice from heaven begins (Rev 18.4–20), all the more dramatically for the fact that from the first it is addressed to ὁ λαός μου, 'my people' (i.e., those who have remained faithful to God), commanding them to leave the city[21] and then informing us of the lamentation of those who have enjoyed its benefits. This is done in direct speech, so that this discourse, nested as it is within another, creates an even greater effect of realism, as the listener/reader hears directly the wailing of the kings (Rev 18.10), the merchants (Rev 18.16–17), and the mariners (Rev 18.18–19), as if in real time. Something similar occurs with Babylon the great, whose words resonate

---

[19] I. J. F. de Jong, *Narrative in Drama: The Art of the Euripidean Messenger-Speech* (Leiden: Brill, 1991), pp. 105–6, 131.

[20] An expression with roots in the Old Testament: Isa 21.9; Jer 28.8. Although scholars tend to consider the aorist ἔπεσεν to be a *perfectum propheticum* (see Beckwith, *Apocalypse*, p. 712; Aune, *Revelation 3*, p. 985; Smalley, *Revelation*, p. 444), I believe that, if we accept as a hermeneutic guideline the fact that the book of Revelation is a narrative of what John saw and heard, then the aorist refers to an action that has already been completed; this explains the song of jubilation (Rev 19.1–8) that comes at the end of these messenger speeches. What is more, this hymn refers explicitly to the smoke rising from the city (Rev 19.3).

[21] The order to leave Babylon, ἐξέλθατε, is an echo of other prophetic passages such as Isa 48.20; 52.11; Jer 51.6, 9. Smalley, *Revelation*, p. 446, shows that this is a recurrent motif in both the OT and the NT (2 Cor 6.14; Eph 5.11; 1 Tim 5.22).

in the scene thanks to the use of the first-person singular (Rev 18,7).[22] What is more, the voice that pronounces this speech is completely involved in what is being told, with the speaker expressing aloud his own opinion of the whore (Rev 18.14). The speech concludes with a cry of jubilation, this time directed to heaven and to the saints who reside there, at the triumphant judgment of God (Rev 18.20).

The speech of the voice from heaven thus completes the angel's announcement, by communicating to the listener/reader what the fall of Babylon was like. Its function is similar to what in classical theatre is known as teichoscopy, a device through which something that is happening out of the audience's sight is described. The illusion is thus created that these events, perceived by the audience through the device of the messenger,[23] are really happening, and this is indeed what the listener/reader of the book of Revelation experiences.

The last of these speeches (Rev 18.21–24) takes place after a brief narrative section in which John describes an angel hurling an enormous stone into the sea (Rev 18.21). Considering the scene of dramatization that is created here, it may be said that Rev 18.21 serves principally as a stage direction that helps the listener/reader to understand the words of the angel.

In his discourse, the angel refers once again to the fall of Babylon, but this time in a highly visual manner. Taking advantage of its deictic power, he uses the adverb οὕτως, 'thus', to illustrate the action he has just performed, which is then repeated textually by means of this word. A comparison is made between the throwing of the stone and the fall of Babylon (Rev 18.21), so that, as the listener/reader visualizes the angel's action, synthesized in οὕτως, they perceive the definitive fall of the great whore. From this moment on, however, the discourse will undergo a change in tone. The angel turns from the listener/reader and addresses Babylon herself, employing the second-person singular to evoke the nearness of the absent interlocutor.[24] The angel thus pronounces his judgment of Babylon in the form of a reproach, which is both tinged with irony and highly lyrical.[25] This is done through a series of parallel

---

[22] His words are reminiscent of those in Isa 47.7–8.

[23] Pavis, *Diccionario*, p. 464, s.v. *teichoscopia*.

[24] De Jong, *Narrative in Drama*, p. 105.

[25] Generally speaking, the lyricism of the messenger speech arises from the character's own emotional involvement with the events being described; see M. Brioso, 'Algunas observaciones sobre el mensajero en el teatro ático clásico', in E. Calderón and A. Morales, *et al.* (eds.), *Koinòs Lógos: Homenaje al profesor José García López*, vol. 1 (Murcia, 2006), p. 117.

statements, one built upon an *amplificatio*: φωνὴ κιθαρῳδῶν καὶ μουσικῶν καὶ αὐλητῶν καὶ σαλπιστῶν, 'the music of the kitharists and the singers, of the flautists and the trumpeters' (Rev 18.22a). This creates a powerful dramatic effect. Others rely on polyptotons: πᾶς τεχνίτης πάσης τέχνης, 'no tradesman in any trade' (Rev 18.22b); φωνὴ νυμφίου καὶ νύμφης, 'the voices of the bridegroom and the bride' (Rev 18.23). These are, in any case, poetic devices that rest upon the narrative's two central pillars: vision and hearing. A new instance of teichoscopy is thus created, through a description of the end of everyday life, reinforced by the *ritornello*: οὐ μὴ ἀκουσθῇ ἐν σοὶ ἔτι, 'will not be heard in you again',[26] in which the double negation, the deictic, and the final adverb, ἔτι, all serve to underscore the fact of Babylon's irremediable destruction.

The reproach concludes with a sentencing and the reason for the city's destruction. Here the angel accuses οἱ ἔμποροί, 'the rich', and all of humanity, πάντα τὰ ἔθνη, 'all of the nations'. In the end, however, there is a shift in interlocutor, and with ἐν αὐτῇ (Rev 18.24) Babylon moves again into the background, as the listener/reader is informed of another reason for the destruction: i.e., that the blood of the saints and the slain is on her hands. The change of interlocutor takes place in the angel's own words. So grave is the accusation that he feels unable to continue addressing Babylon, so great is the contempt that he feels for her,[27] and so the most serious charge is communicated directly to the listener/reader.

d)   *The Chorus*

Another element characteristic of Greek theatre is the use of the chorus, a group of characters who, singing, dancing, and reciting as if they were a single voice, serve a variety of functions within the drama. At times, the chorus acts as a principal character would, participating directly in the action; at others, as if it were the narrator of the story, communicating to the audience what has happened in the past and what will take place in the future;[28] it may even inform the audience of its own reflections on what is

---

[26] Except for Rev 18.22b, 23a, in which εὑρεθῇ and φάνῃ, respectively, are used rather than ἀκουσθῇ, as they refer to visible objects.

[27] Beckwith, *Apocalypse*, p. 719, suggests that this shows the influence of the Psalms and the prophets, in which a change of person within a single poetic composition is frequent: Ps 52.4–6; 62.3–4; 81.10–12; Ezek 32.11–12; Amos 6.3–7.

[28] Goward, *Telling Tragedy*, pp. 13, 22.

happening, offering its own moral judgments[29] or expressing its feelings.[30] In addition, the chorus serves to link together the various episodes of the drama, which may be distinguished by its entrances and exits from the ὀρχήστρα.

Throughout the narrative of the book of Revelation, the listener/reader perceives, thanks to announcements by the narrator, the entrance of various characters: the twenty-four elders, the angels, the multitude, etc., all belonging to the heavenly context. No sooner do they appear than they give praise to God or intone a hymn, creating a scene of dramatization, and so it is easy to establish an analogy between these groups and the chorus of Greek theatre. The only exception is the chorus of the 144,000, whose song we do not hear (Rev 14.3). The reason for this is given by John himself: οὐδεὶς ἐδύνατο μαθεῖν τὴν ᾠδὴν, 'no one could learn the song', and so it was impossible for him to leave a written record of what he heard.

According to Edward W. Benson,[31] seven different choruses may be distinguished:

> 1st chorus: the four living beings and the twenty-four elders (Rev 4.8, 11);
>
> 2nd chorus: the four living beings, the twenty-four elders, the angels, and all living creatures (Rev 5.9–10, 12–14);
>
> 3rd chorus: the saved and the angels (Rev 7.10–12);
>
> 4th chorus: the voices from heaven and the twenty-four elders (Rev 11.15, 17–18);
>
> 5th chorus: the voices from heaven and the 144,000 (Rev 14.2–3);
>
> 6th chorus: the conquerors of the beast (Rev 15.3–4);
>
> 7th chorus: a great multitude together with the twenty-four elders and the four living beings (Rev 19.1–8).

A certain parallel may even be established between the chorus and one specific voice. Once the seventh chorus has begun its song (Rev 19.1–14), there is a short interruption, during which a voice is heard inviting πάντες οἱ δοῦλοι αὐτοῦ, [καὶ] οἱ φοβούμενοι αὐτόν, οἱ μικροὶ καὶ

---

[29] F. Schiller, *Über das pathethische*, p. 251, cited by Pavis, *Diccionario*, p. 98, s.v. *coro. 2b Idealización y generalización*; H. D. F. Kitto, *Greek Tragedy: A Literary Study*, 3rd edn (London: Methuen & Co., 1961), p. 214.

[30] Goward, *Telling Tragedy*, p. 13.

[31] Benson, *The Apocalypse*, pp. 40–1.

οἱ μεγάλοι, 'all of his servants and you who fear him, both great and small' (Rev 19.5) to join in its praise of God. These are then immediately united as the indeterminate ὄχλος, 'multitude', in Rev 19.6–8.

Logically, such analogies between the choruses in the book of Revelation and those of Greek drama rest on the functions they serve within the work, as it is not possible to find similarities in the content of their songs and recitations. In this sense, the book of Revelation does not follow the Greek tradition, but is instead more closely linked to Old Testament texts.[32]

In the book of Revelation, the choruses generally have a dialogical structure reminiscent to some extent of choral singing, with its strophes and antistrophes. Such a structure arises naturally, as the choruses are usually comprised of several characters, so that some begin the song or discourse and others continue it, resorting on occasion to a call-and-response structure. The most representative example of this is the second chorus, where the four living beings and the twenty-four elders begin by intoning a song (Rev 5.9–10) and are then joined first by the angels (Rev 5.11–12) and later by all creatures (Rev 5.13), before concluding with the voices of the four living beings (Rev 5.14).

The dialogued parts usually have different functions. One is to praise, while the other, without renouncing this laudatory purpose completely, is either to complete the narration or to foreshadow what is about to happen, thus serving the various functions of the Greek chorus.[33] And so, for example, the second chorus announces the opening of the seals (Rev 5.9) and its song serves to link the vision of the Lamb with the actual opening of the seals, which is presented in direct speech (Rev 6). In other cases, the song is used to close an episode, as in the first discourse of the seventh chorus, which refers to events that have just taken place, i.e., the judgment of the whore and her destruction (Rev 19.2–3). It is more usual, however, for the songs to announce events that are still to come, in the relatively near future. Thus, the fourth chorus warns of the imminent judgment of the nations (Rev 11.18), while the fifth proclaims that the nations will bow down before God: something that will come to pass at the end of the story (Rev 21.24). The seventh speaks of the wedding of the Lamb (Rev 19.1–8), which will also take place later, in the vision of the New Jerusalem.

---

[32] García Ureña, 'El diálogo dramático', 39–40.
[33] Goward, *Telling Tragedy*, pp. 23–4, 36.

Another relevant aspect of the choruses in the book of Revelation is the place in which each is inserted into the narration, as this is neither accidental nor merely ornamental. The first chorus, for example, concludes the vision of the glory of God and tells of its splendour. Just as the listener/reader was allowed to see by means of the καὶ εἶδον descriptions, they are now able to participate in what was heard there. The first chorus is used to this effect, heightening the sense of realism for the listener/reader, as the narrator disappears to make way for the final heavenly liturgy and the scene is brought to an authentic climax.

The second entrance of the chorus comes after a moment of tension and drama. John is weeping because no one is able to open the book, when he suddenly sees the Lamb (Rev 5.1–8) and hears a new song that announces the opening of the seals (Rev 5.9–14). The use of this song frees the scene from its tension, and brings it to a conclusion in a joyous yet solemn tone.

The third chorus appears after the first six seals have been opened and the resulting catastrophes have occurred. The narration so far has had a tragic tone, with a brief respite when the angels order that the damage to the earth and the sea be stopped for the marking of the chosen (Rev 7.2–3). After their number has been announced (Rev 7.4–8), a song of victory bursts from the mouths of the saved, providing a great relief from the tension that has to this point been building to a climax (Rev 7.10–12).

The subsequent choruses follow a similar pattern. The fourth intones a song of jubilation (Rev 11.15, 17–18) that re-establishes a feeling of joy and harmony after the earthquake and the death of the two witnesses (Rev 11.13). The fifth (Rev 14.2–3) offers still another new song, after the vision of the beasts (Rev 13). The sixth chorus (Rev 15.3–4), singing the song of Moses, appears after the vision of the judgment and its imagery of sowing and harvesting (Rev 14.15–20). Finally, the triumphant songs of the seventh chorus (Rev 19.1–8) put the finishing touches on the messenger speeches that have just announced the destruction of Babylon (Rev 18). The victory of God is thus made explicit.

It may be concluded that the choruses in the book of Revelation generally appear at moments of peak dramatic tension. The prayers and hymns recited by the various choruses serve to relax the mood and restore a positive, optimistic, and victorious vision of the battles being described.

3.1.2 Dramatization and the Epistolary Genre

Mimesis plays such an important role in the book of Revelation that we find it in the narrative from the very beginning. After the first descriptive scene (Rev 1.12–16), John tells us briefly of the impression that the vision has produced in him (Rev 1.17a) and introduces a section of direct speech with the participial form λέγων (Rev 1.17b). The words of Jesus follow (Rev 1.17c-20), and John abandons his role as narrator for that of inter-locutor in order to listen to what Jesus tells him: μὴ φοβοῦ . . ., 'do not be afraid . . . ' (Rev 1.17c); γράψον . . ., 'begin to write . . . ' (Rev 1.19).

However, this scene of dramatization is a peculiar one, as, having received the command to write to the church of Ephesus (Rev 2.1), the seer himself moves into the background and a new interlocutor appears, in the figure of the angel of that church. The second-person singular verb forms, δύνῃ, ἐπείρασας, εὗρες (Rev 2.2) – some in the imperative, μνημόνευε, μετανόησον (Rev 2.5) – will now be addressed to him. Nor is the angel of Ephesus the only interlocutor, as the angels of the other churches – Smyrna, Pergamum, Thyatira, Sardes, Philadelphia, and Laodicea (Rev 1.11) – then appear in succession. The moment of transition to these interlocutors comes after the expression τῷ ἀγγέλῳ τῆς ἐν τῷ δεῖνι ἐκκλησίας γράψον, 'to the angel of the church of . . . begin to write . . . ' (Rev 2.8, 12, 18; 3.1, 7, 14). John becomes in effect a mere ἐπιστολόγραφος, 'secretary', limiting himself to setting down in writing what Jesus dictates to him viva voce.[34]

During the dictation of these messages (Rev 2.3), the dramatic effect is heightened by the use of the form of the literary letter.[35] In the ancient world, the letter was viewed as an intimate, personal conversation that one has with a friend, relative, or distant associate.[36] At times it was even written with the brevity and concision (*Eloc.* 228.231) of a spoken dialogue (*Eloc.* 223.5).[37]

---

[34] In antiquity, letters were written by important figures and dictated to a secretary, who, in turn, wrote them down as quickly as skill would permit. One of Cicero's secretaries is known to have designed a system of shorthand in order to achieve greater speed in transcribing; see H. J. Klauck, *Ancient Letters and the New Testament: A Guide to Context and Exegesis* (Waco, TX: Baylor University Press, 2006), pp. 58–9.

[35] Ramsay, *Letters*; Charles, *Commentary 1*, pp. 37–47; G. B. Caird, *The Revelation of Saint John* (Peabody, MA: Hendrickson, 1999), pp. 27–8; Roloff, *Revelation*, pp. 41–2; Vanni, *Apocalisse*, p. 137; Hemer, *Letters*; J. T. Kirby, 'The Rhetorical Situations of Revelation 1–3', *NTS* 34 (1988), 197; Prigent, *Commentary*, pp. 149–54.

[36] Cicero describes it as such in his correspondence (*Fam.* 12.30; 2.4).

[37] Περὶ ἑρμηνείας is a rhetorical treatise that addresses, among other topics, the precepts of letter writing. The exact date of its composition is unknown, but it is thought to have appeared at some point between the third century BC and the first century AD; see *Demetrio*

Although the letters to the seven churches are not documentary, but literary (and in turn part of a larger literary work), it is striking that they contain the elements that permit both dialogue and dramatization, i.e., an 'I' that addresses a 'you', 'here', and 'now'.[38]

The presence of an 'I' addressing a 'you' can be observed in both the verb forms chosen and in the deixis. Indeed, of the 185 personal verb forms that we find in Rev 2–3, 76.07 per cent are in the first- and second-person. The recurrent use of the first-person singular makes the presence of Jesus strongly felt during the dictation. There is no question that his presence is predominant here. Along with this, the use of the second-person singular and the interjection ἰδού make the absent interlocutor seem closer and more present, to the extent that the listener/reader eventually forgets that John is also present in the scene, as Jesus does not address him directly except to command him to write down the next message.

Deixis is expressed through the constant presence of personal pronouns[39] in the first- and second-person singular.[40] The forms ἐγώ and σύ are alternated in practically equal measure, maintaining the reciprocity proper to a dialogue, except in the letters to Ephesus, Smyrna, and Philadelphia. In the first two of these, 'you' is more prevalent than 'I', which appears only twice in the Ephesus letter (Rev 2.2–7), while in the letter to Philadephia, the 'I' of Jesus appears ten times (Rev 3.8[2], 9, 10[2], 12[5]), as opposed to six times for 'you' (Rev 3.8[2], 9[2], 10, 11).

Ephesus is the first of the churches to which Jesus will write. He begins by mentioning its good works (Rev 2.2–3). The repeated use of the pronoun helps to accentuate this *laudatio* at the same time that it gives a continuous presence to the interlocutor – the angel – in a tone that is personal and intimate: τὰ ἔργα σου, 'your works'; τὴν ὑπομονήν σου, 'your patience' (Rev 2.2). However, the tone of the message soon changes, and with it the function of the deictics. Jesus then addresses the church of Ephesus and confronts it with its errors: ἔχω κατὰ σοῦ, 'I

Sobre el estilo. Longino Sobre lo sublime, intro., trans. and notes by J. García López (Madrid: Gredos, 1996, 1st rep.), pp. 14–20.

[38] Elam, *Semiotics*, p. 130.

[39] Rev 2.3, 6, 13(4), 16, 23, 26, 28(2); 3.2, 4, 5, 8(2), 9, 10(2), 12(5), 16, 18, 19, 20(2), 21 (4), for a total of 33 times.

[40] Rev 2.2(2), 4(2), 5(2), 9, 10, 14, 15, 16, 19(3), 20; 3.1, 2, 3, 8(2), 9(2), 10, 11, 15, 16, 17, 18(3), a total of 30 times.

have [something] against you' (Rev 2.4). The pronominal form here imbues the *vituperatio* with a tone that is even more dramatic and personal. Jesus does not reproach the church only for the loss of 'first love', but of *its* first love (τὴν ἀγάπην σου τὴν πρώτην, Rev 2.4). The deictic possesses such power that it seems to evoke the very gaze of Jesus, filled with disappointment and longing for this lost love as he dictates the letter.[41] Finally, in the *peroratio*, the pronominal forms clustered together in Rev 2.5 increase the dramatic tension by means of the *dativus incommodi*,[42] σοι, and the possessive genitive σου. Exhorted to change, Ephesus itself becomes the central focus of this letter, receiving both praise and recriminations. The 'I' of Jesus is at this point almost nowhere to be found.

Smyrna, on the other hand, is warned that it will be subjected to a test, and encouraged to overcome it. Once again, the protagonist here is the church itself, which is given the praise of Jesus, marked by the personal tone of the pronouns – σου τὴν θλῖψιν καὶ τὴν πτωχείαν, 'your tribulation and your poverty' (Rev 2.9) – and then challenged to pass the test set before it in order to obtain the prize – δώσω σοι, 'I will give you' (Rev 2.10). This explains the absence of the deictic referring to Jesus. However, in this message there also appears, for the first time, a pronominal lexeme referring to the second-person plural: ἐξ ὑμῶν, '[some] of you' (Rev 2.10). This is the first time that Jesus pluralizes his interlocutor, which is now no longer a singular 'you' – i.e., the angel of the church – but the church itself in the plural. Nor will it be the only time, as the second-person plural will reappear in the messages to Pergamum and Thyatira (Rev 2.13, 23[2], 24[2]). The referent in all three cases is clear, as Jesus uses the form to address those members of the community who have behaved in a certain way, some showing their faithfulness and others not. The 'you' addressed by Jesus in the letters is thus clearly a 'you' that includes the constituents of the church. Furthermore, the use of this personal form does much to emphasize the personal and dialogical character of these writings.

The church of Philadelphia is presented as being a community of the faithful (Rev 3.8). In his letter to this church, Jesus pledges his unconditional support. The most important role in the transmission of the message is now that of Jesus, hence the predominance of first-person singular forms. First, the warm, friendly tone of the discourse is underscored:

---

[41] Elam, *Semiotics*, p. 68.
[42] Turner, *Syntax*, p. 238.

ἐτήρησάς μου τὸν λόγον καὶ οὐκ ἠρνήσω τὸ ὄνομά μου, 'you have kept my word and have not denied my name' (Rev 3.8). Next, the love felt by Jesus for this church is stressed – ἐγὼ ἠγάπησά σε, 'I have loved you' (Rev 3.9) – as well as his promise of protection: κἀγώ σε τηρήσω, 'I will keep you' (Rev 3.10). The two pronominal lexemes suggest a tone of voice that is strong and intense, perhaps even accompanied by the placing of the hand on the chest to emphasize the sense of 'I'. This situating of Jesus at the centre of attention is maintained until the end of the letter, where we find the genitive μου repeated five times (Rev 3.12).

The predominance of ἐγώ over σύ or vice versa does not diminish the dialogical character of the letters to Ephesus, Smyrna, and Philadelphia. It serves, rather, to give greater prominence to one or other of the interlocutors.

Lastly, the temporal context of these letters, that of the 'now', underpins their dramatic effect. It is a 'now' in which the action takes place at the moment of speaking, establishing a clear sense of immediacy, similar to the function of the present continuous tense in English. This is done by means of a subtle interweaving that runs through the entire structure of each message.

The nucleus of this interwoven structure is the initial imperative γράψον, 'begin to write', and the expression τάδε λέγει . . ., 'says these things . . . ', of the *superscriptio*. The aorist imperative, γράψον, has an ingressive nuance that indicates the beginning of the action at this precise moment;[43] in this case, it refers to the fact that John must, without delay, begin to write down what Jesus dictates: τάδε λέγει . . .[44]

In the body of the letter, the sense of the 'now' is maintained through the use of the present indicative (62 times)[45] and the imperative (15 times),[46] which, together with the future (used 28 times),[47] are the predominant tenses. The present indicative first appears with the verb form οἶδα, 'I know'. Other instances follow. Imperatives appear in the *peroratio*: μνημόνευε, 'remember' (Rev 2.5); μηδὲν φοβοῦ, 'do not be

---

[43] Blass and Debrunner, *Grammar*, § 337; Mussies, *Morphology*, p. 271.

[44] John was already writing, but not the message to Ephesus; see R. L. Thomas, *Revelation 1–7, An Exegetical Commentary* (Chicago, IL: Moody Press, 1992), p. 154.

[45] 55: Rev 2.2(2), 3, 4, 5, 6(3), 9(2), 10(2), 13(3), 14(2), 15, 16, 20(4), 21, 22, 23, 24(4), 25, 27; 3.1(3), 4(2), 8(2), 9(3), 11(2), 15, 16(2), 17(4), 18, 19(2), 20. The perfect form οἶδα (7) is also included here, because of its present-time value; see *BDAG*, 5205, s.v. οἶδα: Rev 2.2, 9, 13, 19; 3.1, 8, 15.

[46] Rev 2.5(3), 10(2), 16, 25; 3.2(2), 3(3), 11, 19(2).

[47] Rev 2.5, 10(2), 16, 17(2), 23(3), 26, 27, 28; 3.3(2), 4, 5(3), 7, 9(3), 10, 12(2), 20(2), 21.

afraid' (Rev 2.10); μετανόησον οὖν, 'and so, begin to repent' (Rev 2.16); ὁ ἔχετε κρατήσατε, 'begin to preserve what you have' (Rev 2.25); γίνου γρηγορῶν, 'be vigilant' (Rev 3.2); κράτει ὁ ἔχεις, 'keep what you possess' (Rev 3.11); ζήλευε οὖν καὶ μετανόησον, 'and so be earnest and begin to repent' (Rev 3.19). All of these forms give a sense of urgency to the present and further enhance the realism of the message.

The same function is served by the use of future tenses and expressions such as: ἔρχομαί σοι, 'I will come to where you are' (Rev 2.5); ἔρχομαί σοι ταχύ, 'I will come to where you are at once' (Rev 2.16); and ἔρχομαι ταχύ, 'I will come soon' (Rev 3.11), in which the present refers to an imminent future, indicated by ταχύ.[48]

Finally, the letters are closed with the hearing formula, ὁ ἔχων οὖς ἀκουσάτω, 'let the one who has ears, hear',[49] and the expression τί τὸ πνεῦμα λέγει ταῖς ἐκκλησίαις, 'what the Spirit says to the churches', which maintain the dynamic of the immediate present to the very end. The listener/reader is appealed to directly, in order to communicate that it is 'now' that the Spirit is speaking. The type of present established by this commentary of the narrator's has the effect of fixing the reading of the book of Revelation in this same 'now', with the Spirit speaking at the same moment that the listener/reader is 'hearing' the letters.

It may be said in conclusion that John's desire to create mimesis has no limits. Not only does he use the letter form, which is in itself dialogical, but he also dramatizes the epistolary genre, both by representing the moment that the letters are dictated and by appealing directly to the reader/listener.

3.2   The Aural Atmosphere

The events that John sees and the voices that he hears build to a specific climax. As the faithful herald of what he has seen, he attempts to transmit to the listener/reader the aural atmosphere in which these messages are heard. To do this, he recreates through the written word a variety of sounds, tones of voice, music, and even the rumblings of a storm.

---

[48] Blass and Debrunner, *Grammar*, § 323.

[49] The term 'hearing formula' was originated by A. M. Enroth, 'The Hearing Formula in the Book of Revelation', *NTS* 36 (1990), 598–608.

3.2.1   The Sonority of the Lexeme φωνή and Its Nuances

The nominal lexeme φωνή is a recurrent lexeme in the book of Revelation and is in fact the fourth most used.[50] This repetition undoubtedly helps to create the sonic atmosphere in which the narrative plot is enveloped. At times it is used to underscore the presence of the voice, understood as an articulated sound that transmits a message; at others, it conveys a certain acoustic quality, from the roaring sounds that accompany the divine presence to the clamour of war chariots. All of this is immersed in the play of redundancies and alliterations with which these sounds are reproduced and by which the listener/reader is constantly reminded of what John is hearing, and so made to hear it as well.

a)   Φωνή as an Act of Speaking

The nominal lexeme φωνή appears in the narrative when John is listening attentively. This attention is indicated by a formula expression that is built upon a single semantic field, that of hearing:[51]

ἤκουσα + φωνὴν/φωνῆς + λέγουσαν/λέγουσης + direct speech

When the φωνή has been mentioned previously, as is the case for Rev 4.1 and 10.8, this expression is modified to:

ἡ φωνή + ἦν + ἤκουσα + λέγων/λέγουσαν + direct speech

The repetition of these formula expressions throughout the narrative creates a certain sense of sonority, reinforced by the redundant effect that they have at the acoustic and semantic levels. The listener/reader thereby has the sensation of hearing, along with the seer, the various φωναί that tell the story.

In these contexts, the nominal lexeme φωνή functions as both the object of a *verbum audiendi* and the subject of a *verbum dicendi*, with the meaning 'articulated sound that communicates',[52] independently of who might be its originator. Nor is this identification relevant to the narrator; all that matters is that he hears a φωνή, 'voice', an 'articulated sound that communicates', endowed with its own specific characteristics,

---

[50] It is used 55 times in 45 different verses, from Chapters 1 to 21, except for Chapters 2, 13, 15, 17, and 20.

[51] It appears 14 times: Rev 1.10–11; 5.11–12; 6.6, 7; 9.13–14; 10.4; 11.12; 12.10; 14.13; 16.1; 18.4; 19.1, 6; 21.3.

[52] In determining the meaning of the lexeme, the semantic methodology of the *Diccionario Griego-Español del Nuevo Testamento* (FFI2011-26124) has been followed.

as on occasion he accompanies it with the adjectival lexeme μεγάλη. Indeed, John does not use φωνή as a synecdoche, but rather gives it an absolute value. To some extent, he personifies it, giving it autonomy, a life of its own. And so, although he could have used the types of expression that we find in other sections of the narrative – (Rev 6.3; 16.5): 'I heard someone say'; 'I heard what one of the four living beings said'; 'I heard an angel . . . ' – on these occasions he does not.[53] What is most relevant here is not the identity of the character who speaks, but the fact that voices are heard transmitting a message.

Indeed, there frequently appear what may be called undifferentiated voices;[54] that is to say, heavenly voices of which we are only told their origin: ὡς φωνὴν ἐν μέσῳ τῶν τεσσάρων ζῴων, 'like a voice in the midst of the four living beings' (Rev 6.6); φωνὴν μίαν ἐκ τῶν [τεσσάρων] κεράτων τοῦ θυσιαστηρίου, 'a voice from the [four] horns of the altar' (Rev 9.13); φωνὴν ἐκ τοῦ οὐρανοῦ, 'a voice from heaven' (Rev 10.4; 14.13; 18.4); φωνῆς μεγάλης ἐκ τοῦ οὐρανοῦ, 'a loud voice from heaven' (Rev 11.12); μεγάλης φωνῆς ἐκ τοῦ ναοῦ, 'a loud voice from the temple' (Rev 16.1); φωνὴν μεγάλην ἐν τῷ οὐρανῷ, 'a loud voice in heaven' (Rev 12.10); φωνὴ ἀπὸ τοῦ θρόνου, 'a voice from the throne' (Rev 19.5); φωνῆς μεγάλης ἐκ τοῦ θρόνου, 'a loud voice from the throne' (Rev 21.3).

The most significant example of this lack of identification occurs the first time that John mentions one of these voices in the vision's narrative (Rev 1.9–22.16). He makes no attempt to identify it, as we might expect him to do, but describes it with an auditory simile that emphasizes its aural nature: φωνὴν μεγάλην ὡς σάλπιγγος, 'a loud voice like a trumpet' (Rev 1.10). After this, introduced by the participial form λεγούσης, the voice goes on to transmit its message, i.e., the command that John write what he sees and send it to the seven churches (Rev 1.11). John still does not identify the voice, as he is more concerned with emphasizing what is in fact happening, here in his first auditory experience: namely, that he hears an articulated sound transmitting a specific message exclusively to him. This is what he wishes to communicate to the listener/reader, so that the latter will be able to participate in the same experience, which is for the moment only auditory.

Only later does he try to discover whose voice it is. Here he employs a daring twist, with the phrase ἐπέστρεψα βλέπειν τὴν φωνήν, 'I turned to

---

[53] The only instance in which the speaker – the fourth living being – is identified is in Rev 6.7. The reason is a stylistic one: i.e., to break the syntactic monotony maintained up to that point and give added emphasis to the final horse, that of Death.

[54] Aune, *Revelation 2*, p. 561.

see the voice' (Rev 1.12), mixing the visual with the auditory and achieving a sharply synaesthetic effect. Indeed, some exegetes have wondered how exactly it is possible to 'see' a voice.[55] For John, however, there is perhaps not such a sharp contrast between the two senses, as he is simply writing what he sees and hears; what is more, his experience is a continuum of visual and auditory perceptions that succeed each other, intermingle, and eventually blend together. When he finally seeks to identify the φωνή, he has only two ways of ascertaining this: asking, or turning around to look (βλέπειν). From this moment on, John becomes an eyewitness, using καὶ εἶδον and describing what he sees (Rev 1.12–16). This includes the voice, in which he is interested purely for its tone. Its identification will come later, when Jesus finally reveals himself (Rev 1.17–19).

The desire to communicate these various auditory experiences becomes clearer still when the dictation of the letters has concluded. John hears the voice again and repeats the now formulaic expression ἡ φωνὴ ἡ πρώτη ἣν ἤκουσα ὡς σάλπιγγος λαλούσης μετ᾽ ἐμοῦ λέγων, 'the first voice that I heard, like a trumpet, spoke to me saying to me' (Rev 4.1). He also introduces a grammatical anomaly that accentuates what he is saying, a *constructio ad sensum* in which the participle λέγων is masculine but agrees with the feminine φωνή. This is a way of calling attention to the owner of the voice, who is Christ himself.[56]

Thus, the function of φωνή, dependent on ἤκουσα, is to underscore the fact of auditory perception itself. In effect, John is hearing and the listener/reader is hearing along with him.

b)   *Φωνῇ μεγάλῃ or Tone of Voice*

The nominal lexeme φωνή is also used at those moments in the narrative in which a given character speaks. On these occasions, φωνή is used in the dative, whether or not it is preceded by the preposition ἐν, and is always accompanied by the adjectival lexemes μεγάλη or ἰσχυρά. The

---

[55] Aune, *Revelation 1*, p. 87.

[56] Aune (*ibid.*, p. 282) considers the voice in Rev 4.1 to be the same as in Rev 1.10, and identifies it as that of the *angelus interpres*. The reason he gives is that the voice in Rev 4.1 is designated as the first voice and the voice of Christ as the second. However, there is no indication in the text that there is a change of interlocutor, nor does John use the term 'second voice', which would establish a link between the apparition of Christ and the vision of the throne. Scholars in favour of this theory include: Beckwith, *Apocalypse*, p. 436; Beale, *Revelation*, p. 317; Smalley, *Revelation*, p. 113; and Prigent, *Commentary*, p. 224.

phrase [ἐν] φωνῇ μεγάλῃ or ἰσχυρᾷ φωνῇ thus becomes a formula that is repeated 12 times over the course of the narrative: Rev 5.2; 6.10; 7.2, 10; 8.13; 10.3; 14.7, 9, 15, 18; 18.2; 19.17.

In such cases, φωνῇ μεγάλῃ always depends on *verba dicendi*, which may take any of a variety of subjects: an eagle (Rev 8.13); the slain souls (Rev 6.9); the multitude (Rev 7.9); or various angels (Rev 5.2; 7.2; 10.1; 14.7, 9, 15, 18; 18.2; 19.17). Its meaning is one of 'quality, timbre or intensity of sound'. Φωνή thus acquires an instrumental sense, which emphasizes its acoustic quality.

The adjective μεγάλη underscores a voice's intensity. However, as the *verba dicendi* themselves express the idea of 'speaking aloud',[57] it is somewhat difficult for the modern reader to grasp the nuance added by the adjective. This will, in any case, be clarified by the narrative itself when, in Rev 10.3, the seer describes what he means by ἔκραξεν φωνῇ μεγάλῃ, saying: ὥσπερ λέων μυκᾶται, 'like a lion roaring'. Since it is known that the roar of a lion can be heard from a great distance,[58] the image grants vividness to the sonority expressed by φωνῇ μεγάλῃ: that is, a tone of voice that is so loud, so deafening, that it can be heard far from its source. Therefore, μεγάλη, in qualifying φωνή, endows it with the connotation of 'deafening, noisy, clamorous'. As a result, the expression φωνῇ μεγάλῃ serves also to heighten the tension of the moments at which these messages are transmitted.

John has once again made use of a redundant structure, built upon the semantic field of hearing and used repeatedly to introduce a section of direct speech:[59]

Verbum dicendi + [ἐν] φωνῇ μεγάλῃ + λέγων + direct speech

With these types of structure, what is being emphasized is the way in which each character communicates their message, i.e., loudly and with solemnity. The presence of [ἐν] φωνῇ μεγάλῃ serves to reinforce the acoustic effect and creates a climax of expectation and tension that the listener/reader perceives with clarity.

---

[57] Λέγω, 'to say' (Rev 8.13; 14.7, 9); κήρυσσω, 'to transmit an official announcement' (Rev 5.2); κράζω, 'to cry out' (Rev 6.10; 7.2, 10; 10.3; 14.15; 18.2; 19.17); or φωνέω, 'to speak aloud' (Rev 14.18).

[58] Ryken, *et al., Dictionary*, s.v. *lion*. The lion's roar is so emblematic that allusions to it are frequent in Old Testament texts: Song 21.14; Prov 19.12; 28.15; Jer 2.15; Hos 11.10.

[59] As usual where the style of the book of Revelation is concerned, there are always exceptions. In the case of Rev 10.3, it is not direct speech that is introduced, but a simile. However, from the context it is clear that the words have been pronounced, as the thunder echoes a response (Rev 10.3b).

c)   *The Lexical Group Ἀστραπαὶ καὶ Φωναὶ καὶ Βρονταί: The Storm*

The nominal lexeme φωνή is also found in the context of the cata-strophes, which I will refer to here as the *cataclysmic context*. It is here used in the plural, φωναί, and accompanied by a series of other nominal lexemes, plural or singular, by which visual and tangible perceptions (ἀστραπαί, 'flashes of lightning'; σεισμός, 'earthquake') are alternated with auditory ones (βρονταί, 'thunderclaps'), or intermingled with them (χάλαζα, 'hail'):[60] ἀστραπαὶ καὶ φωναὶ καὶ βρονταί (Rev 4.5; 16.18);[61] βρονταὶ καὶ φωναὶ καὶ ἀστραπαὶ καὶ σεισμός (Rev 8.5); and ἀστραπαὶ καὶ φωναὶ καὶ βρονταὶ καὶ σεισμὸς καὶ χάλαζα μεγάλη (Rev 11.19).

Again, John uses a formulaic expression to transmit to the listener/reader what he is hearing and, in this case, seeing, although here it is the auditory atmosphere that takes precedence. What he hears, and tries to make the listener/reader hear, is specifically the clamour of the storm, as well as various other atmospheric and seismic phenomena. To do so, he enumerates them, linking them with the conjunction καί and preceding the list with the personal form of the verb on which it depends. The structure used for this, with slight variations in the order of the phenom-ena presented, is as follows:

Καὶ + verb + ἀστραπαὶ + καὶ + φωναὶ + καὶ + βρονταί

This lexical group also helps to create in the listener/reader a certain feeling of fear with regard to the events taking place, as they echo phrases appearing in both Old Testament (Isa 29.6; Esth 11.5) and pseudepigra-phal texts (Jub 2.2) and therefore seem familiar. In any case, in the book of Revelation, the formula is intensified by the use of polysyndeton, which gives it both a repetitive, rhythmic aspect and an air of solemnity. To this is added the onomatopoeic effect of alliterating occlusive and vowel sounds.

---

[60] I omit the translation of the phrases that follow, so as not to offer an interpretation in advance.

[61] R. Bauckham, *The Climax of Prophecy: Studies on the Book of Revelation* (Edinburgh: T & T Clark, 1999, rep. 2005), p. 202, and Aune, *Revelation 2*, p. 902, include in the list: καὶ σεισμὸς ἐγένετο μέγας and καὶ χάλαζα, which are found in Rev 16.21. However, neither σεισμός nor χάλαζα form part of the list strictly speaking, as no enumera-tion proceeds from them. Each lexeme has its own personal verb: ἐγένετο (Rev 16.18) and καταβαίνει (Rev 16.21). The enumeration is here finally interrupted as John slows down the narration by explaining in detail the last two calamities – the earthquake and the hailstorm – produced by the opening of the seventh seal.

In these contexts, the nominal lexeme φωνή depends on verbs that indicate some type of atmospheric phenomenon: ἐγένοντο, 'there were' (Rev 8.5; 11.19; 16.18); ἐκπορεύονται, 'came out' (Rev 4.5). Thus, when φωνή is used in reference to such phenomena, or, in a wider sense, to nature (a contextual factor), it has the meaning of 'unarticulated and unpleasant sound', which may be understood as 'noise, clamour, racket'. At the same time, φωναί is closely related to βρονταί, 'thunderclaps', and is never separated from that lexeme, which would seem to suggest hendiadys. Hence, φωναί καὶ βρονταί can be taken to mean 'rumblings of thunder'.[62] This hendiadys, specific to the formulaic expression, allows the rhythm of the locution, with its polysyndeton and alliteration, to be maintained, while transmitting to the listener/reader a feeling of the deafening sound of a great cataclysm. It also has an allusive function, so that the listener/reader, recognizing the expression and connecting it to the cataclysm, will unconciously be reminded of the noise of these events once John has begun to enumerate them.

d)   *Φωνή and its Descriptive Similes*

The lexeme φωνή is also used to describe each φωνή itself. The description is addressed to the listener/reader, who experiences along with John the acoustic effect and sensation it produces. It may be said that, in these cases, the description does not have as an objective the goal of *ante oculos ponere* that Cicero spoke of in *De inventione*, but rather that of *adesse*: of making present – or, more precisely, audible – to the listener/reader what John hears and how he hears it. It forms a sort of auditory parallel of the descriptive effect. To achieve this, John describes each φωνή using a variety of similes, always introduced by ὡς. The description typically consists of the nominal lexeme φωνή and an expansion effected by three predicate groups that are different but that all belong to the semantic field of hearing:

1.   ὡς φωνή and phenomena of nature;
2.   ὡς φωνή and elements of war;
3.   ὡς φωνή and musical instruments.

---

[62] In Rev 10.3, βρονταί is also accompanied by φωνή, but as the object of its verb ἐλάλησαν: ἐλάλησαν αἱ ἑπτὰ βρονταὶ τὰς ἑαυτῶν φωνάς. In this case, argues Robertson, *Comentario*, p. 741, φωνάς is used as a kind of internal accusative of the verb λαλέω. Its presence is simply to explain. It is yet another of the author's literary devices, an etymological figure used to indicate that he is not referring to the rumbling of thunder *per se*, but to the message being transmitted by it.

The predicate group 'ὡς φωνή and phenomena of nature' is comprised of similes that attempt to capture in words the powerful, resonant sound of natural phenomena, such as rushing water or, again, thunder: ἡ φωνὴ αὐτοῦ ὡς φωνὴ ὑδάτων πολλῶν, 'his voice was like the roar of vast waters' (Rev 1.15); ἤκουσα ἑνὸς ἐκ τῶν τεσσάρων ζῴων λέγοντος ὡς φωνὴ βροντῆς, 'I heard the first of the four living beings saying, like the rumbling of thunder' (Rev 6.1); ἤκουσα φωνὴν ἐκ τοῦ οὐρανοῦ ὡς φωνὴν ὑδάτων πολλῶν καὶ ὡς φωνὴν βροντῆς μεγάλης, 'I heard a voice from heaven like the roar of vast waters and like the rumbling of loud thunder' (Rev 14.2a); ἤκουσα ὡς φωνὴν ὄχλου πολλοῦ καὶ ὡς φωνὴν ὑδάτων πολλῶν καὶ ὡς φωνὴν βροντῶν ἰσχυρῶν, 'I heard the voice of an innumerable multitude like the roar of vast waters and like the rumbling of loud thunder' (Rev 19.6).

In these descriptions, the nominal lexeme φωνή may appear either in the denomination (Rev 1.15; 14.2a) or in the expansion. It is, in effect, a use that is redundant at the auditory level. What is more, there are times when it is employed again and again, without any fear of overaccumulation. Thus, φωνή appears twice in Rev 1.15 and four times in Rev 14.2ab. As a result, the narrative is framed within a completely aural atmosphere that demands the listener/reader's participation.

The predicate groups φωνὴ ὑδάτων πολλῶν, 'roar of vast waters', and φωνὴ βροντῆς, 'rumbling of thunder', both suggest the presence of a φωνή whose sonority is such that no other sound can be heard. Indeed, they impose themselves so completely upon the listener/reader that they produce a sensation of fear. At the content level, the difference between the two similes is that while φωνὴ ὑδάτων πολλῶν, 'roar of vast waters', evokes a continuous sound, φωνὴ βροντῆς implies one that is brief and fleeting.

In terms of form, the φωνὴ ὑδάτων πολλῶν group remains unchanged in the various pericopes in which it appears. This is not the case, however, of φωνὴ βροντῆς, which incorporates different adjectival lexemes (μέγας, ἰσχυρός) that further intensify the acoustic sensation. Not only do we hear ὡς φωνὴ βροντῆς, 'like the rumbling of thunder' (Rev 6.1), but βροντῆς μεγάλης, 'of loud thunder' (Rev 14.2a), and βροντῶν ἰσχυρῶν, 'of mighty thunderclaps' (Rev 19.6).

Another peculiarity here is that John seems to have no reservations about applying the same simile to different voices. Curiously, all of these belong to the heavenly context, and so the repeated use of these similes does not seem coincidental, but rather to be a way of informing the listener/reader that what they are hearing has a specific origin: that is, that it comes from heaven. This is an example of what later on I will refer to as an 'identity formula'.

The heavenly context is also made present by the fact that these similes have their roots in the Old Testament, and in contexts connected with theophanies. Indeed, ὡς φωνὴν ὕδατος πολλοῦ and ὡς φωνὴ βροντῆς are both used in the OT to describe the voice of God (Ezek 43.2;[63] Ps 76.19; 103.7).

It may be concluded that the 'ὡς φωνή and phenomena of nature' similes serve not only to express an acoustic image, but also to inform the listener/reader that the characters speaking belong to the heavenly context and have a close relationship with God, as their voices are described much as the voice of the Lord is described in the OT. The difference lies in the fact that the image is not applied directly, but always through a simile introduced by ὡς, so that, while the voices appear similar to God's, they are not actually identified as his. This is a clear example of the force of intertextuality and analogy.

As for the 'ὡς φωνή and instruments of war' predicate groups, such an auditory simile is used to describe the φωνή of the locusts (Rev 9.9b). The nominal lexeme φωνή appears in both the denomination and the expansion and, in this case, with the same meaning in both cases: 'noise'. An effect of redundancy is thus created at both the phonic and semantic levels, while at the same time the assonance of 'o' helps to recreate, to a certain extent, the sounds of war chariots speeding towards the line of battle:

> ἡ φωνὴ τῶν πτερύγων αὐτῶν ὡς φωνὴ ἁρμάτων ἵππων πολλῶν τρεχόντων εἰς πόλεμον (Rev 9.9b).

> The noise of their wings was like the noise of chariots with teams of many warhorses rushing into battle.

In this way, the Ciceronian *adesse* is given form, and so what John hears is made audible and highly realistic to the listener/reader. It also creates a certain feeling of uneasiness, which is all the greater if one is able to perceive the connotations of the image itself. War chariots are one of the three types of chariots mentioned in the OT, and the noise they produced as they rolled into battle[64] was such that the image is a recurrent

---

[63] In this case, it is the Hebrew version that uses the simile; the LXX avoids it as an anthropomorphism.

[64] Ryken, *et al., Dictionary*, s.v. *chariot*.

one in the visions of the prophets (Neh 3.2; Jer 29.3[65]). Especially emblematic in this sense is that of Joel, who, when he prophesies the day of YHWH, uses the expression ὡς φωνὴ ἁρμάτων . . ., 'like the noise of chariots . . . ', and, shortly afterwards, ὡς λαὸς πολὺς καὶ ἰσχυρὸς παρατασσόμενος εἰς πόλεμον, 'like a large and mighty throng drawn up for battle' (Joel 2.5), a description that we find echoed in Rev 9.9b.

Consequently, the simile of chariots is not only a traditional image, but one that connotes a catastrophe that occurs as a divine punishment. Through this simile, the listener/reader is made to feel the terrifying noise of the wings of the locusts and the imminence of catastrophe. Indeed, the sense of unease produced in the listener/reader is overpowering and, upon hearing this sound, they are made to feel the nearness of divine retribution.

3.2.2   The Recreation of Music

In this world of vision and hearing, music cannot be absent. Indeed, melody pervades the narrative, enriching the aural atmosphere that John aims to reproduce. The devices he uses to achieve this effect are occasionally similes; at other times, there are direct mentions of ᾠδή, 'song', or musical instruments such as the σάλπιγξ, 'trumpet', and κιθάρα, 'kithara'. The contexts in which such instruments appear, however, do not always have the same implications. The σάλπιγξ, 'trumpet', is mentioned in contexts where cries of οὐαί, 'woe', are also heard, whereas the κιθάρα, 'kithara', is the instrument used to accompany the ᾠδαί, 'songs of jubilation', that we find in the book of Revelation.

a)   Σάλπιγξ, *'Trumpet'*

The sound of the σάλπιγξ is characterized above all by its clarity. In Israel, in accordance with the commandments given by God to Moses, it was used not only in military contexts to announce the beginning or the end of a battle (2 Chron 13.14) or a victory (2 Chron 20.28), but also in the worship of God. The trumpet is known to have been played at offerings (Num 10.10), at the dedication of temples (2 Chron 5.13), and at feasts (Lev 23.24). In the OT, the sounding of trumpets often

---

[65] Jer 29.3 corresponds to Jer 47.3 in the MT and the Vulgate, as the Greek text of Jeremiah is shorter by one-sixth than the Masoretic Text. This shorter version of Jeremiah pre-dates that of the MT; see Fernández Marcos, *Introducción*, p. 91–2.

precedes a theophany (Exod 19.16).[66] The instrument appears in similar contexts in the book of Revelation.

The trumpet simile, ὡς σάλπιγγος, 'like a trumpet' (Rev 1.10), is in fact used to open the narrative. John employs it to describe the first voice that he hears, and then again to describe the one that precedes the great theophany in Rev 4.1.

When the φωνή, 'voice', is described as ὡς σάλπιγγος, the expansion unfolds in two ways. On the one hand, it is described in terms of its acoustic dimension – it is as loud and clear as the sound of a trumpet – and, on the other, as a sign to the listener/reader, who, through the familarity of the simile, is reminded both of the heavenly context and, more specifically, of an impending theophany. This is in fact what happens next: first, the resurrected Christ appears (Rev 1.13–20), followed by the vision of God in his glory (Rev 4.2–11). This may be the reason that John repeats ὡς σάλπιγγος (Rev 1.10; 4.1). The simile thus establishes a link between the God of Sinai, the resurrected Christ, and the One seated upon the throne, as the sound that precedes all three is similar: ὡς σάλπιγγος.

Although the sound of the σάλπιγξ, 'trumpet', is the first musical sound alluded to in the book of Revelation, the literal sounding of trumpets will not occur until somewhat later. The instrument itself will be mentioned again in Rev 8.2, when the trumpets are given to the seven angels. As they are yet to be sounded, the narrator takes advantage of this to build to a sort of climax.

After a discourse by an elder, who explains to John who the ὄχλος πολύς, 'innumerable multitude', is (Rev 7.13–17), the seventh seal is opened, leading to a σιγή, 'silence', which lasts ὡς ἡμίωρον, 'for about half an hour', and gives rise to a period of tense waiting (Rev 8.1).[67] During this silence, John's visions continue. First, he witnesses the trumpets being given to the seven angels (Rev 8.2), after which one angel infuses the altar with smoke and fragrant perfume from his censer. It is only when the angel hurls the burning embers from the altar of God onto the earth that the silence turns to noise: ἐγένοντο βρονταὶ καὶ φωναὶ

[66] G. Friedrich, '† σάλπιγξ, † σαλπίζω, † σαλπιστής', *TDNT* 7, 71–88; J. Braun, *Music in Ancient Israel/Palestine: Archaeological, Written, and Comparative Sources*, trans. D. W. Stott (Grand Rapids, MI – Cambridge: William B. Eerdmans, 2002), pp. 26–9; Y. Kolyada, *A Compendium of Musical Instruments and Instrumental Terminology in the Bible*, trans. by the author and D. J. Clark (Oakville, CT – London: Equinox, 2009), pp. 73–4.

[67] J. Lambrecht, 'The Opening of the Seals (Rev 6.1–8.6)', *Bib* 79 (1998), 198–221.

καὶ ἀστραπαὶ καὶ σεισμός, 'there were rumblings of thunder and flashes of lightning and an earthquake' (Rev 8.5). The angels then ready themselves to σαλπίζειν, 'sound the trumpets' (Rev 8.6), which must be played very loudly in order to be heard.

The framework within which the sounding of the trumpets will take place has thus been laid out in detail: first, a prolonged silence; then a tremendous clamour; finally, the sounding of the first trumpet, which seems to rise above the noise of the storm and the earthquake. John is playing here with the listener/reader's acoustic perception and with the effect of suspense produced by this unexpected change of sounds, as these ringing trumpet blasts seem to be announcing something.

The sounding of the trumpets is not described, however, nor are we told what type of announcement is being made. Furthermore, we hear only the isolated sound of each trumpet, as the angels play them one at a time. The succession of trumpet blasts is expressed through the repeated use of the verbal lexeme σαλπίζω, inserted into a simple structure that concludes each blast with a pause:

Καὶ ὁ δεύτερος ἄγγελος ἐσάλπισεν·
Conj. + Subject + Verb + Pause

Thus, this structure, which I will refer to as σαλπίζειν, becomes a device for making the successive sounding of the trumpets audible to the listener/reader (Rev 8.7, 8, 10, 12; 9.1, 13; 11.15). It is also a way of expressing the distinctively loud and clear sound of the instrument itself.

The σαλπίζειν structure arouses a variety of emotions in the listener/reader. After the sounding of the first four trumpets (Rev 8.7a, 8a, 10a, 12a), they already know that after the sounding of each trumpet there will be a catastrophe: the plague of fire and hail (Rev 8.7c); the mountain-like object that crashes down upon the earth and the sea (Rev 8.8b–9); the falling star (Rev 8.10b–11); and the darkening of the sun and celestial bodies (Rev 8.12c). The trumpet, therefore, is used by the angels to announce imminent catastrophe. This is so consistently the case that, each time John employs the σαλπίζειν structure, the listener/reader perceives the same acoustic sensation and feels the same terror at what is about to happen. This terror increases still more with the omen of the eagle and its lamentation of the triple οὐαί, 'woes', with the next three trumpet blasts (Rev 8.13; 9.12; 11.14). Indeed, if the listener/reader has felt overwhelmed by the events that have taken place thus far, they are all the more so when they hear the eagle bemoaning the impending fate of humanity. At this point, however, and to the listener/reader's great surprise, the sounding of the seventh trumpet announces the triumph of God, drawing the acclamation of the twenty-four elders (Rev 11.15–18) and transforming the dramatic tension in this scene into joy and hope.

b)   Κίθαρα, *'Kithara', and* ᾠδαί, *'Songs'*

The soothing sound and music of the kithara also make an appearance in the book of Revelation. Although this was an instrument known to have been used in rituals of worship, it was not restricted exclusively to this context. It was also played for entertainment at family gatherings and celebrations (Gen 31.27; Job 21.12; Isa 24.8), a custom that we find mentioned in the New Testament as well (1 Cor 14.7). There is also a reference to music in this context in the book of Revelation, when it is remarked that no music was heard during the fall of Babylon (Rev 18.22).

In the book of Revelation, the κίθαρα, 'kithara', and ᾠδαί, 'songs', appear within a specific context: the heavenly. Indeed, this context includes both those who make music (the four living beings and the twenty-four elders, in Rev 5.8; the voice from heaven, in Rev 14.2; and the conquerors of the beast, in Rev 15.2) and those to whom the songs are dedicated (God and the Lamb, Rev 5.6–7; 15.3–4). There is even a moment in which the kitharas are said to be τοῦ θεοῦ, 'of God' (Rev 15.2). Therefore, both the melodies played on them and the songs associated with them are closely linked to the worship of God.

Logically, the melodies offered in services of worship are designed to reflect the feelings of the worshippers in relation to the mystery being celebrated: joy, sorrow, repentance, and so forth. The songs themselves are in fact given different denominations according to whether they express sorrow or joy. Thus, the prophet Amos would remark, μεταστρέψω ... πάσας τὰς ᾠδὰς ὑμῶν εἰς θρῆνον, 'I will turn ... all your songs into lamentations' (Amos 8.10).

In the Septuagint, the term ᾠδή indicates a song of jubilation,[68] which, when it refers to God, becomes a joyful song of praise and thanksgiving. The LXX thus designates as ᾠδαί the song of Moses after he has crossed the Red Sea (Exod 15.1–18), the song that David dedicates to the Lord upon being freed from Saul (2 Sam 22.1–51), and the various hymns of

---

[68] Lust, *et al., Lexicon,* p. 676, s.v. ᾠδή; T. Muraoka, *A Greek–English Lexicon of the Septuagint: Chiefly of Pentateuch and Twelve Prophets* (Louvain – Paris: Peeters, 2002), p. 609, s.v. ᾠδή.

praise that are sung in the temple (2 Chron 5.13). In these contexts, the feeling of joy is explicit: consider ἐν εὐφροσύνῃ καὶ ἐν ᾠδαῖς, 'with joy and singing' (2 Chron 23.18).

For this reason, the use of ᾠδή in the book of Revelation connotes jubilation: the joy with which one praises God. This same joy is likewise transmitted by the sound of the κίθαρα, 'kithara', which accompanies the ᾠδή, 'song'. Indeed, mention of the κίθαρα invariably precedes this song (Rev 5.8; 15.2), just as in the real world musical notes are played to establish the pitch before a song is sung. This order is maintained even when what we hear is not exactly the instrument itself, but a voice resembling it:

> ἡ φωνὴ ἣν ἤκουσα ὡς κιθαρῳδῶν κιθαριζόντων ἐν ταῖς κιθάραις αὐτῶν (Rev 14.2).

The voice I heard was like that of kitharists playing songs on their kitharas.

The acoustic effect of the Greek simile is remarkable. To a great extent, this is achieved through the polyptoton formed by the verbal lexeme κιθαρίζω and the two nominal lexemes, κιθαρῳδός, 'kitharist',[69] and κιθάρα, 'kithara'. The first refers to the act of playing the kithara, the second to the singer/musician, and the third to the instrument itself. John enables the listener/reader to hear the speaker's voice as if it were the delicate music of the kithara.

As on other occasions, there seems to be a fixed structure, which, by its repetition (Rev 5.8–9; 14.2–3; 15.2.3), gains a striking evocative power:

κιθάρας + καὶ + ᾄδουσιν τὴν ᾠδὴν + Determination

Thus, on hearing the kitharas, the listener/reader is already calling to mind a special song offered to God and sung within the heavenly context.

John's insistence that the listener/reader experience a musical atmosphere that is real – i.e., what he himself has heard – does not end here. It will also manifest itself in the way that these songs are described: καινή, 'new' (Rev 5.9; 14.3), and τὴν ᾠδὴν Μωϋσέως τοῦ δούλου τοῦ θεοῦ καὶ τὴν ᾠδὴν τοῦ ἀρνίου, 'the song of Moses, servant of God, and the song of the Lamb' (Rev 15.3).

---

[69] Two terms are used for the player of this instrument: κιθαριστής, one who plays the kithara; and κιθαρῳδός (κιθάρα, ἀοιδός), one who plays and sings to the kithara. The first plays the melody by plucking it on the kithara, while the second strums the instrument to accompany his own singing; see *BDAG*, 4239, s.v. κιθαρῳδός.

Καινή, 'new', can be found in the Septuagint – principally in the book of Psalms (Ps 32.3; 39.4; 97.1; 143.9) – modifying ᾠδή or ᾆσμα ('song, hymn'). Given the diversity of the psalms in which it appears and their contexts, it is evident that ᾆσμα καινόν does not refer to a specific canticle, but rather expresses the desire of the worshipper to sing to the Lord in a new way, whether to thank God for the blessing they have received (Ps 39.4; 143.9) or to praise the goodness of God (Ps 32.3; 97.1). Logically, this new song will be sung to different melodies according to the psalm in which it is contained. Thus, the expression ᾠδὴ καινή would have been familiar to the listener/reader of the book of Revelation and would have evoked in them the various melodies to which the psalms were sung.[70]

As for the second description, the double structure τὴν ᾠδὴν Μωϋσέως . . . καὶ τὴν ᾠδὴν τοῦ ἀρνίου has led some exegetes to conclude that this canticle is a combination of two different songs.[71] However, after this double direct object, there appears the verb form λέγοντες, and with it, the text of a specific song, which would indicate that John had in mind a single canticle.[72]

Although its content is an amalgam of texts taken mostly from the Psalter, it would seem that the allusion to the sea, as well as the mention of τὴν ᾠδὴν Μωϋσέως τοῦ δούλου τοῦ θεοῦ and the victory, are in some way echoes of Exod 15, i.e., the song of Moses and the crossing of the Red Sea.[73] This song was incorporated into the acts of cult worship celebrated in the temple and sung on the afternoon of the Sabbath to accompany the sacrifice.[74] As S. Moyise[75] has pointed out, Philo of Alexandria, in *De vita contemplativa*[76] and *De agricultura* (although

---

[70] On the other hand, Bauckham, *Climax*, p. 230, proposes that ᾠδὴ καινή may be identified as a song of victory sung at the end of a battle (2 Chron 20.28) and views the terminology as being proper to a holy war. However, in the light of what has been explained here and of the meaning of καινός in the NT, such a thesis does not appear to be sustainable.

[71] Swete, *Apocalypse*, p. 192.

[72] Beckwith, *Apocalypse*, p. 677. Smalley, *Revelation*, p. 385, sees the presence of the second καί, which he considers to be epexegetic, as maintaining the overall unity of the song.

[73] Aune, *Revelation 2*, pp. 872–5; S. Moyise, 'Singing the Song of Moses and the Lamb: John's Dialogical Use of Scripture', *AUSS* 42 (2004), 350–4.

[74] Charles, *Commentary 2*, p. 36.

[75] Moyise, 'Singing the Song', 354.

[76] *Contempl.* 83.3–86.6. In this work, reference is made to the *therapeutae*; i.e., those who have embraced the contemplation of nature and live for the soul (*ibid.*, 90.1–3).

here only allegorically),[77] indicates that Exod 15 was a song that was used as a model and, in its day, was sung by a mixed chorus of men and women. It was, then, a song that was well known, and so this allusion to the song of Moses may have recalled to the listener/reader its familiar melody. In this sense, John is making the listener/reader 'hear' the content of the lyric, and at the same time evoking its accompanying music.

It may be concluded that, by transmitting the melodies of the kithara and its songs to the listener/reader, John is expressing a clear intention to make heard this joyful music offered to God, associated with melodies that were very familiar to the audience – i.e., the community – and drawn from OT liturgy. By echoing the Old Testament in this way, John is reviving in the memory of the listener/reader not only that context, but, in particular, the music of its liturgy. Thus, the listener/reader of the time was made to hear the same melody that John heard, as they would have recalled the choral singing of their own assemblies, in which they would probably have participated – an association that unfortunately cannot be recaptured by their modern-day counterparts.

3.3   The Oral Style of the Herald

As can be deduced from the opening beatitude, μακάριος ὁ ἀναγινώσκων καὶ οἱ ἀκούοντες τοὺς λόγους τῆς προφητείας, 'blessed is he who reads aloud and those who hear the words' of this prophecy' (Rev 1.3), John is aware that his text will be read aloud. This fact, while it has its benefits – the text, as it speaks for itself, will stir the emotions of its audience[78] – also carries with it certain risks in transmitting the revelation. As it is proclaimed in this way, it is possible that the listener will not listen attentively to what is being said, or may be distracted and leave off listening altogether. This may explain the use of devices that are characteristic of the oral style in the book of Revelation.

What is meant by the oral style is that which is 'destined to be heard'.[79] It characterizes those works that are designed to be read aloud and

---

[77] *Agric.* 81.1–82.3.

[78] Callahan, 'Language of Apocalypse', 461.

[79] M. Frenk, *Entre la voz y el silencio* (Alcalá de Henares, Madrid: Centro de Estudios Cervantinos, 1997), p. 95.

received through attentive listening.[80] It was a common practice in antiquity for audiences to listen to the public recitation of a poet's work. In the terminology of modern-day literary theory, it could be said that the poet was conscious of the 'poetic performance'; that is to say, the action by which a poetic message is simultaneously transmitted and perceived, here and now.[81]

Such a performance implies the adoption of a series of strategies that facilitate the listener/reader's reception of the text, both to make the experience a pleasant one and to ensure that the story can be followed and its message understood. Such strategies include formulas, repetitions, additive structures, enumerations, and comments addressed by the narrator to the audience.[82]

3.3.1   Formulas

The use of formulas is a specific characteristic both of literary compositions that are oral in nature and lack the support of a written form and of written texts that are received through being read aloud, as in the case of the book of Revelation. Such formulas provide rhythm to the discourse and serve a mnemotechnical function, much like that of fixed expressions that are spread by word of mouth.[83] They also facilitate communication with the audience, thanks to their clarity and the predictability of their diction.[84]

The first definition of such a formula comes from Milman Parry: 'a group of words which is regularly employed under the same metrical conditions to express a given essential idea'.[85] However, despite the inarguable influence of this theory, other ideas about the concept of the formula have developed successively over time, to the point that there is still no definition capable of condensing the many diverse manifestations

---

[80] J. A. Russo, 'Oral Theory: Its Development in Homeric Studies and Applicability to Other Literatures', in M. E. Vogelzang and H. L. J. Vanstiphout, *Mesopotamian Epic Literature: Oral or Aural?* (Lewiston, NY: Edwin Mellen Press, 1992), p. 21.

[81] P. Zumthor, *Introduction à la poésie orale* (Paris: Seuil, 1983), p. 32.

[82] W. J. Ong, *Orality and Literacy: The Technologizing of the Word* (London – New York, NY: Routledge, 1982, rep. 1990), pp. 33–77.

[83] *Ibid.*, p. 35.

[84] J. A. Russo, 'Is Oral or Aural Composition the Cause of Homer's Formulaic Style?', in B. A. Stolz and R. S. Shannon (eds.), *Oral Literature and the Formula* (Ann Arbor, MI: University of Michigan, 1976), p. 49.

[85] M. Parry, *The Making of Homeric Verse: The Collected Papers of Milman Parry* (Oxford: Oxford University Press, 1971), p. 272.

of formulaic language.[86] In any case, the concept of the formula recently proposed by the Dutch scholar Egbert J. Bakker, based on discourse theory, may well be the best suited to the book of Revelation, as, like the Homeric epics, it is evidently a text intended to be read aloud.

Bakker defines a formula as a 'stylized intonation unit'.[87] That is to say, it is a unit that is: semantic (a group of words that transmit a message); recurrent (the expression must appear at least three times); and communicated by means of an intonation unit, whose length and duration depends on the listener's ability to process the information (two or three seconds). The formula, therefore, may consist of a clause, a prepositional or nominal group, and so on.[88]

Given the variety of formulas that appear in the book of Revelation,[89] I will examine here only those that play a relevant role in the narrative in transmitting the story. These are the formulas of designation, identity, and antagonism. Lastly, I will address those that have a traditional character.

a)   *Designation Formulas*

I use the term 'designation formulas' for those formulas which designate the various characters that figure in the narrative. Considering the general absence of proper names in the book of Revelation, the use of formulas to name characters enables the listener/reader to identify them, principally when they appear as collectives.

According to Walter J. Ong, the use of formulaic numerical groupings is common in oral-style compositions and is a device that is mnemotechnically useful to the listener/reader.[90] Examples include the Seven against Thebes, the Three Graces, and the Three Fates (the Moirai).

---

[86]   J. A. Russo, 'The Formula', in I. Morris and B. Powell (eds.), *A New Companion to Homer* (Leiden – New York, NY: Brill, 1997), p. 259; M. Taft, *The Blues Lyric Formula* (New York, NY: Routledge, 2006), p. 29.

[87]   E. J. Bakker, *Poetry in Speech: Orality and Homeric Discourse* (Ithaca, NY: Cornell University Press, 1996), p. 53; *Pointing at the Past: From Formula to Performance in Homeric Poetics* (Cambridge, MA: Harvard University Press, 2005), p. 47.

[88]   Bakker, *Poetry in Speech*, pp. 49, 52.

[89]   Detailed lists of expressions repeated in the book of Revelation and their variations may be found in Bauckham, *Climax*, pp. 22–9 and S. W. Pattemore, 'Repetition in Revelation: Implications for Translation', *BT* 53 (2002), 425–41. Neither one, however, establishes a distinction between formula and repetition.

[90]   Ong, *Orality*, p. 70.

A clear example of the designation formula is that of the four living beings. When John sees them for the first time (Rev 4.6), he identifies them as τέσσαρα ζῷα, 'four living beings', and, after they are described as such, each time they reappear in the narrative they are referred to as τὰ τέσσαρα ζῷα, 'the four living beings' (Rev 5.6, 8, 14; 6.1, 6; 7.11; 14.3; 15.7; 19.4). Thus, τὰ τέσσαρα ζῷα becomes a formula by which this group of characters is named. The same occurs with οἱ εἴκοσι τέσσαρες πρεσβύτεροι, 'the twenty-four elders' (Rev 4.4, 10; 5.8; 11.16; 19.4), also referred to as οἱ πρεσβύτεροι (Rev 5.5, 6, 11, 14; 7.11, 13; 14.3), and the seven angels who are called οἱ ἑπτὰ ἄγγελοι οἱ ἔχοντες τὰς ἑπτὰ φιάλας, 'the seven angels who hold the seven bowls' (Rev 16.1; 17.1; 21.9).

At other times, such designation formulas are constructed on the pattern of the name–epithet formulas that we find in Homer, such as κρείων Ἀγαμέμνων, 'mighty Agamemnon' (*Il.* 1.102, 130, 285, etc.) or γλαυκῶπις Ἀθήνη, 'owl-eyed Athena' (*Il.* 2.172, 279, 446, etc.). This is the case for Βαβυλὼν ἡ μεγάλη, 'Babylon the great' (Rev 14.8; 16.19; 17.5; 18.2). The proper name, however, may sometimes be substituted by a collective noun: ὄχλος πολύς, 'an innumerable multitude' (Rev 7.9; 19.1, 6).

Not all of these designation formulas are specific to the book of Revelation, as some also appear in the OT. Βαβυλὼν ἡ μεγάλη, for example, is found in Dan 4.30, while βασιλεῖς τῆς γῆς, 'the kings of the earth' (Rev 1.5; 6.15; 17.2, 18; 18.3, 9; 19.19; 21.24), appears in the book of Psalms (Ps 2.2; 75.13; 88.28; 101.16; 137.4; 148.11) and other biblical texts (Josh 12.1; 1 Kings 5.14; 2 Chron 9.23; etc.). The same is true of the formulas used to refer to God.

Ὁ καθήμενος ἐπὶ τοῦ θρόνου, 'the One seated upon the throne', is a formula that John uses once he has recognized that the character he sees is in fact God.[91] From this moment on, the expression becomes fixed and is spoken by a variety of characters: the narrator (Rev 4.9, 10; 5.1, 7; 19.4; 20.11; 21.5); the choruses (Rev 5.13; 7.10); the kings of the earth (Rev 6.16); and the elder (Rev 7.15). The formula itself has its origin in the Old Testament, but in this case the common root is not the LXX, but rather the Hebrew version of the book of Psalms. It is in the Psalter that

---

[91] Curiously, in this formula the preposition ἐπί takes different cases, depending upon the case of the participle; see Swete, *Apocalypse*, p. cxxxii. Thus, if the participle is in the genitive or dative, ἐπί will require that it be genitive or dative, respectively. If the participle is in the nominative, the genitive (Rev 7.15) is alternated with the dative (Rev 20.11).

we find the verb יָשַׁב used to refer to God (Ps 2.4; 9.8; 55.20; 80.2; etc.). This specific verbal lexeme has the meaning of 'to sit, to be seated on a throne, to occupy a throne',[92] and is the word through which the sovereignty of God over the world is emphasized in the Psalms.[93] The Septuagint, however, being reluctant to present an anthropomorphic image of God,[94] avoids the formula and instead employs other devices, such as the use of the verbal lexemes κατοικέω, 'to inhabit' (Ps 2.4; 122.1), κατοικίζω, 'to settle' (Ps 67.7), and ὑπάρχω, 'to exist' (Ps 54.20). Only on one occasion do we find ὁ καθήμενος (Ps 79.2), but without the context-specific ἐπὶ τοῦ θρόνου.

Κύριος ὁ θεός, 'the Lord God' (Rev 1.8; 18.8; 22.5, 6), is used 971 times in the Septuagint (Gen 2.8; Lev 2.13; Num 10.10; Deut 1.6; etc.). It is the formula used to translate the various Hebrew names of God: יהוה, אֱלֹהִים ... It also appears in the NT (Matt 4.7; Mark 12.29, 30; Luke 1.16, 32, 68; Heb 2.39).

Κύριος ὁ θεὸς ὁ παντοκράτωρ, 'the Lord God Almighty' (Rev 4.8; 11.17; 15.3; 16.7; 19.6; 21.22) is a formula common in the books of the prophets (Hos 12.6; Amos 5.8, 14, 15, 16; Nah 3.5; Zech 10.3). It reappears, although with less frequency, in the Pseudepigrapha (3 Bar 1.3; Sol_A 3.5).

Lastly, there is the use of ὁ παντοκράτωρ θεός, 'Almighty God' (Rev 16.14; 19.15), which appears sporadically in both the Septuagint (2 Mac 8.18; 3 Mac 6.2; Jer 3.19) and the Pseudepigrapha (SibOr. 2.330; Sol_A 6.8; Aristeas 185).

The use of formulaic language like this is not casual, but rather one of the means used to capture the attention of the listener/reader, as it has an evocative power that recalls OT texts.[95] Indeed, thanks to such formulas, the listener/reader recognizes the God of the Old Testament in the God of the book of Revelation. They are one and the same, as is made clear not only in the way in which each is decribed, but through the names by which each is designated.

---

[92] Alonso Schökel, *Diccionario*, p. 340, s.v. יָשַׁב.
[93] H. J. Kraus, *Teología de los Salmos*, trans. V. Martínez de Lapera (Salamanca: Sígueme, 1985), p. 31.
[94] J. Trebolle, *La Biblia Judía y la Biblia Cristiana: Introducción a la Historia de la Biblia* (Madrid: Trotta, 1993), p. 463.
[95] This is one of the characteristics of the formula: it enables the listener to recognize the similarities between present and past contexts, and to discover why they are being used; see Bakker, *Poetry in Speech*, p. 159.

b) *Identity Formulas*

Identity formulas are those that establish links of association relating to the identity of the characters. In some cases, they allow the identification of a character who appears in different guises; in others, they connect characters to their particular contexts.

The most representative example of the way in which formulaic language is used to identify a given character is that of Jesus. In John's visions, Jesus is presented as ὅμοιον υἱὸν ἀνθρώπου, 'like a son of man' (Rev 1.13); ἀρνίον, 'a Lamb' (Rev 5.6); ἐπὶ τὴν νεφέλην καθήμενον, 'seated upon the cloud' (Rev 14.14); and, finally, as ὁ καθήμενος ἐπ' αὐτόν, 'the one mounted upon it' (Rev 19.11). In none of these representations, however, is it explicitly declared that John is referring to the same person in each case. It is through the use of formulaic language that he indicates this to the listener/reader.

After the opening vision, John discovers that the person he had described initially as ὅμοιον υἱὸν ἀνθρώπου, 'like a son of man' (Rev 1.13), is none other than the resurrected Christ. Indeed, it is through the words that Jesus addresses to him that this is made clear (Rev 1.17–18). Later, the figure who appears ἐπὶ τὴν νεφέλην καθήμενον, 'seated upon the cloud' (Rev 14.14), is described in the same manner as the resurrected Christ: ὅμοιον υἱὸν ἀνθρώπου (Rev 1.13; 14.14). The rider also has the gaze of Jesus – οἱ δὲ ὀφθαλμοὶ αὐτοῦ ὡς φλὸξ πυρός, 'his eyes like a flame of fire' (Rev 1.14; 19.12) – and one of the titles – πιστὸς καὶ ἀληθινός, 'faithful and true' (Rev 19.11) – used by Jesus in the *superscriptio* of the letter to Laodicea (Rev 3.14). Finally, an intimate connection is established between the Lamb and the rider, as both are referred to as κύριος κυρίων καὶ βασιλεὺς βασιλέων (Rev 17.14; 19.16).[96] It can thus be concluded that both the Lamb and the rider are in fact Jesus in different manifestations.

Something similar occurs in the heading of the letters to the seven churches. Their author, Jesus, does not use his own name, but instead employs expressions that the listener/reader has just heard, and which eloquently reveal the writer's identity. Thus, for example, the expression οἱ δὲ ὀφθαλμοὶ αὐτοῦ ὡς φλὸξ πυρός, 'his eyes like a flame of fire', which we find in the description of Jesus in Rev 1.14, appears again in the *superscriptio* of the letter to Thyatira (Rev 2.18). A similar function is served by ῥομφαία δίστομος ὀξεῖα, 'sharp, double-edged sword' (Rev 1.16), οἱ ἑπτὰ ἀστέρες, 'the seven stars' (Rev 1.20), and ὁ μάρτυς ὁ

---

[96] The formula appears in the book of Daniel (Dan OG 4.37).

πιστός, 'the faithful witness' (Rev 1.5), which reappear, respectively, in the *superscriptio* of the letters to Pergamum (Rev 2.12), Ephesus (Rev 2.1), and Sardis (Rev 3.1), and in the letter to Laodicea (Rev 3.14). However, as these expressions appear only twice each, they cannot be included within the formula concept as strictly defined.

As for the use of identity formulas to group characters within a shared context, a significant example is that of κεφαλαὶ ἑπτὰ καὶ κέρατα δέκα, 'seven heads and ten horns' (Rev 12.3; 13.1; 17.3). Three different animals are described as having these features: the dragon, the beast that rises from the sea, and the beast upon which the woman is seated. The formula, in this case, indicates to the listener/reader that all three of these figures belong to the context of evil.

c)   Antagonism Formulas

This type of formula points to a common trait shared by characters belonging to opposing contexts: the heavenly versus the evil. At times, this opposition shows how characters of the evil context in some way imitate those of the heavenly. For example, the Lamb appears ὡς ἐσφαγμένον, 'as though slaughtered' (Rev 5.6), and is later referred to as τὸ ἀρνίον τὸ ἐσφαγμένον, 'the slaughtered Lamb' (Rev 13.3). However, the beast that rises from the sea, and which belongs to the context of evil, is also said to appear ὡς ἐσφαγμένην, 'as though slaughtered' (Rev 13.3). In this case, the formula is used to present the beast as a parodic mirror image of the Lamb.[97]

At other times, the repetition of opposites highlights the difference between the heavenly and evil contexts. For example, the expression ἐκ τοῦ οἴνου τοῦ θυμοῦ, 'of the wine of wrath', is applied both to the great whore and to God. In the case of the whore, the full phrase is ἐκ τοῦ οἴνου τοῦ θυμοῦ τῆς πορνείας, 'of the wine of the wrath of her fornication' (Rev 14.8; 18.3), while for God it is ἐκ τοῦ οἴνου τοῦ θυμοῦ τοῦ θεοῦ, 'of the wine of God's wrath' (Rev 14.10; 16.19; 19.15).

d)   Traditional Formulas

I will call 'traditional formulas' those that form part of the broad tradition of language that dates from the very first written compositions to the

---

[97] E. Schüssler Fiorenza, *Revelation: Vision of a Just World* (Minneapolis, MN: Fortress Press, 1991), p. 83.

present day. In the words of Paul Zumthor, there are preserved within tradition a series of formulas that are available to the poet who truly knows his art.[98] The author of the book of Revelation has no reservations about drawing upon some of these and sprinkling them through his narrative. This is the case for polar expressions such as ἡμέρα καὶ νύξ, 'day and night', and οἱ μικροὶ καὶ οἱ μεγάλοι, 'great and small', or formulas that have become part of the liturgy, such as εἰς τοὺς αἰῶνας τῶν αἰώνων, 'for ever and ever'; δόξα καὶ τιμή, 'glory and honour', and so forth.

The polar expression ἡμέρα καὶ νύξ appears with some frequency, in both the heavenly context (Rev 4.8; 7.15) and the evil context (Rev 12.10; 14.11; 20.10). It is used to express the uninterrupted nature of the worship of God (Rev 4.8; 7.15); the devil's accusation of God is similarly uninterrupted (Rev 12.10), as is the adoration of the beast (Rev 14.11) and the punishment it will receive (Rev 20.10). The formula is used in the Septuagint in several different contexts,[99] but always with the same meaning: that of having uninterrupted duration. It is also found in the NT and the Pseudepigrapha.[100]

Οἱ μικροὶ καὶ οἱ μεγάλοι is a formula that John uses in the enumerations to communicate a sense of totality to his audience (Rev 11.18; 13.16; 19.5, 18). It is used in the same way in the LXX,[101] the NT,[102] and the Pseudepigrapha.[103]

---

[98] Zumthor, *Introduction*, p. 118.

[99] These are: care of and observances in the temple (1 Chron 9.33; 2 Chron 6.20); form of prayer (Josh 1.8; 1 Kings 8.29[2], 59; Neh 1.6; Esth 4.16; Jdth 11.17; 2 Mac 13.10; Ps 1.2; Odes 8.71; Dan 3.71); defence or vigilance (Neh 4.3); misfortune (Ps 31.4; 41.4; 54.11; Isa 34.10; Jer 8.23; 14.17; Lam 2.18); among others (Gen 8.22; Lev 8.35; Num 9.21; Deut 28.66; 1 Sam 25.16; 3 Mac 5.11; Isa 60.11).

[100] In the NT, it is used in the same contexts as in the LXX: form of prayer (Luke 2.37; 18.7; Heb 26.7; 1 Thess 3.10; 1 Tim 5.5; 2 Tim 1.3); defence (Heb 9.24); and other scenes of everyday life (Matt 4.27; Mark 5.5; Heb 20.31; 1 Thess 2.9; 2 Thess 3.8). In the Pseudepigrapha, although the formula appears in the context of worship and prayer (Sol_A 1.5; Rechab 11.4), it is also used in that of vigilance (Sedr 8.1; Sol_A 7.5) and various others (1 Enoch 18.6; 23.2; 104.8; Sedr. 11.6; Sol_A 4.12; 10.8; Pseudo_Hecat 6.18).

[101] Examples include: Deut 25.13, 14; 1 Sam 20.2; 1 Chron 22.31; 1 Chron 12.15. Some variants also appear: κατὰ τὸν μικρὸν καὶ κατὰ τὸν μέγαν (Deut 1.17; 1 Chron 25.8; 26.13); μικρὸν ἢ μέγα (Num 22.18; 1 Sam 22.15; 25.36); ἀπὸ μικροῦ ἕως μεγάλου (Gen 19.11; 1 Sam 5.9; 30.2, 19; etc.).

[102] Heb 26.22. The variant ἀπὸ μικροῦ ἕως μεγάλου is found in Heb 8.10 and 8.11.

[103] SibOr 2.323; Abraham_B 8.10.

The formula εἰς τοὺς αἰῶνας τῶν αἰώνων appears at the end of some antiphons or acclamations (Rev 1.6; 5.13; 7.12), and is spoken by various characters with reference to the eternity of God (Rev 4.9, 10; 10.6; 11.15; 14.11; 15.7; 19.3; 20.10; 22.5) or Jesus (Rev 1.18). Its origins can be traced back to the Septuagint, where it is used predominantly in the singular.[104] The New Testament corpus inherited this formula in the plural, and it is generally found in doxologies.[105] Significant examples also appear in pseudepigraphal texts.[106]

Lastly, δόξα καὶ τιμή is found in songs and acclamations addressed to God (Rev 4.9, 11; 5.12, 13; 7.12), with the exception of Rev 21.26, where it is applied to the New Jerusalem. In the LXX, the formula appears in a context of worship and reverence to the king.[107] It is frequent in the NT, as well as the Pseudepigrapha,[108] although in different contexts.

3.3.2   Repetitions

Repetition is another of the strategies that help the listener/reader follow the story, at the same time that it permits the author to influence his audience intellectually.[109] It is a frequently used device in the book of Revelation. Enumerations (e.g., of the social classes of the inhabitants of the earth in Rev 6.15, 13.16, and 19.18), expressions (βύσσινον ... καθαρόν, Rev 19.8, 14), and individual lexemes are all repeated.

One of the most significant examples of this, for the meaning it evokes, is the recurrent use of the numerical adjective ἑπτά, 'seven'. Cropping up from the beginning of the work (Rev 1.4) until nearly the end (Rev 21.9), ἑπτά appears 55 times. It is in fact the third most used adjectival lexeme in the book of Revelation, after μέγας, 'great' (80 times) and πᾶς, 'all' (59 times). It is usually accompanied by a nominal lexeme, thus forming part of a lexical group. Curiously, these groups, generally headed by ἑπτά, are

---

[104]   4 Mac 18.24; Ps 83.5; Dan OG 3.90. In the LXX, there is a preference for the singular form: εἰς τὸν αἰῶνα τοῦ αἰῶνος (Ps 9.6, 37; 44.7, 18; 47.15; 51.10; 60.9; etc.).

[105]   It appears in Heb 1.8 and in seven doxologies (Gal 1.5; Eph 3.21; Phil 4.20; 1 Tim 1.17; 2 Tim 4.18; Heb 13.21; 1 Pet 4.11).

[106]   1 Enoch 10.12; Esdr 7.16; Sedr 16.3, 7; 3 Bar 17.4; Abraham_B 14.9; Sol_A 26.9; Adam_Eve 43.4; Prayer_Jac 8.

[107]   Exod 28.2, 40; 2 Chron 32.33; 1 Mac 14.21; Ps 8.6; 28.1; 95.7; Job 37.22; 40.10; Dan OG 2.37.

[108]   NT: Rom 2.7, 10; 1 Tim 1.17; Heb 2.7, 9; 1 Pet 1.7; 2 Pet 1.17. Pseudepigrapha: 1 Enoch 3.1; 14.16; 98.3; 99.1; Abraham_B 14.9; Adam_Eve 43.4.

[109]   Lausberg, *Retórica literaria 2*, p. 97, § 608.

introduced into the text gradually, in small clusters, repeated successively in specific sections, and grouped together into 'bunches'.

There are even points at which these nominal groups accumulate and then disappear from the text altogether. At the very beginning, for example, two lexical groups are mentioned: αἱ ἑπτὰ ἐκκλησίαι, 'the seven churches', and τὰ ἑπτὰ πνεύματα, 'the seven spirits' (Rev 1.4). Shortly afterwards, αἱ ἑπτὰ ἐκκλησίαι is repeated (Rev 1.11), and then later repeated again two more times (Rev 1.20). Apart from these two lexical groups, Rev 1.20 also includes αἱ ἑπτὰ λυχνίαι, 'the seven menorahs' (Rev 1.12), and αἱ ἑπτὰ ἀστέρες, 'the seven stars' (Rev 1.16). And so, from an aural perspective,[110] Rev 1.20 is a compendium of the various septenary lexical groups that have already appeared in the text. After this, one of the groups in Rev 1.20, αἱ ἑπτὰ ἀστέρες, 'the seven stars', will continue to be repeated (Rev 2.1; 3.1) and associated with the aforementioned τὰ ἑπτὰ πνεύματα, 'the seven spirits' (Rev 3.1), which will appear again in Rev 4.5 and Rev 5.6. The sound of ἑπτά, then, is interwoven into the narrative, regardless of whether it is applied to characters or objects of the heavenly context (αἱ ἑπτὰ ἐκκλησίαι, 'the seven churches'; αἱ ἑπτὰ ἀστέρες, 'the seven stars'; etc.), the evil context (οἱ ἑπτὰ βασιλεῖς, 'the seven kings', Rev 17.9), or that of the cataclysms (αἱ ἑπτὰ βρονταί, 'the seven thunderclaps', Rev 10.3, 4).

This recurrent use of ἑπτά becomes a kind of background music in the narrative and, as such, transmits a specific message. As Walter J. Ong has pointed out, the sound of the word has the ability to communicate more precisely than its written counterpart, as the spoken word has a greater power to express an intended meaning.[111]

The frequent use of the number ἑπτά is, once again, not exclusive to the book of Revelation, but deeply rooted in biblical tradition. In the OT, it is used 351 times and, if the contexts in which it appears are analyzed, one comes to the conclusion that ἑπτά signifies completeness, or the totality loved by God – a meaning that we find in other cultures as well.[112]

---

[110] In the field of philological research, the terms 'oral' and 'aural' are used with different meanings. Orality is understood as the means of accessing the original elocution. Aurality, on the other hand, refers to the acoustic effects inherent in the text, created to facilitate its comprehension or to engage its audience.

[111] W. J. Ong, *The Presence of the Word: Some Prolegomena for Cultural and Religious History* (Minneapolis, MN – Oxford: University of Minnesota Press, 1981), p. 115.

[112] K. H. Rengstorf, 'ἑπτά, † ἑπτάκις, † ἑπτακισχίλιοι, ἕβδομος, ἑβδομήκοντα, † ἑβδομηκοντάκις. The NT Usage', *TDNT* 2, 200–69.

This concept of totality is evident in the way the adjectival lexeme is used in Old Testament texts: God created the world in seven days (Gen 1.1–2, 3; Exod 20.11); God will avenge Cain seven times should anyone harm him (Gen 4.15); the menorah has seven lamps (Exod 25.37); blood is sprinkled seven times during sacrifices to indicate complete purification (Lev 16.14, 19); seven animals are given to God as burnt offerings (Job 42.8; Ezek 45.23); God views the world through seven eyes (Zech 4.10).[113]

The same connotation of totality is maintained in the NT.[114] The recurrent use of ἑπτά throughout the book of Revelation, therefore, transmits to the listener/reader a very specific message; i.e., the idea of the totality loved by God, or of a complete reality. This concords with a narrative that is presented as the revelation of Jesus Christ. Just as the works of God are perfect, it is logical that the totality loved by God will be one of the motifs developed in such a narrative.

3.3.3   Additive Structures: The Conjunction καί

One of the specific characteristics of compositions in the oral style is a preference, at the syntactic level, for accumulative structures rather than hypotaxis. It is well known that subordination implies written discourse, as the transmission of meaning has the support only of the linguistic structures themselves; in contrast, compositions destined to be read in public use other devices to establish communication, such as tone of voice, rhythm, gestures, and so on.[115] This explains the presence of the additive style in the book of Revelation, observable in the constant use of the coordinating conjunction καί.

Καί is the second most used term in the text. It is employed 1,128 times, to link phrases, to begin clauses, or as a nexus of union between the various lexemes, nominal, adjectival, and so forth. According to a study undertaken by David E. Aune, the book of Revelation contains a total of

[113] E. D. Schmitz, 'Number. s.v. ἑπτά', *NIDNTT* 2, 690; J. Mateos and F. Camacho, *Evangelio, figuras y símbolos*, 3rd edn (Córdoba: El Almendro, 1999), pp. 87–8; M. Lurker, *Diccionario de imágenes y símbolos de la Biblia*, trans. R. Godoy (Córdoba: El Almendro, 1994), p. 213, s.v. *siete*.

[114] The adjective is used in the NT (excluding the book of Revelation) 33 times.

[115] Ong, *Orality*, pp. 37–8; E. A. Havelock, *The Muse Learns to Write: Reflections on Orality and Literacy from Antiquity to the Present* (New Haven, CT: Yale University Press, 1986), pp. 65, 71–2.

337 clauses. Of these, 245 begin with καί: that is to say, 73.79 per cent.[116]
Rev 6.8 provides a representative example of this recurrent use:

> καὶ εἶδον, καὶ ἰδοὺ ἵππος χλωρός, καὶ ὁ καθήμενος ἐπάνω αὐτοῦ
> ὄνομα αὐτῷ [ὁ] θάνατος, καὶ ὁ ᾅδης ἠκολούθει μετ᾽ αὐτοῦ καὶ
> ἐδόθη αὐτοῖς ἐξουσία ἐπὶ τὸ τέταρτον τῆς γῆς ἀποκτεῖναι ἐν
> ῥομφαίᾳ καὶ ἐν λιμῷ καὶ ἐν θανάτῳ καὶ ὑπὸ τῶν θηρίων τῆς γῆς.

And I saw, behold, a pale greenish grey horse, and the rider
[had] the name of Death, and Hades followed him, and to these
were given the power to kill one fourth of the world with sword
and with hunger and with death and with the wild beasts of the
earth.

In this particular pericope, we find καί used eight times. The first
heads the clause, as is characteristic of the Septuagint;[117] the second,
in the phrase καὶ ἰδοὺ ἵππος, introduces a construction showing
semitic influence in the nominative; the third, in καὶ ὁ καθήμενος,
links this term with ἵππος – that is, it links parts of the same clause;
the fourth, in καὶ ὁ ᾅδης, and the fifth, in καὶ ἐδόθη, are used to
coordinate clauses; while the three final instances of καί provide
a clear example of polysyndeton, which is frequent in such
enumerations.

The conjunction καί becomes an ideal aural device, thanks to its
constant presence in the text. The listener/reader perceives the conjunction as an element that is inseparable from the book of
Revelation and gives continuity to the narration. This is so much
the case that, were one to be distracted, the conjunction would make
it a simple matter to pick up the story again. Indeed, on many
occasions, such as in the enumerations, καί is devoid of any specific
semantic content.[118]

Finally, it does not seem that the use of the copulative conjunction stems
from the book of Revelation being a Greek translation of an originally
Hebrew or Aramaic text,[119] but rather that its author is writing a text
designed to be read aloud. He therefore employs the additive structures
that characterize this type of writing.

---

[116] Aune, *Revelation 1*, p. cxcii. Cf. Pattemore, 'Repetition', 426.
[117] Aune, *Revelation 1*, p. cxcii.
[118] Pattemore, 'Repetition', 426.
[119] Aune, *Revelation 1*, pp. cxci–cxcii, examines this proposal in detail.

3.3.4   Αὔξεσις and the Enumerations

Αὔξεσις, or *amplificatio*, is a device employed in the oral style to create fluidity and variety in a discourse. In addition, it enables the listener to remain in sync with the lector or, in the event that he loses this synchronization, to regain it easily.[120]

One of the figures of diction that support *amplificatio* is that of enumeration. This is characterized by the accumulation of parts that together comprise a whole, organized reciprocally and equally, and either linked syndetically or juxtaposed.[121] Enumeration tends to slow down plot development, while at the same time highlighting some aspect that the narrator wants to emphasize. The listener/reader, upon hearing this enumeration, focuses their attention on what is being enumerated, as the successive listing of words introduces a tranquil rhythm into the reading, a cadence that allows them to listen calmly and reflect upon what they are hearing. As a result, the listener/reader reacts emotionally to the message.

Three types of enumeration can be distinguished, according to the semantic field predominant in each. These are enumerations of materials, characters, and circumstances.

a)   Enumerations of Materials

Enumerations of materials are found scattered throughout the narrative (Rev 9.17; 17.4; 21.19–20). Some form part of descriptions and help to develop their expansion. I will here look at one such example, which I consider representative in terms of its emotional impact on the listener/reader. This is the enumeration of merchandise found in Rev 18.12–13:

> γόμον χρυσοῦ καὶ ἀργύρου καὶ λίθου τιμίου καὶ μαργαριτῶν καὶ βυσσίνου καὶ πορφύρας καὶ σιρικοῦ καὶ κοκκίνου, καὶ πᾶν ξύλον θύϊνον καὶ πᾶν σκεῦος ἐλεφάντινον καὶ πᾶν σκεῦος ἐκ ξύλου τιμιωτάτου καὶ χαλκοῦ καὶ σιδήρου καὶ μαρμάρου, [13] καὶ κιννάμωμον καὶ ἄμωμον καὶ θυμιάματα καὶ μύρον καὶ λίβανον καὶ οἶνον καὶ ἔλαιον καὶ σεμίδαλιν καὶ σῖτον καὶ κτήνη καὶ πρόβατα, καὶ ἵππων καὶ ῥεδῶν καὶ σωμάτων, καὶ ψυχὰς ἀνθρώπων.

---

[120] Ong, *Orality*, pp. 39–40.
[121] Lausberg, *Retórica literaria 2*, p. 135, § 669.

merchandise of gold and silver, and of precious stones and pearls; and fine linen cloth, purple and silk and scarlet; and all citron wood, and all types of ivory objects and all types of objects of the most costly woods, and of bronze and of iron and marble; [13] and cinnamon and amomum,[122] and perfumes, and myrrh and incense; and wine and oil, and flour and wheat; and beasts of burden and sheep, and horses and carriages, and slaves; that is to say,[123] human beings.

This pericope is part of one of the messenger speeches (Rev 18.4–20), in which, by enumeration, the listener/reader is informed of the goods that will no longer be sold in Babylon. Once again, description is the means of achieving Cicero's goal of *ante oculos ponere* and thus affecting the audience. In the terminology of description, γόμος corresponds to denomination or *pantonyme*, and the enumeration to the expansion, properly speaking.

The expansion here consists of a list of nominal lexemes presented in a specific order, i.e., by type of merchandise.[124] A variety of commercial sectors are mentioned – metalworking, textiles, carpentry and handicrafts, spices and perfumes, food and livestock[125] – the perception of which involves the entire spectrum of human senses: vision, touch, hearing, smell, and taste. Thus, as the listener/speaker is presented with a succession of 33 different lexemes, they not only admire these sumptuous goods, but experience them as a sort of feast for the senses. This helps to create the particular aural quality of the enumeration, as well as its fluid, uninterrupted rhythm, achieved by polysyndeton (the copulative conjunction καί is repeated 28 times) and the cadence created by the names of the merchandise being catalogued.

These acoustic effects awaken a sense of awe in the listener/reader at the splendour and magnificence of the markets of Babylon, where one could find basic staples such as wine, oil, and wheat[126] alongside luxury

---

[122] As the identification of ἄμωμον, 'amomum', is uncertain, it is preferable, as Beckwith proposes, *Apocalypse*, p. 716, to transcribe the term rather than to offer a translation.

[123] I consider καί to have an epexegetic value; hence the translation, 'that is to say'.

[124] *NT-IGLESIAS*, Rev 18.12, notes 12–13.

[125] Detailed studies of the origin and use of each of the elements in this enumeration may be found in: Swete, *Apocalypse*, pp. 229–31; Bauckham, *Climax*, pp. 352–66; Aune, *Revelation 3*, pp. 998–1002.

[126] I exclude σεμίδαλις, as it was a finer-quality flour; see *BDAG*, 6622, s.v. σεμίδαλις. Indeed, Masyngberde Ford, *Revelation*, p. 305, demonstrates that this is the term used by the LXX in Leviticus to designate the flour used for offerings.

goods, such as gold, purple cloth, citron wood, and cinnamon.[127] The unhurried flow of lexemes helps to depict the sumptuousness that ruled the city of Babylon. The luxury is further highlighted by the fact that the enumeration is not hierarchical but instead passes from objects of opulence – precious stones, fine cloth, woods, spices, and perfumes – to objects of basic necessity – foodstuffs, etc. – concluding with articles of great luxury that were reserved for the upper classes: καὶ ἵππων καὶ ῥεδῶν καὶ σωμάτων, καὶ ψυχὰς ἀνθρώπων, 'and horses and carriages, and slaves; that is to say, human beings'. The last two terms, however, σωμάτων and καὶ ψυχὰς ἀνθρώπων, have a special resonance for the listener/reader, through which the splendour of Babylon is somewhat tarnished.

Initially, perhaps, the presence of σώματα, 'slaves',[128] in this list would not have been surprising to the listener/reader, as in antiquity slavery was a deeply rooted custom in many cultures; indeed, in the first century AD, Rome was the world's leading slave market.[129] However, the fact that σώματα closes the enumeration of animals and, at the same time, is followed by ψυχαὶ ἀνθρώπων, has a powerful effect on the listener/reader as a result of the contrast it creates. The σώματα, 'slaves', although treated and considered as animals (and enumerated as simply one more type of merchandise), are in reality ψυχαὶ ἀνθρώπων, 'human beings'. John takes this occasion to instruct his audience on the injustice of slavery, i.e., of people being reduced to the condition of animals. In this way, the enumeration carries a paraenetic tone, through which the luxury of Babylon appears dimmed by the existence of slaves.

It may be concluded, then, that this enumeration of merchandise has a double function: referential, as it informs the listener/reader of the splendour and ostentation of Babylon; and appellative, as it exhorts by warning them of the horrors of slavery.

---

[127]   Citron was a highly valued wood in antiquity, according to Pliny, *NH* 37.204. The same is true of spices, which, as imported goods, were also very costly; see Aune, *Revelation 3*, pp. 999, 1001.

[128]   This meaning of σῶμα appears already to have been in use in the first century AD; see L. García Ureña, 'La Septuaginta, testigo de un proceso de lexicalización: σῶμα de cuerpo a esclavo', in A. Agud, *et al.*, *Séptimo centenario de los estudios orientales en Salamanca* (Salamanca: Ediciones Universidad de Salamanca, 2013), pp. 271–382.

[129]   Aune, *Revelation 3*, p. 1003.

b)   *Enumerations of Characters*

Character enumerations are typified by a fairly wide range of adjectival and nominal lexemes, linked by the copulative conjunction καί and thus giving rise to polysyndeton. The uninterrupted succession of lexemes followed by καί gives a certain rhythm to the text in these passages, by which the listener/reader is made to pay precise attention to those affected by the events described. These enumerations are coupled with a strongly paraenetic aspect, reinforced by the hyperbole that characterizes this particular literary device.

Such enumerations include that of the seven churches (Rev 1.11) and those that enumerate characters. Grouped by categories that are both social (Rev 6.15; 13.16; 19.18) and moral, they include the 144,000 (Rev 7.4–8), the allies of the Lamb (Rev 17.14), the sinners (Rev 2.8; 22.15), and the new inhabitants of Babylon (Rev 18.2). Of these, the most notable for its formal and aural perfection, as well as its evocative power, is the enumeration of the 144,000:

> ἐκ φυλῆς Ἰούδα δώδεκα χιλιάδες ἐσφραγισμένοι, ἐκ φυλῆς Ῥουβὴν δώδεκα χιλιάδες, ἐκ φυλῆς Γὰδ δώδεκα χιλιάδες, [6] ἐκ φυλῆς Ἀσὴρ δώδεκα χιλιάδες, ἐκ φυλῆς Νεφθαλὶμ δώδεκα χιλιάδες, ἐκ φυλῆς Μανασσῆ δώδεκα χιλιάδες, [7] ἐκ φυλῆς Συμεὼν δώδεκα χιλιάδες, ἐκ φυλῆς Λευὶ δώδεκα χιλιάδες, ἐκ φυλῆς Ἰσσαχὰρ δώδεκα χιλιάδες, [8] ἐκ φυλῆς Ζαβουλὼν δώδεκα χιλιάδες, ἐκ φυλῆς Ἰωσὴφ δώδεκα χιλιάδες, ἐκ φυλῆς Βενιαμὶν δώδεκα χιλιάδες ἐσφραγισμένοι (Rev 7.5–8).

> From the tribe of Judah, twelve thousand were marked; from the tribe of Ruben, twelve thousand; from the tribe of Gad, twelve thousand; [6] from the tribe of Asher, twelve thousand; from the tribe of Naphtali, twelve thousand; from the tribe of Manasseh, twelve thousand; [7] from the tribe of Simeon, twelve thousand; from the tribe of Levi, twelve thousand; from the tribe of Issachar, twelve thousand; [8] from the tribe of Zebulon, twelve thousand; from the tribe of Joseph, twelve thousand; from the tribe of Benjamin, twelve thousand were marked.

The enumeration here appears in a well-defined context. After the sixth seal is opened, the voice of an angel is heard, asking that the next plague not be unleashed until the servants of God have first been marked (Rev 7.3). This statement captures the attention of the listener/reader by

sparking their curiosity as to who these servants are, especially considering that just before this they have heard an enumeration of the various
social classes afflicted by the earthquake (Rev 6.15). The listener/reader
then hears καὶ ἤκουσα τὸν ἀριθμὸν τῶν ἐσφραγισμένων, 'and I heard the
number of those who were marked' (Rev 7.4). In this case, however, it is
not the voice that gives the number, as occurs elsewhere, but John
himself: ἑκατὸν τεσσαράκοντα τέσσαρες χιλιάδες, ἐσφραγισμένοι ἐκ
πάσης φυλῆς υἱῶν Ἰσραήλ, 'one hundred and forty-four thousand
marked, from all the tribes of the sons of Israel'. John does not tell us
who these servants are, but rather their number,[130] and here begins the
enumeration, which is no less than a detailed expansion of the 144,000
marked.

In fact, it is an elaborate construction built on the anaphoric repetition
of two elements, the circumstantial object and a number, within which is
inserted the name of each of the tribes of Israel:

	Ἰούδα, 'of Judah',	
	Ῥουβὴν, 'of Ruben',	
	Γὰδ, 'of Gad',	
	Ἀσὴρ, 'of Asher',	
	Νεφθαλὶμ, 'of Naphtalí',	
φυλῆς, 'from the tribe',	Μανασσῆ, 'of Manasseh',	δώδεκα χιλιάδες, '12,000'
	Συμεὼν, 'of Simeon',	
	Λευὶ, 'of Levi',	
	Ἰσσαχὰρ, 'of Issachar',	
	Ζαβουλὼν, 'of Zebulon',	
	Ἰωσὴφ, 'of Joseph',	
	Βενιαμὶν, 'of Benjamin',	

At first, this locution creates a feeling of suspense in the listener/
reader, but this is gradually transformed into satisfaction when he
hears that the marked are of the twelve tribes and that all of the
tribes have the same number of saved. This effect is emphasised by
the enumeration's opening and closing with the term ἐσφραγισμένοι,
'marked' (Rev 7.5a, 8c). The repetition here is perhaps due to the
fact that the seer goes on to say that following the Lamb he saw
a multitude whose number no one could count (Rev 7.9). In this
way, with a certain irony, he communicates to the listener/reader

---

[130] This is perhaps an attempt to answer speculation as to the exact number of those who
will be saved (Luke 13.23: εἰ ὀλίγοι οἱ σῳζόμενοι, 'Are only a few to be saved?').

that, although the ἐσφραγισμένοι number 144,000, the followers of the Lamb are too many to count: ὃν ἀριθμῆσαι αὐτὸν οὐδεὶς ἐδύνατο.

The enumeration of the 144,000, given its anaphoric repetition, acquires an unhurried but constant rhythm. This serves to imbue the message with a dramatic power that the text otherwise lacks, because of the absence of the voice that gave John the number.

Before concluding, it should not be forgotten that the listener/reader of the time would probably have noticed the deviations from popular usage that appear in the list of tribes. When the book of Revelation was written, two types of lists were used, which are now classified as 'A' and 'B'. The first was a classification by patronymic, originating from the birth of the sons of Jacob. The second was geographical and referred to the areas occupied by particular tribes. The difference between them is that the 'A' lists generally include Levi and Joseph, while the 'B' lists do not, adding, in their place, two of Jacob's adopted sons: Ephraim and Manasseh (Gen 48.5).[131]

While such lists usually begin with the firstborn son, Ruben, the list in the book of Revelation opens with Judah. The reason for choosing him over the firstborn son is perhaps that the Lamb is presented as ὁ λέων ὁ ἐκ τῆς φυλῆς Ἰούδα, 'the lion of the tribe of Judah' (Rev 5.5).[132] As with group 'A', Levi and Joseph are also included, as is Manasseh, who belonged to group 'B', while Ephraim and Dan are omitted.[133] Considering that, over time, both of the latter tribes fell into idolatry (Jdg 17.1–13; 18.14–31), and that it is precisely such idolatry that is excluded from the presence of God (Rev 21.8; 22.15), it is logical that these two tribes are likewise excluded from the enumeration of the 144,000.[134]

c)   Enumerations of Circumstances

Enumerations of circumstances are less frequent in the book of Revelation and are characterized by their simplicity. They are generally comprised of three nominal lexemes linked by the copulative conjunction καί or sometimes οὔτε. Their function is to highlight a particular message

---

[131] C. H. J. de Geus, 'Gad [Person]', *ABD* 2, 864–6.

[132] Prigent, *Commentary*, p. 286.

[133] Thomas, *Revelation 1–7*, pp. 480–2, synthesizes the reasons behind this exclusion.

[134] Thomas, *Revelation 1–7*, p. 482.

and to influence the listener/reader emotionally. In this group we find: the presentation of John (Rev 1.9); the works of the churches of Ephesus (Rev 2.2), Smyrna (Rev 2.9), and Thyatira (Rev 2.19); the calamities caused by Death (Rev 6.8); and the description of the dwelling of God among men (Rev 21.4). I will analyse the last of these more closely, with regard to its expressiveness and evocative power.

The description of the dwelling of God with men (Rev 21.4) is part of what is pronounced by φωνὴ μεγάλη ἐκ τοῦ θρόνου, 'a loud voice from the throne' (Rev 21.3), after the apparition of the New Jerusalem. The voice explains to John the characteristics of the new dwelling of God among men by means of an enumeration:

> καὶ ὁ θάνατος οὐκ ἔσται ἔτι οὔτε πένθος οὔτε κραυγὴ οὔτε πόνος οὐκ ἔσται ἔτι . . .

> And death will no longer exist, nor weeping, nor lamentation, nor even pain . . .

The expressive power of this particular enumeration lies not only in the accumulation of nominal lexemes drawn from the semantic field of pain (θάνατος, πένθος, κραυγὴ, πόνος), but also from its being built upon litotes. This is a rhetorical device which expresses the full dramatic force of a particular thought through a combination of emphasis and irony, the author knowing full well that what will be understood is more than what he says.[135] This is very much the case in Rev 21.4. The voice we hear from the throne tells John that, when God comes to dwell with men, all of their longings for happiness will be fulfilled, as death, sorrow, and pain will have disappeared. This is reinforced by the circular structure of the enumeration itself, which concludes just as it began, with οὐκ ἔσται ἔτι. The listener/reader thus has the certainty that the afflictions of this life will disappear with the coming of the holy city.

Furthermore, both the vocabulary used and its context suggest to the listener/reader more than what the text itself seems at first to be saying, as Rev 21.4 is in effect recalling the words that God spoke through Isaiah about the restoration of Jerusalem (Isa 65.17–19). Isaiah also speaks of a new heaven and a new earth, the same that John has just seen, and concludes by affirming: μὴ ἀκουσθῇ ἐν αὐτῇ φωνὴ κλαυθμοῦ οὐδὲ φωνὴ κραυγῆς, 'and there will no longer be heard there any voice of weeping or cry of sorrow' (Isa 65.19). These similarities explain the impact of this

---

[135] B. Mortara Garavelli, *Manuale di retorica*, 7th edn (Milan: Tascabili Bompiani, 2003), p. 177; Lausberg, *Retórica literaria 2*, pp. 86–7, § 586.

enumeration on the listener/reader, not only for what is being affirmed, but because it makes clear that the prophecy of Isaiah is being fulfilled in John's visions and auditions. The reaction of the listener/reader is therefore one of joy and hope that the longings of men will soon be over.

3.3.5   The Narrator's Comments

The narrator's comments make plain his desire to keep alive the contact he has established with the listener/reader and involve them directly in the plot. References to the audience of this kind are not exclusive to the book of Revelation; indeed, traces of this technique are found in other New Testament texts, and in other contemporary[136] and later[137] texts.

John intends, above all, to communicate what he has seen and heard to the listener/reader and, at the same time, make them a participant in these experiences. Hence the use of the interjection ἰδού, which implicates the listener/reader in the visions, or the formula of hearing ὁ ἔχων οὖς ἀκουσάτω, which impels them to listen, or John's attempt to prove the veracity of his story, or to oblige the listener/reader to reflect on it, or simply to know what the author feels about what he sees. In this sense, each time it is read, the book of Revelation becomes an account of visions that have not only taken place in the past, but are in some way happening now, at the moment the story is being read.

In the field of narratology, interruptions from the narrator of this kind are referred to as explicit comments, and may take one of two forms: an apostrophe (when the narrator speaks directly to the reader), or an explicative gloss (when it completes information that is considered to be insufficient).[138]

a)   Apostrophe

Apostrophe is the most direct method of narrator intrusion. In the book of Revelation, it takes three different forms: the use of the interjection ἰδού, 'behold'; the hearing formula; and the makarisms or beatitudes.

---

[136] An example from Catullus: *prodeas, nova nupta, si/iam videtur, et audias/nostra verba*, 'Go out, new wife, if it now seems right, and listen to my words' (61.92–4); and another from Horace: *auditis? an me ludit amabilis/insania*? 'Do you hear? Or is pleasant poetic exaltation playing games with me?' (*Carm.* 3.4.5).

[137] Frenk, *Entre la voz*, pp. 22–3 and Ong, *Orality*, p. 158.

[138] Marguerat and Bourquin, *Per leggere*, p. 106.

The interjection ἰδού, 'behold', has an obvious appellative and deictic function that establishes a direct connection with the listener/reader.[139] The clearest examples of the use of the interjection ἰδού as an apostrophe addressed to the listener/reader are:

Ἡ οὐαὶ ἡ μία ἀπῆλθεν· ἰδοὺ ἔρχεται ἔτι δύο οὐαὶ μετὰ ταῦτα (Rev 9.12).

The first woe has passed. Behold! There are still two more woes to come after these things.

Ἡ οὐαὶ ἡ δευτέρα ἀπῆλθεν· ἰδοὺ ἡ οὐαὶ ἡ τρίτη ἔρχεται ταχύ. (Rev 11.14)

The second woe has passed. Behold! The third woe is coming soon.

In these two parallel-structured pericopes, after an initial informative statement (ἡ οὐαὶ ἡ μία/δευτέρα ἀπῆλθεν), John immediately addresses and captures the attention of his interlocutor. He does so by means of the interjection ἰδού, so that the listener/reader is not distracted, but remains alert to the imminent arrival of the next woes.

This device of speaking to the listener/reader can be observed in other parts of the narrative as well, in both the descriptions and the discourses. In the former, the interjection ἰδού is used at the moment that John begins to describe the vision he has had: μετὰ ταῦτα εἶδον, καὶ ἰδοὺ θύρα, 'after these things I saw, and behold, a door' (Rev 4.1); εὐθέως ἐγενόμην ἐν πνεύματι· καὶ ἰδοὺ θρόνος, 'immediately I fell into ecstasy, and behold, a throne' (Rev 4.2); καὶ εἶδον, καὶ ἰδοὺ ἵππος, 'and I saw, and behold, a horse' (Rev 6.2, 5, 8); μετὰ ταῦτα εἶδον, καὶ ἰδοὺ ὄχλος πολύς, 'after these things I saw, and behold, an innumerable multitude' (Rev 7.9); καὶ ὤφθη ἄλλο σημεῖον ἐν τῷ οὐρανῷ, καὶ ἰδοὺ δράκων, 'and another sign was seen in heaven, and behold, a dragon' (Rev 12.3); καὶ εἶδον, καὶ ἰδοὺ τὸ ἀρνίον, 'and I saw, and behold, the Lamb' (Rev 14.1); and so forth.

It is in these cases that the narrative is unexpectedly interrupted for a moment as John exhorts the listener/reader to share his vision. Thus, the interjection ἰδού is generally preceded by εἶδον (Rev 6.2, 5, 8; 14.1, 14; 19.11) or the syntagma μετὰ ταῦτα εἶδον (Rev 4.1; 7.9). It is as if John

---

[139] John recreates the past by transforming it into the here-and-now reality of his audience, much as the Homeric epic had done earlier; see Bakker, 'Discourse and Performance: Involvement, Visualization and "Presence" in Homeric Poetry', *Classical Antiquity* 12 (1993), 19.

were saying: 'I saw, but look with me, there before you is a door/a throne/ etc.' It is an attempt to make the past of the vision visible in the present of the reader, so that they contemplate it *ante oculos*, here and now, at the moment that they are reading the book.

As for the use of ἰδού in the discourses, it appears with some frequency (13 times). However, in these cases, it is not so clear that the narrator is speaking to the listener/reader, as the interjection appears within a dialogue or in one of the letters, which have their own interlocutor, usually John (Rev 1.18; 5.5; 21.3, 5; 22.7, 12) or the churches (Rev 1.7; 2.10, 22; 3.8, 9, 20). There is, however, one instance where this is indisputable, as the interjection ἰδού creates a rupture in the narrative, and this is Rev 16.15. We have been hearing the consequences of the pouring of the sixth bowl, when suddenly the narration breaks off and the interjection ἰδού appears, introducing a section of direct speech that leads finally to one of the book of Revelation's beatitudes:

> Ἰδοὺ ἔρχομαι ὡς κλέπτης. μακάριος ὁ γρηγορῶν καὶ τηρῶν τὰ ἱμάτια αὐτοῦ, ἵνα μὴ γυμνὸς περιπατῇ καὶ βλέπωσιν τὴν ἀσχημοσύνην αὐτοῦ (Rev 16.15).

> Behold! I am coming like a thief. Blessed is he who is vigilant and keeps his clothing on, so that he may not go about naked and his shame be seen.

On this occasion, it does not seem to be the voice of John that is speaking but that of Jesus, as the verse repeats expressions of his that appeared earlier, addressed to the church of Sardis: ἐὰν οὖν μὴ γρηγορήσῃς, ἥξω ὡς κλέπτης, 'if you are not vigilant, I will come like a thief' (Rev 3.3). Indeed, ὡς κλέπτης may be a repetition that is employed here deliberately to identify the speaker as Christ.[140] In any case, regardless of whose voice it is, there is a clear exhortation here for the listener/reader to reflect, examine their life, and adopt an attitude of vigilance.

The second type of apostrophe found in the book of Revelation is the hearing formula, which serves an important function through its two

---

[140] The identity of this voice has been disputed. Those in favour of its being Jesus include: Robertson, *Comentario*, p. 753; Aune, *Revelation 1*, p. 221; Smalley, *Revelation*, p. 411. Among those in opposition are Beckwith, *Apocalypse*, p. 684, who is inclined to think that it is John himself, and Charles, *Commentary 1*, p. 49, who feels that it is an interpolation added by someone other than the author.

variants: εἴ τις ἔχει οὖς ἀκουσάτω, 'if anyone has ears, let him hear', and ὁ ἔχων οὖς ἀκουσάτω, 'let the one who has ears hear'.[141] Rev 13.9–10 is perhaps the clearest example of this desire on the narrator's part to speak directly to the listener/reader:

> Εἴ τις ἔχει οὖς ἀκουσάτω. [10] εἴ τις εἰς αἰχμαλωσίαν, εἰς αἰχμαλωσίαν ὑπάγει· εἴ τις ἐν μαχαίρῃ ἀποκτανθῆναι αὐτὸν ἐν μαχαίρῃ ἀποκτανθῆναι. Ὧδέ ἐστιν ἡ ὑπομονὴ καὶ ἡ πίστις τῶν ἁγίων (Rev 13.9–10).

> If anyone has ears, let him hear: [10] if someone is destined to captivity, to captivity shall he go; if someone must die by the sword, so will he die by the sword. Here is the patience and the faith of the saints.

The context in which it appears is as follows: John has just concluded the story of the beast by saying that its followers will be excluded from the book of life (Rev 13.8). It is here that the narrator's intrusion occurs, breaking into the story and addressing the listener/reader directly. These words carry a powerful impact, not only because they are spoken *ex abrupto* and through the presence of the lexeme ὧδέ, but because to a certain extent they reproduce the words of Jeremiah, adapted to the calamities which threaten John's own community.[142] The listener/reader cannot help but reflect upon what they hear and take stock of what it means to be faithful to the Lamb.

Other examples of this type of apostrophe, expressed as ὁ ἔχων οὖς ἀκουσάτω, 'let the one who has ears hear', appear at the end of some of the letters to the seven churches (Rev 2.7, 11, 17, 29; 3.6, 13, 22). However, the formula is not addressed to the direct interlocutor of these messages, i.e., the community, as the familiar form of 'you' has either just been used (Rev 2.6, 10, 15), or, if a third person is indicated, it conceals a similar 'you', as it has specific members of the community as antecedents (Rev 2.26; 3.5, 12, 20–21). Therefore, the interlocutor is none other than the listener/reader themselves. By speaking to them like this, John arouses their attention through a method that is certainly paraenetic; that is, by exhorting them to listen to what Jesus has said to the various churches, he will enable them, if they should find themselves in a similar situation, to behave correctly. The content of the messages

---

[141]   Both forms are found in the NT: Matt 11.15; 13.9, 43; Mark 4.9, 23; Luke 8.8; 14.35.
[142]   Smalley, *Revelation*, p. 344.

thus acquires a more universal dimension, one not restricted to the communities to which Jesus directed the letters.

A final example of apostrophe is that of the makarisms. These express a positive wish addressed to a third person by means of the adjectival lexeme μακάριος. An example of this, especially relevant for the way it bursts into the narrative *ex abrupto*, is:

> μακάριος καὶ ἅγιος ὁ ἔχων μέρος ἐν τῇ ἀναστάσει τῇ πρώτῃ· ἐπὶ τούτων ὁ δεύτερος θάνατος οὐκ ἔχει ἐξουσίαν, ἀλλ᾽ ἔσονται ἱερεῖς τοῦ θεοῦ καὶ τοῦ Χριστοῦ καὶ βασιλεύσουσιν μετ᾽ αὐτοῦ [τὰ] χίλια ἔτη (Rev 20.6).

> Blessed and holy is he who takes part in the first resurrection. Over these, the second death will have no power, and instead they will be the priests of God and Christ, and will reign with him for a thousand years.

Rev 20.6 comes nearly at the end of the narrative, after John has finished telling us that the devil has been taken captive and the thousand-year kingdom of Christ established. Once again, without warning, John proclaims this beatitude, and thereby encourages the listener/reader to reflect upon what it affirms.

The other beatitudes in the narrative (Rev 1.9–22.16) are either preceded by the interjection ἰδού or form part of a direct-speech discourse. The former (Rev 16.15; 22.7) are inserted into a context dominated beforehand by an apostrophe, as they begin with a direct allusion to the listener/reader. The beatitude, in these cases, helps to maintain and prolong the effect of this direct appeal to the audience.

As for the beatitudes given in direct speech, these do not interrupt the text so abruptly. The fact that we know who is being addressed greatly weakens the impact of the apostrophe on the listener/reader, even though its influence over them is in some sense undeniable: καὶ ἤκουσα φωνῆς ἐκ τοῦ οὐρανοῦ λεγούσης· γράψον· μακάριοι οἱ νεκροὶ . . ., 'and I heard a voice from heaven saying, "Write: blessed are the dead . . . "' (Rev 14.13); καὶ λέγει μοι· γράψον· μακάριοι οἱ εἰς τὸ δεῖπνον τοῦ γάμου τοῦ ἀρνίου κεκλημένοι . . ., 'and said to me, "Write: blessed are those who are invited to the wedding feast of the Lamb . . . "' (Rev 19.9); μακάριοι οἱ πλύνοντες τὰς στολὰς αὐτῶν . . ., 'blessed are those who wash their robes . . . ' (Rev 22.14).

b)   The Explicative Gloss

An explicative gloss is a device that allows the narrator to speak about, explain, or judge some aspect or action of the story.[143] Such glosses appear scattered throughout the text of the book of Revelation and may be divided into three groups: the ἤκουσα τὸν ἀριθμόν glosses; the ὧδε glosses; and the glosses relating to the New Jerusalem.

The ἤκουσα τὸν ἀριθμόν glosses may be seen as interruptions of the narrative with the aim of informing the listener/reader about the source of a given number. Such interjections are not a usual occurrence in the narration. More commonly, the number of the objects or persons described is given without their origin being specified. Even when John does not know the exact number, he tries to provide an approximate figure. Thus, for example, when he has just witnessed the glory of God and hears a choir of angels, he explains that ἦν ὁ ἀριθμὸς αὐτῶν μυριάδες μυριάδων καὶ χιλιάδες χιλιάδων, 'their number was myriads of myriads and thousands of thousands' (Rev 5.11); similarly, when he later refers to the army of Satan, he states that ὁ ἀριθμὸς αὐτῶν ὡς ἡ ἄμμος τῆς θαλάσσης, 'their number is like the sands of the sea' (Rev 20.8). For this reason, it is striking that, in two specific moments, John not only gives the number, but adds a brief comment: that is to say, the gloss: ἤκουσα τὸν ἀριθμόν, 'I heard the number'. This is the case both in Rev 7.4 and 9.16:

> Καὶ ἤκουσα τὸν ἀριθμὸν τῶν ἐσφραγισμένων, ἑκατὸν τεσσαράκοντα τέσσαρες χιλιάδες, ἐσφραγισμένοι ἐκ πάσης φυλῆς υἱῶν Ἰσραήλ (Rev 7.4).

> And I heard the number of the marked, one hundred and forty-four thousand, marked from all the tribes of the sons of Israel.

> καὶ ὁ ἀριθμὸς τῶν στρατευμάτων τοῦ ἱππικοῦ δισμυριάδες μυριάδων, ἤκουσα τὸν ἀριθμὸν αὐτῶν. (Rev 9.16)

> And the number of cavalry was two hundred million; I heard their number.

These asides are addressed to the listener/reader so that they know that the number mentioned is not a mere approximation, but rather an exact figure, because this is what John heard. That is to say, the seer has this information not because he has been able to count this number of persons with his own eyes, but because it has been communicated to him. The

---

[143]   Marguerat and Bourquin, *Per leggere*, p. 110.

allusion to hearing here serves to prove the veracity of what he is telling, as well as being a device to capture the listener/reader's attention. Upon hearing the expression ἤκουσα τὸν ἀριθμόν, the listener/reader feels that it is they who are being addressed by John and accept the figure that is given as a true one.

The ὧδε glosses break into the plot through the use of that particular adverbial lexeme. Its function is to inform the listener/reader of some aspect of the story that remains incomplete, but at the same time to make them think, given that they are informed through a kind of riddle (Rev 13.18; 14.12; 17.9). I will examine Rev 13.18 more closely, in terms of its influence on the reception of the work:

> Ὧδε ἡ σοφία ἐστίν. ὁ ἔχων νοῦν ψηφισάτω τὸν ἀριθμὸν τοῦ θηρίου, ἀριθμὸς γὰρ ἀνθρώπου ἐστίν· καὶ ὁ ἀριθμὸς αὐτοῦ ἑξακόσιοι ἑξήκοντα ἕξ.
>
> Here is wisdom! Let the one who has understanding calculate the number of the beast, as it is the number of a man: his number is six hundred and sixty-six.

The adverbial lexeme ὧδε itself expresses the proximity of the speaker,[144] and so the narration shifts from being an account in the third-person singular, in which the actions of the beast of the earth are described (Rev 13.11–17), to a foreground view.[145] It is from this perspective that the narrator, John, addresses his interlocutors directly, 'as if they were by his side',[146] and challenges them with a riddle. By doing this, he manages to bring the plot, synthesized in ὧδε, closer to the real lives of his interlocutors.

John does not answer the riddle in this gloss, however. Instead, he impels the listener/reader to discover for himself who exactly 666 is, as, rather than the neuter gender that would have allowed the number to agree with τὸ θηρίον, he employs the masculine.[147] It is not known whether John succeeded in inspiring his own audience to try to decipher the enigma, but we do know that he achieved this objective for later listener/readers, as demonstrated by the ample bibliography that exists on

---

[144] LOUW and NIDA, 83.1, s.v. ὧδε.

[145] In this sense, Vanni, 'Liturgical Dialogue', 366, argues that ὧδε refers directly to this point in the reading of the text: that is to say, this point in the book.

[146] Prigent, *Commentary*, p. 445.

[147] This is a case of attraction to the gender of the preceding noun, ἀριθμός; see Mussies, *Morphology*, p. 225.

the identity of 666.[148] Even so, as Pierre Prigent states, these studies are still no more than hypotheses.[149] The riddle was still unresolved in the time of Irenaeus, another native of Asia Minor.[150]

Finally, there are the glosses about the New Jerusalem, which appear almost at the end of the narrative (Rev 21.24–27; 22.3–5). Of their insertion into the description of the holy city, which I have already discussed, I will here briefly comment on two aspects.

Unlike in the earlier comments by the narrator, in these John uses no element (interjection, imperative, etc.) that indicates the beginning of the gloss, or that addresses the listener/reader directly. He passes from the description to the comment very naturally and spontaneously. Were it not for the appearance of the future tense in the verb forms, the fact that John is presenting an explicative gloss would not in fact be perceptible. It is only this future tense (περιπατήσουσιν, ἔσται, οἴσουσιν, ὄψονται) that shows that the seer is leaving his ecphrasis in order to involve the listener/reader as a participant in something that is not seen, but rather known: that is, the identity of those who will reside in the holy city (Rev 21.24–27) and details of what they will do there (Rev 22.3–5).

As on other occasions, John here uses a device that has the effect of multiplying his message for his interlocutors. This is his use of allusion to Old Testament texts, specifically to some of the salvation oracles of Isaiah and Zechariah (Isa 60; Zech 14.7, 11).

The content of the oracle of Isaiah is very similar to Rev 21.24–7. In it, the prophet describes a Jerusalem that is dazzling for the glory of God reflected in it, as well as welcoming to pilgrims (both commoners and kings) from all corners of the world. John says much the same of the New Jerusalem: the holy city will be illuminated by the presence of God and the Lamb, will receive the peoples and kings of the earth, and will be open day and night. Nor does the similarity end at the level of content; it is also found in specific expressions, such as:

---

[148] Studies synthesizing the three great lines of interpretation of the number 666 – Pythagorean arithmetic, gematria, and symbolism – may be found in: Aune, *Revelation 2*, pp. 770–3; Prigent, *Commentary*, pp. 426–8; Biguzzi, *Apocalisse*, pp. 140–52; Smalley, *Revelation*, pp. 351–2.

[149] Prigent, *Commentary*, p. 428.

[150] Irenaeus would dedicate part of his work *Adversus Haereses* to showing that the figure could refer to several different names – ΕΥΑΝΘΑΣ, ΛΑΤΕΙΝΟΣ, ΤΕΙΤΑΝ (5.30) – albeit with the caveat that he did not know to which it actually corresponded.

καὶ περιπατήσουσιν τὰ ἔθνη διὰ τοῦ φωτὸς αὐτῆς, καὶ οἱ
βασιλεῖς τῆς γῆς φέρουσιν τὴν δόξαν αὐτῶν εἰς αὐτήν (Rev
21.24).

the nations will walk in its light, and the kings of the earth will
render to it their glory.

καὶ πορεύσονται βασιλεῖς τῷ φωτί σου καὶ ἔθνη τῇ λαμπρότητί
σου (Isa 60.3).

and the kings will walk in your light and the nations in your
splendour.

καὶ οἱ πυλῶνες αὐτῆς οὐ μὴ κλεισθῶσιν ἡμέρας, νὺξ γὰρ οὐκ
ἔσται ἐκεῖ (Rev 21.25).

its gates will never close, because there will be no night there.

καὶ ἀνοιχθήσονται αἱ πύλαι σου διὰ παντός ἡμέρας καὶ νυκτὸς
οὐ κλεισθήσονται (Isa 60.11).

your gates will be open – not by day nor by night will they close.

In this way, John not only provides us with information about the New
Jerusalem, but inspires his interlocutors to undertake their own pil-
grimages to the city.[151]

The passage in Zechariah is shorter (Zech 14.7, 11), but its echo, in content
and form, is once again perceptible in both Rev 21.27 and Rev 22.3, 5:

καὶ οὐ μὴ εἰσέλθῃ εἰς αὐτὴν πᾶν κοινὸν καὶ [ὁ] ποιῶν βδέλυγμα καὶ ψεῦδος ... (Rev 21.27) Nothing unclean will enter into it, nor any who commit abomination and lie	καὶ οὐκ ἔσται ἀνάθεμα ἔτι (Zech 14.11) there will no longer be any curse
καὶ πᾶν κατάθεμα οὐκ ἔσται ἔτι (Rev 22.3) there will be no longer be any curse	
καὶ νὺξ οὐκ ἔσται ἔτι (Rev 22.5). night will be no more	καὶ οὐχ ἡμέρα καὶ οὐ νύξ (Zech 14.7). there will be no day and no night

However, perhaps the statement that moves the interlocutor most is
the simple phrase, ὄψονται τὸ πρόσωπον αὐτοῦ, 'they will see his face'
(Rev 22.4). Its impact may be traced to the constant longing to

151 Smalley, *Revelation*, p. 561.

contemplate the face of God that we find expressed in the Psalms (Ps 16.15; 26.8–9), in the knowledge that this is, at the same time, completely forbidden. Not even John in his visions ever sees the face of God, but only the radiance it emits (Rev 4.3).

With these explicative glosses, the listener/reader, absorbed in the seer's vision of the New Jerusalem, is profoundly moved when John completes the record of what he has seen with what he announces, drawing upon the writings of the prophets to do so.

3.4   Other Reading Guidelines for the Modern Reader

The first listeners/readers of the book of Revelation, that community to whom John would address his text, belonged to a socio-cultural context in which the strategies used to communicate τὸν λόγον τοῦ θεοῦ καὶ τὴν μαρτυρίαν Ἰησοῦ Χριστοῦ, 'the word of God and the testimony of Christ' (Rev 1.2), were universally familiar. The use of direct speech was common in biblical stories, and the dramatic devices of Greek theatre formed part of the cultural substratum. Nor was the oral style grating or strange to John's audience. Indeed, the book of Revelation was a text that was read aloud. Furthermore, it was as easy for the listener/reader to recognize the constant echo of the scriptures as it was for them to recall the melodies of the psalms. Finally, the narrator's continually calling the listener/reader's attention would move the latter to reflection and deep emotion, as they felt themselves to be one of οἱ δοῦλοι, 'the servants', of God (Rev 1.11) – that is to say, a true recipient of the revealed message that John was transmitting to them.

The modern-day reader does not experience the book of Revelation in the same way. In the first place, they are generally only a reader, and only rarely assume the role of listener. The oral strategies employed therefore seem to them monotonous and repetitive. When they open the pages of the book of Revelation and begin to read, they come face to face with the abyss separating them from the work. Nor do they feel that the revelation is addressed to themselves; they are instead merely the reader of a strange book whose message is difficult to decipher. Not only do they generally overlook the work's Hellenistic influences, but, with some notable exceptions, they also find it difficult to recognize the echo of earlier biblical texts, let alone the melodies of the canticles.

Nevertheless, having arrived at this point in the present study, the reader will now possess the tools necessary for uncovering the literary strategies employed in this work and will be able to understand something of its rhythm and language. Only one further step remains: that of feeling oneself to be, in fact, the recipient of the revelation: in effect, either the 'lector', ὁ ἀναγινώσκων, or one of 'the ones who hear', οἱ ἀκούοντες, so that they can allow the voice of John to speak to them, in the here and now. Only then will their reading of the text be truly effective.

EPILOGUE

Throughout these pages, and following the lines of Luis Alonso Schokel, I have in effect been 'disassembling' the book of Revelation with the aim of creating a model that explains its harmony and its dissonances. The time has come, then, to reassemble it and determine whether it meets these expectations.

The model begins to emerge with the reading guidelines set forth in the prologue (Rev 1.1–3). First, the book is presented as the revelation of Jesus, to which John is the visual and auditory witness (Rev 1.1–2). Second, the revelation itself does not take place in order to benefit its witness, but rather to be transmitted to a designated group of recipients: the δοῦλοι τοῦ θεοῦ, 'servants of God' (Rev 1.1). This is the reason for its being put into writing: τὰ γεγραμμένα (Rev 1.3). In consequence, the work is taken to be true because it is the revelation of Jesus and because it transmits what John saw and heard (Rev 1.1–2). Finally, it appears to be a work intended to be read aloud before a community (Rev 1.3).

These guidelines are not independent of each other, but are closely linked, creating a narrative structure of great unity and cohesion. The fact that John presents himself as a visual and auditory witness to the revelation also leads to a number of specific narrative strategies. Outstanding among these is the choice of a homodiegetic narrator, which allows him to function both as witness to the story and as a character within it, thus heightening the veracity of his narrative.

Moreover, the narrator adopts two strategies that enable him to highlight his own role as visual and auditory witness: description and direct-speech discourse. The use of description allows him to create, in the manner of classical rhetoric, the effect of *ante oculos ponere* for the listener/reader, while direct speech, to paraphrase Cicero, gives him the power of *ad aures ponere*, at the same time that it allows him to portray himself as a mere auditor of what he himself hears.

The other two guidelines – that the work is addressed specifically to believers and that it was conceived to be read aloud within a community – explain the presence of the oral style, as well as the apparent heterogeneity of textual forms: a prologue (Rev 1.1–3); an introductory liturgical dialogue (Rev 1.4–8); the account of visions and auditory revelations (Rev 1.9–22.16); and a final liturgical dialogue (Rev 22.17–21).

The liturgical dialogues at the beginning and end of the work, with their distinct alternating voices, give it a form that demands that it be read aloud in an assembly, with a reader reciting and the assembly responding. In addition, the use of a heading (Rev 1.4) and a final epistolary closing (Rev 22.21) to open and close the work make the book of Revelation resemble a letter, suggesting that it be read by the community in the same way as the Pauline letters; that is, collectively.

As for the narrative it recounts (Rev 1.9–22.16), two parts may be clearly differentiated: Rev 1.9–22.5, the narration of visions and auditory revelations; and Rev 22.6–16, the process of the book's own authentification, which reaffirms the veracity of what is written and of the idea that John was the visual and auditory witness of the revelation.

Rev 1.9–22.16 is highly analogous to the short-story form, as it pays particularly strong attention to its receiver. This aspect constitutes one of the key guidelines for reading the work. In addition, what is relevant in the short story is not what is narrated, but what is transmitted through the narration itself; much the same is true of the book of Revelation. There is likewise a similarity in plot development and in the techniques employed, as in both the short story and the book of Revelation the coordinates of time and space are given a flexibility not seen in other narrative forms, while qualifying adjectives are used not only to provide information about the goodness or wickedness of the characters they describe, but to jar the sensibilities of the listener/reader. Equally, the description and direct-speech discourse that we find in the book are not mere ornamentation, but ways of making the revelation visible and audible. The two strategies complement each other to the point that the description practically creates the setting and the voices required for mimesis, and that mimesis, in turn, through its dramatization, helps to flesh out the significance of the visions and advance the storyline. Thus, both description and direct-speech discourse contribute to the overall effectiveness of the story. It does not seem, then, that either description or direct speech pose any sort of obstacle to drawing this analogy between Rev 1.9–22.16 and the short-story form. As the short story is the literary form that best adapts to the demands of the author, especially with regard to involving the listener/reader, Rev 1.9–22.16 can be seen as having a literary form that is indeed close to that of the short story.

The model proposed here for reading the book of Revelation succeeds in explaining the work's apparent dissonances and in revealing the harmony of this complex, heterogeneous text. In any case, the twenty-first-century reader should keep in mind that, although the text may be brought up to date and revived, one's modern-day experience of it will in part be marred by a lack of familiarity with the textual, oral, and liturgical tradition in which it was originally conceived and read.

Lastly, I would not like to overlook the considerable literary skills of its author. While previous scholars have pointed out his mastery in adapting the Greek tongue to the demands of the text, the present study testifies to his extraordinary ability to transmit his story, as if it were taking place at the moment of its narration. To do so, he would draw upon a wealth of literary strategies, whether of his own invention or taken from the literature of his time, in both the Hellenistic tradition and that of the Old Testament, to which he is clearly indebted.

BIBLIOGRAPHY*

Accordance Bible Software® version 12.0.2: Oaktree Software, Inc., 2016
Allo, E. B., *L'Apocalypse* (Paris: Lecoffre, 1933)
Alonso Schökel, L., *Diccionario bíblico hebreo-español* (Madrid: Trotta, 1994)
  Treinta Salmos: Poesía y oración (Madrid: Cristiandad, 1981)
Alonso Schökel, L. and C. Carniti, *Salmos: Traducción, introducciones y comentario*, 2 vols. (Estella: Verbo Divino, 1992–6)
Alvar Ezquerra, J. (ed.), *Diccionario Espasa Mitología Universal* (Madrid: Espasa-Calpe, 2000)
Ammianus Marcellinus, *Ammiani Marcellini Rerum Gestarum Libri qui supersunt*, W. Seyfarth, ed., vol. 1 (Stuttgart: B. G. Teubner, 1999)
Anderson Imbert, E., *Teoría y técnica del cuento* (Barcelona: Ariel, 1992)
Aristotle, *Ars poetica: Poética*, V. García Yebra, ed. (Madrid: Gredos, 1974, rep. 1999)
Aune, D. E., 'A Latinism in Revelation 15:2', *JBL* 110 (1991), 691–2
  Revelation 1–5 (Dallas, TX: Word Books, 1997)
  Revelation 6–16 (Nashville, TN: T. Nelson, 1998)
  Revelation 17–22 (Nashville, TN: T. Nelson, 1998)
Austin, J. L., *Palabras y acciones: Cómo hacer cosas con palabras*, compiled by J. O. Urmson, trans. G. R. Carrio and E. A. Rabossi (Buenos Aires: Paidós, 1971)
Bachmann, H., et al., *Vollständige Konkordanz zum Griechischen Neuen Testament*, 3 vols. (Berlin – New York: Gruyter, 1978–83)
Bakker, E. J., 'Discourse and Performance: Involvement, Visualization and "Presence" in Homeric Poetry', *Classical Antiquity* 12 (1993), 1–29
  Poetry in Speech: Orality and Homeric Discourse (Ithaca, NY: Cornell University Press, 1996)
  Pointing at the Past: From Formula to Performance in Homeric Poetics (Cambridge, MA: Harvard University Press, 2005)
Bal, M., *Teoría de la narrativa (Una introducción a la narratología)*, trans. J. Franco, 5th edn (Madrid: Cátedra, 1998)

---

* The fact that some of these works have been studied electronically has at times made it impossible to specify the exact page numbers consulted. However, the complete bibliographical data for these works is given here, with an indication as to whether they have been referred to electronically.

Baquero Goyanes, M., *Qué es la novela. Qué es el cuento* (Murcia: Universidad de Murcia, 1988)

Barr, D. L., *Tales of the End: A Narrative Commentary on the Book of Revelation* (Santa Rosa, CA: Polebridge Press, 1998)

'The Apocalypse of John as Oral Enactment', *Int* 40 (1986), 243–56

'The Story John Told: Reading Revelation for its Plots', in D. L. Barr (ed.), *Reading the Book of Revelation: A Resource for Students* (Leiden – Boston: Brill, 2004), pp. 11–23

Bauckham, R., *The Climax of Prophecy: Studies on the Book of Revelation* (Edinburgh: T & T Clark, 1999, rep. 2005)

Bauer, W., *A Greek–English Lexicon of the New Testament and Other Early Christian Literature* 5th edn (1958), trans. and expanded rev. F. W. Gingrich and W. Danker (Chicago, IL: University of Chicago Press, 1979) [Electronic resource: Accordance]

Beale, G. K., 'Revelation', in D. A. Carson and H. G. M. Williamson (eds.), *It Is Written: Scripture Citing Scripture. Essays in Honour of Barnabas Lindars, S.S.F.* (Cambridge: Cambridge University Press, 1988), pp. 318–36

The Book of Revelation: A Commentary on the Greek Text (Grand Rapids, MI – Cambridge, UK– Carlisle: The Paternoster Press, 1999)

Beckwith, I. T., *The Apocalypse of John: Studies in Introduction with a Critical and Exegetical Commentary* (Eugene, OR: Wipf and Stock, 1919, rep. 2001)

Benson, E. W., *The Apocalypse: An Introductory Study of the Revelation of St John the Divine* (London: Macmillan and Co., 1900)

La Bible de Jérusalem, ed. L'École Biblique de Jerusalem, new rev. edn (Paris: Cerf, 1998)

Biblia Hebraica Stuttgartensia, K. Elliger and W. Rudolph, eds. (Stuttgart: Deutsche Bibelgesellschaft, 1967–77; last printing to date: 1997)

Biblia Sacra iuxta Vulgatam Versionem, B. Fischer and R. Weber, eds., 5th edn (Stuttgart: Deutsche Bibelgesellschaft, 2007)

Biguzzi, G., *L'Apocalisse e suoi enigmi* (Brescia: Paideia, 2004)

Blass, F. and A. Debrunner, *A Greek Grammar of the New Testament and Other Early Christian Literature*, trans. and rev. R. W. Funk (Chicago, IL – London: University of Chicago Press, 1961)

Blevins, J. L., *Revelation as Drama* (Nashville, TN: Broadman Press, 1984)

Bonheim, H., *The Narrative Modes: Technique of the Short Story* (Woodbridge: Brewer, 1982)

Boring, M. E., *Revelation: Interpretation. A Bible Commentary for Teaching and Preaching* (Louisville, KY: John Knox Press, 1989)

Bowman, J. W., *The Drama of the Book of Revelation: An Account of the Book with a New Translation in the Language of Today* (Philadelphia, PA: The Westminster Press, 1955)

'The Revelation to John: Its Dramatic Structure and Message', *Int* 9 (1955), 436–53

Brant, J. A. A., *Dialogue and Drama: Elements of Greek Tragedy in the Fourth Gospel* (Peabody, MA: Hendrickson, 2004)

Braun, J., *Music in Ancient Israel/Palestine: Archaeological, Written, and Comparative Sources*, trans. D. W. Stott (Grand Rapids, MI – Cambridge, UK: William B. Eerdmans, 2002)

Brioso, M., 'Algunas observaciones sobre el mensajero en el teatro ático clásico', in E. Calderón, *et al.* (eds.), *Koinòs Lógos: Homenaje al profesor José García López*, vol. 1 (Murcia: Universidad de Murcia, 2006), pp. 111–20

Brown, C. (ed.), *The New International Dictionary of New Testament Theology*, 3 vols. (Grand Rapids, MI: The Paternoster Press – Zondervan, 1975–8)

Brown, F., *et al.* (eds.), *A Hebrew and English Lexicon of the Old Testament* (Oxford: Oxford University Press, 1907, rep. 1962)

Bruns, J. E., 'The Contrasted Women of Apocalypse 12 and 17', *CBQ* 26 (1964), 459–63

Caird, G. B., *The Revelation of Saint John* (Peabody, MA: Hendrickson, 1999)

Callahan, A. D., 'The Language of Apocalypse', *HTR* 88 (1995), 453–70

Cancik, H., *et al.* (eds.), *Brill's New Pauly* (Leiden – Boston, MA: Brill Online, 2007)

Cardona, G. R., *Diccionario de lingüística*, trans. M. T. de Cabello (Barcelona: Ariel, 1991)

Catullus, *Catulli C. V. Carmina*, R. A. B. Mynors, ed. (Oxford: Clarendon Press, 1958, rep. 1960)

Charles, R. H., *A Critical and Exegetical Commentary on the Revelation of St. John: Introduction, Notes and Indices, Also the Greek Text and English Translation*, 2 vols. (Edinburgh: T & T Clark, 1920)

Charlesworth, J. H. (ed.), *The Old Testament Pseudepigrapha: Apocalyptic Literature and Testaments*, 2 vols. (Garden City, NY: Doubleday, 1983–5) [Electronic resource: Accordance]

Cheyne, T. K. and J. Sutherland Black (eds.), *Encyclopedia Biblica: A Dictionary of the Bible. A Critical Dictionary of the Literary, Political and Religious History, the Archaeology, Geography and Natural History of the Bible*, vol. 3 (London: Macmillan & Co., 1902)

Cicero, M. T., *De l'invention*, ed. and trans. G. Achard (Paris: Les Belles Lettres, 1994)

Ciceronis M. T. Epistulae, W. S. Watt, ed. (Oxford: Clarendon Press, 1982)

Clement of Alexandria, *Clemens Alexandrinus [Werken des]*, O. Stählin, L. Früchtel and U. Treu, eds., vol. 3 (Berlin: Akademie – Verlag, 1970)

Collins, J. J., *The Apocalyptic Imagination: An Introduction to Jewish Apocalyptic Literature*, 2nd edn (Grand Rapids, MI – Cambridge, UK: William B. Eerdmans, 1998)

Dansk, E., *The Drama of the Apocalypse* (London: Fisher Unwin, 1894)

De Jong, I. J. F., *Narrative in Drama: The Art of the Euripidean Messenger-Speech* (Leiden: Brill, 1991)

Delebecque, E., '"Je vis" dans l'Apocalypse', *RevThom* 3 (1998), 460–6

Demetrius of Phalerum and Cassius Longinus, *Demetrio Sobre el estilo. Longino Sobre lo sublime*, intro., trans. and notes J. García López (Madrid: Gredos, 1979, rep. 1996)

Di Berardino, A. (ed.), *Diccionario patrístico y de la antigüedad cristiana*, 2 vols., trans. A. Ortiz García and J. M. Guirau (Salamanca: Sígueme, 1991–2)

Didaché: Doctrina apostolorum. Epístola del Pseudo-Bernabé, intro., trans. and notes J. J. Ayán Calvo (Madrid: Ciudad Nueva, 1992)

D'Souza, J. D., *The Lamb of God in the Johannine Writings* (Allahabad: St Paul Publications, 1968)

Eco, U., *Lector in fabula: La cooperazione interpretativa nei testi narrativi* (Milan: Bompiani, 1979)

Elam, K., *The Semiotics of Theatre and Drama*, 2nd edn (London: Routledge, 2002)

Enroth, A. M., 'The Hearing Formula in the Book of Revelation', *NTS* 36 (1990), 598–608

Estébanez Calderón, D., *Diccionario de términos literarios* (Madrid: Alianza, 1996)

Fernández Marcos, N., *Introducción a las versiones griegas de la Biblia* (Madrid: CSIC, 1998)

Fokkelman, J., *Reading Biblical Narrative: A Practical Guide*, trans. I. Smit (Leiden: Deo Publishing, 1999)

Freedman, D. N. (ed.), *The Anchor Bible Dictionary*, 6 vols. (New York, NY: Doubleday, 1992) [Electronic resource: Accordance]

Frenk, M., *Entre la voz y el silencio* (Alcalá de Henares, Madrid: Centro de Estudios Cervantinos, 1997)

Gaffiot, F., *Dictionnaire illustré latin–français* (Paris: Librairie Hachette, 1984)

García Barrientos, J. L., *Cómo se comenta una obra de teatro: Ensayo de método* (Madrid: Síntesis, 2003)

García Barrientos, J. L. (ed.), *Análisis de la Dramaturgia: Nueve obras y un método* (Madrid: Fundamentos, 2007)

García Berrio, A. and T. Hernández Fernández, *Crítica literaria: Iniciación al estudio de la literatura* (Madrid: Cátedra, 2004)

García Landa, J. Á., *Acción, relato, discurso: Estructura de la ficción narrativa* (Salamanca: Ediciones Universidad de Salamanca, 1998)

García Martínez, F. (ed.), *Qumran and Apocalyptic: Studies on the Aramaic Texts from Qumran* (Leiden: E. J. Brill, 1992)

Textos de Qumrán, 4th edn (Madrid: Trotta, 1993)

García Ureña, L., 'Colour Adjectives in the New Testament', *NTS* 61 (2015), 219–38

'El diálogo dramático en el Apocalipsis: De Ezequiel, el Trágico, a Juan, el vidente de Patmos', *Greg* 92 (2011), 23–56

'El rigor del método. Una ayuda para el exegeta y traductor', in L. Roig Lanzillotta and I. Muñoz Gallarte (eds.), *Liber amicorum en honor del profesor Jesús Peláez del Rosal* (Córdoba: El Almendro, 2013), pp. 53–63

'La Septuaginta, testigo de un proceso de lexicalización: σῶμα de cuerpo a esclavo', in A. Agud, *et al.* (eds.), *Séptimo centenario de los estudios orientales en Salamanca* (Salamanca: Ediciones Universidad de Salamanca, 2012), pp. 371–82

Garrido Domínguez, A., *El texto narrativo* (Madrid: Síntesis, 1996)

Garrido Gallardo, M. Á., *Nueva introducción a la teoría de la literatura*, 3rd edn (Madrid: Síntesis, 2004)

Genette, G., *Figures III* (Paris: Editions du Seuil, 1972)

'Frontières du récit', in *Figures II* (Paris: Seuil 1969), pp. 49–69. Later published as: 'Fronteras del relato' in R. Barthes, *et al.* (eds.), *Análisis estructural del relato*, trans. B. Dorriots (U. Eco's text) and A. N. Vaisse (dossier) (México: Coyoacán, 1996, rep. 1998), pp. 199–213

Seuils (Paris: Editions du Seuil, 1987)

González de Gambier, E., *Diccionario de terminología literaria* (Madrid: Síntesis, 2002)

Gould, E. P., *The Gospel According to St Mark* (Edinburgh: T & T Clark, 1948)

Goward, B., *Telling Tragedy: Narrative Techniques in Aeschylus, Sophocles and Euripides* (London: Duckworth, 1999)

Halliday, M. A. K. and R. Hasan, *An Introduction to Functional Grammar*, 2nd edn (London: Edward Arnold, 1994)

Cohesion in English (London: Longman, 1976)

'Dimensions of Discourse Analysis: Grammar', in T. Van Dijk (ed.), *Handbook of Discourse Analysis*, vol. 2 (London: Academic Press, 1985), pp. 29–56

Hamon, P., *Introduction à l'analyse du descriptif* (Paris: Hachette, 1981)

La description littéraire: De l'Antiquité à Roland Barthes. Une anthologie (Paris: Macula, 1998)

Le personnel du roman (Geneva: Droz, 1983)

'Pour un statut sémiologique du personnage', in R. Barthes, *et al.* (eds.), *Poétique du récit* (Paris: Seuil, 1977), pp. 115–80. Previously published in *Littérature* 6 (1972), 86–110

'Qu'est-ce qu'une description?', *Poetique* 12 (1972), 465–85

Harrington, W. J., *Revelation* (Collegeville, MI: The Liturgical Press, 1993)

Harrisville, R. A., 'The Concept of Newness in the New Testament', *JBL* 74 (1955), 69–79

Hatch E. and H. A. Redpath, *A Concordance to the Septuagint and the Other Greek Versions of the Old Testament (Including the Apocryphal Books)*, 2 vols. (Graz, Austria: Akademische Druck – u. Verlagsanstalt, 1954)

Havelock, E. A., *The Muse Learns to Write: Reflections on Orality and Literacy from Antiquity to the Present* (New Haven, CT: Yale University Press, 1986)

Hemer, C. J., *The Letters to the Seven Churches of Asia in Their Local Setting* (Sheffield: JSOT Sheffield, 1986)

Herodotus, *Herodoti Historiae*, K. Hude, ed., 3rd edn, vol. 1 (Oxford: Clarendon Press, 1963)

Hoffmann, M. R., *The Destroyer and the Lamb: The Relation Between Angelomorphic and Lamb Christology in the Book of Revelation* (Tübingen: Mohr Siebeck, 2005)

Homer, *Homeri opera*, D. B. Monro and T. W. Allen, eds., 3rd edn, vol. 2 (Oxford: Clarendon Press, 1962)

Horace, *Horati Flacci Q. Opera*, E. C. Wickham, ed., 2nd edn (Oxford: Clarendon Press, 1963)

Hornblower, S. and A. Spawforth (eds.), *The Oxford Classical Dictionary*, 3rd edn (Oxford: Clarendon Press, 1996)

The Oxford Companion to Classical Civilization (Oxford: Oxford University Press, 1998)

Irenaeus, *Irénée de Lyon Contre les hérésies. V.2. Texte et traduction*, A. Rousseau, *et al.*, eds. (Paris: Éditions du Cerf, 1969)

Jiménez, J. R., *Platero y yo* (Madrid: Biblioteca Nueva, 1997)

Johns, L., *The Lamb Christology of the Apocalypse of John: An Investigation into Its Origins and Rhetorical Force* (Tübingen: Mohr Siebeck, 2004)

Justin Martyr, *Dialogue avec Tryphon*, crit. edn, trans. and commentary P. Bobichon (Fribourg: Academic Press Fribourg, 2003)

Kavanagh, M. A., *Apocalypse 22: 6–21 as Concluding Liturgical Dialogue* (Rome: Pontifical Gregorian University, 1984)

Kiddle, M., *The Revelation of St. John*, 7th edn (London: Hodder and Stoughton, 1963)

Kirby, J. T., 'The Rhetorical Situations of Revelation 1–3', *NTS* 34 (1988), 197–207

Kittel, G. and G. Friedrich (eds.), *The Theological Dictionary of the New Testament*, 10 vols. (Grand Rapids, MI: William B. Eerdmans, 1964–1976) [Electronic resource: Logos Research Systems]

Kitto, H. D. F., *Greek Tragedy: A Literary Study*, 3rd edn (London: Methuen & Co, 1961)

Klauck, H. J., *Ancient Letters and the New Testament: A Guide to Context and Exegesis* (Waco, TX: Baylor University Press, 2006)

Koehler, L. and W. Baumgartner, *A Bilingual Dictionary of the Hebrew and Aramaic Old Testament, English and German* (Leiden – Cologne – New York, NY: Brill, 1998)

Kolyada, Y., *A Compendium of Musical Instruments and Instrumental Terminology in the Bible*, trans. by the author and D. J. Clark (Oakville, CT – London: Equinox, 2009)

Korner, R. J., '"And I Saw … " An Apocalyptic Literary Convention for Structural Identification in the Apocalypse', *NT* 42 (2000), 160–83

Kovacs, J. and C. Rowland, *Revelation: The Apocalypse of Jesus Christ* (Malden, MA: Blackwell, 2004)

Kraus, H. J., *Teología de los Salmos*, trans. V. Martínez de Lapera (Salamanca: Sígueme, 1985)

Ladrière, J., 'La performatividad del lenguaje litúrgico', *Concilium* 82 (1973), 215–29

Lambrecht, J., 'The Opening of the Seals (Rev 6.1–8.6)', *Bib* 79 (1998), 198–221

Lausberg, H., *Manual de retórica literaria*, trans. J. Pérez Riesgo, vol. 2 (Madrid: Gredos, 1967)

Lenski, R. C. H., *The Interpretation of St. John's Revelation* (Minneapolis, MN: Augsburg, 1963)

Lewis, C. S., *An Experiment in Criticism* (Cambridge: Cambridge University Press, 1961, rep. 1995)

Liddell, H. G., *et al.* (eds.), *A Greek–English Lexicon with a Supplement 1968*, 9th edn with a revised supplement (Oxford: Clarendon Press, 1996)

Louw, J. P. and E. A. Nida, *Greek–English Lexicon of the New Testament Based on Semantic Domains*, 2 vols. (New York, NY: United Bible Societies, 1988) [Electronic resource: Accordance]

Lurker, M., *Diccionario de imágenes y símbolos de la Biblia*, trans. R. Godoy (Córdoba: El Almendro, 1994)

Lust, J., *et al.* (eds.), *A Greek–English Lexicon of the Septuagint* (Stuttgart: Deutsche Bibelgesellschaft, 2003)

Luzárraga, J., *Cantar de los Cantares: Sendas del amor* (Estella: Verbo Divino, 2005)

Malbon, E. S., 'Narrative Criticism: How Does the Story Mean?', in J. C. Anderson and S. D. Moore (eds.), *Mark and Method: New Approaches in Biblical Studies* (Minneapolis, MN: Fortress, 1992), pp. 23–49

Mann, C. S., *Mark: A New Translation, with Introduction and Commentary* (New York, NY: Doubleday, 1986)

Marguerat, D. and Y. Bourquin, *Per leggere i racconti biblici: La Bibbia si racconta. Iniziazione all'analisi narrativa*, trans. M. Zappella (Rome: Borla, 2001)

Márquez Rowe, I., 'Inscripciones reales cuneiformes del II y I milenio a. de C.', *Aula Orientalis* 15 (1997), 69–98

Marshall, I. H., *et al.* (eds.), *New Bible Dictionary*, 3rd edn (Leicester – Downers Grove, IL: InterVarsity Press, 1996) [Electronic resource: Accordance]

Massyngberde Ford, J., *Revelation: Introduction, Translation and Commentary* (New York, NY: Doubleday, 1975)

Mateos, J., *Método de análisis semántico* (Córdoba: El Almendro, 1989)

Mateos, J. and F. Camacho, *El Hijo del Hombre: Hacia la plenitud humana* (Córdoba: El Almendro, 1995)

Evangelio, figuras y símbolos, 3rd edn (Córdoba: El Almendro, 1999)

Mateos, J. and J. Peláez (eds.), *Diccionario griego-español del Nuevo Testamento Análisis semántico de los vocablos*, 4 vols. (Córdoba: El Almendro, 2000–10)

Metzger, B. M., *A Textual Commentary on the Greek New Testament: A Companion Volume to the United Bible Societies' Greek New Testament*, 2nd edn (Stuttgart: Deutsche Bibelgesellschaft, 2002)

Migne, J. P. (ed.), *Patrologia Latina Database* (Alexandria, VA: Chadwyck-Healey, Inc., 1995)

Miller, G. A., 'Some Problems in the Theory of Demonstrative Reference', in R. J. Jarvella and W. Klein (eds.), *Speech, Place, and Action: Studies of Deixis and Related Topics* (Chichester – New York, NY: Wiley, 1982), pp. 61–72

Moldenke, H. N. and A. L. Moldenke, *Plants of the Bible* (Waltham, MA: Chronica Botanica, 1952)

Montanari, F., *Vocabolario della lingua greca (greco-italiano)* (Turin: Loescher, 1995)

Mortara Garavelli, B., *Manuale di retorica*, 7th edn (Milan: Tascabili Bompiani, 2003)

Moulton, J. H. and N. Turner, *A Grammar of New Testament Greek, Syntax*, vol. 3 (Edinburgh: T & T Clark, 1963)

Mounce, R. H., *The Book of Revelation* (Grand Rapids, MI: William B. Eerdmans, 1977)

Moyise, S., 'Singing the Song of Moses and the Lamb: John's Dialogical Use of Scripture', *AUSS* 42 (2004), 347–60

Muraoka, T., *A Greek–English Lexicon of the Septuagint: Chiefly of Pentateuch and Twelve Prophets* (Louvain – Paris: Peeters, 2002)

Mussies, G., *The Morphology of Koine Greek, As Used in the Apocalypse of St. John: A Study in Bilingualism* (Leiden: Brill, 1971)

Novum Testamentum Graece, E. Nestle and K. Aland, eds., 28th rev. edn (Stuttgart: Deutsche Bibelgesellschaft, 2012)

Nueva Biblia Española, L. Alonso Schökel and J. Mateos, eds. (Madrid: Cristiandad, 1975, rep. 1993)

Nuevo Testamento, M. Iglesias, ed. (Madrid: Encuentro, 2003)

Nuevo Testamento Trilingüe, J. M. Bover and J. O'Callaghan, eds. (Madrid: BAC, 1977, rep. 2005)

Ong, W. J., *Orality and Literacy: The Technologizing of the Word* (London – New York, NY: Routledge, 1982, rep. 1990)

   The Presence of the Word: Some Prolegomena for Cultural and Religious History (Minneapolis, MN – Oxford: University of Minnesota Press, 1981)

Origen, *Origène Commentaire sur Saint Jean. I, Livres I–V*, ed., trans. and notes C. Blanc (Paris: Éditions du Cerf, 1966)

   Origène Contre Celse. III, Livres V et VI, intro., crit. edn, trans. and notes M. Borret (Paris: Éditions du Cerf, 1969)

   Origène Contre Celse. IV, Livres VII et VIII, intro., crit. edn, trans. and notes M. Borret (Paris: Éditions du Cerf, 1969)

Parry, M., *The Making of Homeric Verse: The Collected Papers of Milman Parry* (Oxford: Oxford University Press, 1971)

Pattemore, S. W., 'Repetition in Revelation: Implications for Translation', *BT* 53 (2002), 425–41

Pavis, P., *Diccionario del teatro: Dramaturgia, estética, semiología*, trans. J. Melendres (Barcelona: Paidós, 1998)

Philo of Alexandria, *Philon d'Alexandrie (Les oeuvres de). 9, De agricultura*, intro., trans. and notes J. Pouilloux (Paris: Éditions du Cerf, 1961)

   Philon d'Alexandrie (Les oeuvres de). 29, De vita contemplativa, intro. and notes F. Daumas; trans. P. Miquel (Paris: Éditions du Cerf, 1963)

Pineda, V., 'La invención de la écfrasis', in C. Pérez Romero (ed.), *Homenaje a la profesora Carmen Pérez Romero* (Cáceres: Universidad de Extremadura, Servicio de Publicaciones, 2000)

Pliny the Elder, *Pline l'Ancien, Histoire naturelle. Livre XVIII*, ed. and trans. H. Le Bonniec and A. Le Boeuffle (Paris: Belles Lettres, 1972)

Pliny the Younger, *Plini Caecili Secundi C. Epistularum libri decem*, R. A. B. Mynors, ed. (Oxford: Clarendon Press, 1963)

Porter, S. E., *Verbal Aspect in the Greek of the New Testament with Reference to Tense and Mood* (New York, NY: P. Lang, 1989, rep. 2003)

Pozuelo Yvancos, J. M., 'Escritores y teóricos: La estabilidad del cuento', in C. Becerra, *et al.* (eds.), *Asedios ó conto* (Vigo: Universidad de Vigo, 1999), pp. 37–48

Prigent, P., *Commentary on the Apocalypse of St. John*, trans. W. Pradels (Tübingen: Mohr Siebeck, 2001)

Ramsay, W. M., *The Letters to the Seven Churches*, rev. edn (Peabody, MA: Hendrickson, 1994)

Real Academia de la Lengua Española, *Diccionario de la lengua española*, CD-ROM, 22nd edn (Madrid: Espasa-Calpe, 2003)

Reis, C. and A. C. M. Lopes, *Diccionario de narratología*, trans. Á. Marcos de Dios, 2nd edn (Salamanca: Almar, 2002)

Resseguie, J. L., *Revelation Unsealed: A Narrative Critical Approach to John's Apocalypse* (Leiden – Boston – Cologne: Brill, 1998)

Richards, I. A., *The Philosophy of Rhetoric* (New York, NY: Oxford University Press, 1967)

Ricoeur, P., *Tiempo y narración II: Configuración del tiempo en el relato de ficción*, trans. A. Neira (Madrid: Cristiandad, 1987)

Rivas Carmona, M. M., 'El concepto de cohesión', in G. Álvarez, *et al.* (eds.), *Comunicación y discurso* (Seville: Mergablum, 2003), pp. 48–57

Robertson, A. T., *Comentario al texto griego del Nuevo Testamento*, trans. and notes S. Escuain (Terrassa: Clie, 2003)

Rodríguez Adrados, F. (ed.), *Diccionario griego-español*, 7 vols. (Madrid: CSIC, 1980–2009)

Roloff, J., *The Revelation of John: A Continental Commentary*, trans. J. E. Alsup (Minneapolis, MN: Fortress Press, 1993)

Romero González, D., *El adjetivo en el Nuevo Testamento: Clasificación semántica*. *Tesis Doctoral* (Córdoba: Universidad de Córdoba, 2007). Available at: https://helvia.uco.es/xmlui/handle/10396/3535

Russo, J. A., 'Is Oral or Aural Composition the Cause of Homer's Formulaic Style?', in B. A. Stolz and R. S. Shannon (eds.), *Oral Literature and the Formula* (Ann Arbor, MI: University of Michigan, 1976), pp. 31–71

'Oral Theory: Its Development in Homeric Studies and Applicability to Other Literatures', in M. E. Vogelzang and H. L. J. Vanstiphout (eds.), *Mesopotamian Epic Literature: Oral or Aural?* (Lewiston, NY: Edwin Mellen Press, 1992), pp. 7–21

'The Formula', in I. Morris and B. Powell (eds.), *A New Companion to Homer* (Leiden – New York, NY: Brill, 1997), pp. 238–60

Ryken, L., *et al.* (eds.), *Dictionary of Biblical Imagery: An Encyclopedic Exploration of the Images, Symbols, Motifs, Metaphors, Figures of Speech and Literary Patterns of the Bible* (Downers Grove, IL: InterVarsity, 1998) [Electronic resource: Accordance]

Saffrey, H. D., 'Relire l'Apocalypse à Patmos', *RB* 82 (1975), 385–417

Sagrada Biblia, Profesores de la Facultad de Teología de la Universidad de Navarra, eds., 5 vols. (Pamplona: EUNSA, 1999–2004)

Schmid, J., *Studien zur Geschichte des Griechischen Apocalypse-Textes*, 2 vols. (Munich: Karl Zink, 1955–6)

Scholes, R. and R. Kellogg, *The Nature of Narrative* (Oxford: Oxford University Press, 1966)

Schüssler Fiorenza, E., *Revelation: Vision of a Just World* (Minneapolis, MN: Fortress Press, 1991)

Septuaginta: Id est Vetus Testamentum graece iuxta LXX interpretes, A. Rahlfs, ed., 2 vols. (Stuttgart: Privilegierte Württembergische Bibelanstalt, 1935 and reps.)

Serra, E., *Tipología del cuento* (Madrid: Cupsa, 1978)

Sicre, J. L., *Profetismo en Israel: El profeta: Los profetas: El mensaje* (Estella: Verbo Divino, 1992)

Smalley, S. S., *The Revelation to John: A Commentary on the Greek Text of the Apocalypse* (London: SPCK Publishing, 2005)

Thunder and Love: John's Revelation and John's Community (Milton Keynes: Word Publishing, 1994)

Spang, K., *Persuasión: Fundamentos de retórica* (Pamplona: EUNSA, 2005)

Teoría del drama: Lectura y análisis de la obra teatral (Pamplona: EUNSA, 1991)

Spitzer, L., 'The "Ode on a Grecian Urn", or Content vs. Metagrammar', in A. Hatcher (ed.), *Essays on English and American Literature* (Princeton, NJ: Princeton University Press, 1962), pp. 67–97

Stanislas, S., 'The Slaughtered and Standing Lamb in the Book of Revelation', *IndTheolStud* 43 (2006), 471–94

Stott, W., 'A Note on the Word ΚΥΡΙΑΚΗ in Rev 1:10', *NTS* 12 (1965–6), 70–5

Strabo, *Estrabón Geografía. V, Libros XI-XIV*, intro., trans. and notes M. P. Hoz García-Bellido (Madrid: Gredos, 2001)

Swete, H. B., *The Apocalypse of St. John: The Greek Text with Introduction, Notes and Indices* (Eugene, OR: Wipf and Stock, 1906, rep. 1999)

Taft, M., *The Blues Lyric Formula* (New York, NY: Routledge, 2006)

Tertullian, *Adversus Marcionem*, ed. and trans. E. Evans, vol. 2 (Oxford: Clarendon Press, 1972)

Thayer, J. H., *A Greek–English Lexicon of the New Testament: Being Grimm's Wilke's Clavis Novi Testamenti* (Edinburgh: T & T Clark, 1889) [Electronic resource: Accordance]

Thomas, R. L., *Revelation 1–7: An Exegetical Commentary* (Chicago, IL: Moody Press, 1992)

Revelation 8–22: An Exegetical Commentary (Chicago, IL: Moody Press, 1995)

Thucydides, *Thucydidis Historiae*, H. S. Jones ed., critical apparatus and expansion J. E. Powell (Oxford: Clarendon Press, 1966)

Tolkien, J. R. R., 'On Fairy-Stories', in C. Tolkien (ed.), *The Monsters and the Critics and Other Essays* (London – Boston – Sydney: Allen & Unwin, 1983), pp. 109–61

Trebolle, J., *La Biblia Judía y la Biblia Cristiana: Introducción a la Historia de la Biblia* (Madrid: Trotta, 1993)

Vanni, U., 'Il Simbolismo nell'Apocalisse', *Greg* 61 (1980), 461–506

L'Apocalisse: Ermeneutica, esegesi e teologia (Bologna: Dehoniane, 1988)

Lectura del Apocalipsis: Hermenéutica, exégesis, teología, trans. H. Rey (Estella: Verbo Divino, 2005)

'Liturgical Dialogue as a Literary Form in the Book of Revelation', *NTS* 37 (1991), 348–72

'Un esempio di dialogo liturgico in Ap 1,4-8', *Bib* 57 (1976), 453–67

Villanueva, D., 'Glosario de narratología', in *Comentario de textos narrativos: La novela* (Gijón: Ediciones Júcar, 1989), pp. 181–201. Available at: https:// glosarios.servidor-alicante.com/narratologia/tiempo-de-la-historia

Vitruvius, *Vitrubio Pollione M. De architectura. Libri X*, ed. and trans. F. Bossalino and V. Dazzi (Rome: Kappa, 2002)

Yarbro Collins, A., 'Early Christian Apocalypticism', *Semeia* 36 (1986), 1–11

'Numerical Symbolism in Jewish and Early Christian Apocalyptic Literature', *ANRW II.21.2* (Berlin – New York, NY: De Gruyter, 1984), pp. 1222–87

The Apocalypse (Collegeville, MN: Liturgical Press, 1979, rep. 1990)

Zimmermann, R., 'Nuptial Imagery in the Revelation of John', *Bib* 84 (2003), 153–83

Zohary, M., *Plants of the Bible* (Cambridge: Cambridge University Press, 1982)

Zorell, F., *Lexicon Graecum Novi Testamenti* (Paris: Lethielleux, 1931)

Zumthor, P., *Introduction à la poésie orale* (Paris: Seuil, 1983)

INDEX OF ANCIENT SOURCES

The Old Testament[1]

[1] The Septuagint canon is followed, as Greek is the language used in the Book of Revelation.

The New Testament

SUBJECT INDEX